AF271327

Folding Ideas
for cards & envelopes

折り方のアイディア：カード、封筒

Faltideen für Karten und Umschläge

Ideas para plegar tarjetas y sobres

Idées de pliage pour cartes et enveloppes

Piegare con arte: idee la creazione di biglietti e buste

Laurence K. Withers

The Pepin Press • Agile Rabbit Editions

Amsterdam & Singapore

the pepin press
agile rabbit editions
Janneke Rijpkema account manager
sales@pepinpress.com
Postal Address:
P.O. Box 10349
1001 EH Amsterdam, The Netherlands
Street Address:
Lauriergracht 50,
1016 VT Amsterdam, The Netherlands
Tel +31 20 4202021
Fax +31 20 4201152
www.pepinpr

Dégustation
Roussillon

HAPPY VALENTINE'S DAY!
Grazie...
GET WELL SOON!
the pepin press

Summer Jams
Club Bird
friday evenings
Arabian Nights Music
call me for a drink...
Yvonne

Something to keep you dry during the Monsoon!

Introduction in English   **19**

日本語による序文   23

Introduction en français   27

Introducción en español   31

Introduzione in italiano   35

Einleitung auf Deutsch   39

Simple Folds   **43**

簡単な折り • Pliages simples • Pliegues simples • Cartotecnica semplice • Einfache Faltideen

Cards   **73**

カード • Cartes • Cartas • Biglietti • Karten

Frames and Windows   **127**

フレーム、窓 • Cadres et fenêtres • Marcos y ventanas • Cornici e finestre • Fenster und Rahmen

Locking Devices   **205**

固定部品 • Systèmes de fermeture • Sistemas de cierre • Sistemi di chiusura • Verschlüsse

Pop-ups   **259**

ポップアップ • Dépliages • Desplegables • Biglietti pop-up • Pop-ups

Envelopes   **357**

封筒 • Enveloppes • Sobres • Buste • Umschläge

Miscellaneous   **387**

その他 • Divers • Varios • Varie • Sonstiges

Free CD-Rom inside the back cover

The Pepin Press | Agile Rabbit Editions
P. O. Box 10349
1001 EH Amsterdam

Tel +31 20 4202021
Fax +31 20 4201152
mail@pepinpress.com
www.pepinpress.com

Concept & drawings: Laurence K. Withers
Template correction: Jakob Hronek for The Pepin Press
Series editor & designer: Pepin van Roojen
Layout assistant: Margreet Mulder

ISBN 978 90 5768 128 8

10   9   8   7   6   5   4   3   2
2014   13   12   11   10   09

Printed in Singapore

GET WELL
SOON!

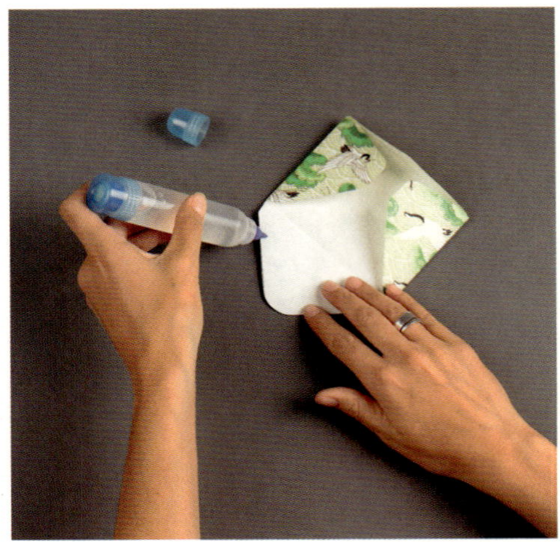

 Example 例 Exemple Ejemplo Esempio Beispiel 1

 Example 例 **Exemple** Ejemplo **Esempio** Beispiel **2**

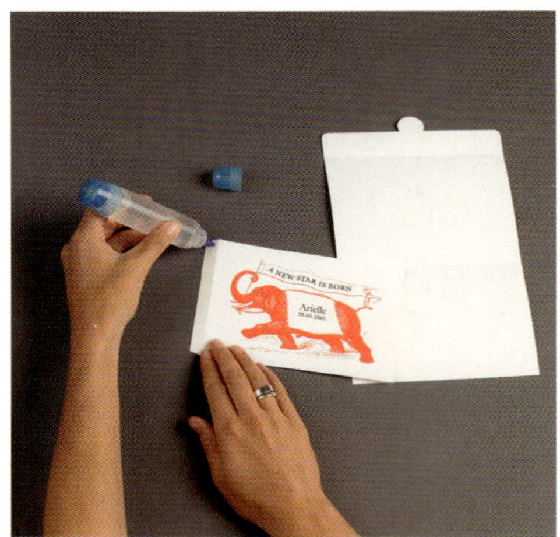

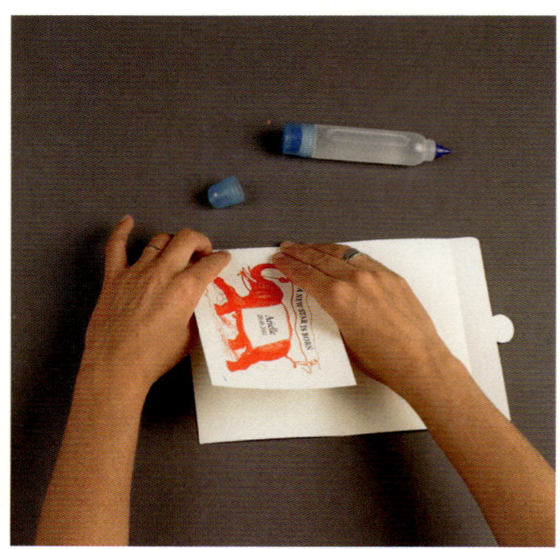

Example 例 **Exemple** Ejemplo **Esempio** Beispiel **3**

A NEW STAR IS BORN
Arielle
28.05.2001

Introduction

序文
Introduction
Introducción
Introduzione
Einleitung

Folding Ideas is a collection of card and envelope design ideas that has been compiled as a source of inspiration for hobbyists and designers at all levels. Each design is accompanied by a template that can be used to personalise the card or envelope. All of these designs are included as PDF files on the enclosed CD.

The easiest programme to use to open and print a PDF file is Acrobat Reader. If you want to decorate a design before printing it, you can import the design as an image into another document using a word processing programme, for example. After you have placed the design, you can add text, pictures or patterns as you wish. Designers can also import the PDF files as images into advanced layout programmes or open the files directly in vector-editing software, which allows you to create your own variations.

The ornaments and patterns used in the photographs throughout this book (plus many more) are also on the CD for your use. These images have been chosen from a selection of books published by The Pepin Press. For more information, please visit our website at www.pepinpress.com.

Paper and envelope sizes

Most of the designs included in this book appear on the CD in two formats. These have been arranged in two separate folders on the CD.

Templates in folder FI-A are exactly as they appear in the book. These are ideal for graphic designers and those who have access to large format printers. Most of these will fit on A3 or Tabloid paper but some are even larger. Larger paper sizes can be printed at most copy/print shops.

Templates in folder FI-B have been adapted for use by those who only have access to a standard paper printer. Here, the large designs in the book have been split into smaller pieces and arranged so that they can be printed on standard paper (either A4 or US Letter). Glue tabs have been added so that the separate pieces can be assembled easily. See pages 14 and 15 for an example of how these templates can be assembled.

Most of the cards in this collection have been designed to fit standard international envelope sizes. Some of the cards have been designed with matching envelopes.

All designs can, of course, be reduced in size to fit on smaller paper but this will reduce the size of the final card/envelope.

Using the design templates

There are countless ways of using these designs to create your own unique cards and envelopes.

Example 1

The easiest way to customise a design is to print the design on fancy paper and assemble it. When using this technique, it is best to print on the back of the paper (page 10). After the design is cut out, it only needs to be folded and glued. The photograph on page 11 shows the result of how the envelope design from page 367 was printed on paper with a beautiful Japanese print.

Example 2

More personalised cards can be made by printing a design on plain paper or card stock, then decorating it by hand. If using card stock or heavier papers, folds will be easier and neater if the paper is creased first. An easy way to do this is to run the dull (back) side of a kitchen knife along the fold line, using a ruler to keep the line straight. It may seem strange, but the crease needs to be made on the side of the paper that will end up being on the outside of the fold. The photographs on page 12 show how to do this. The paper used in this example is 220 gsm (US 80 lb), a weight that works well with the card designs in this book.

Once the design has been printed, almost anything can be used to decorate a card or envelope—pencils, markers, paint, glitter, stickers ... the possibilities are endless.

Example 3

You can also do some or all of the decorating on your computer. This option works well if you want to produce a set of cards or envelopes. The best way to work with a design template on the computer will depend on the programme you are using. The example on page 14 shows some of the ways decorations and text can be added to the design templates.

When the design is complete, it can be printed on the paper of your choice. If the design requires assembly (templates in folder FI-B on the CD), the separate pieces need to be glued together, using the glue tabs, as shown on pages 14 and 15.

CD and image rights

The templates in this book are stored on the accompanying CD and can be used for inspiration or as a graphic resource. The names of the files on the CD correspond with the page numbers in the book. The CD is provided free with the book and is not for sale separately. The files on Pepin Press/Agile Rabbit CDs are sufficiently large for most applications. However, larger files are available for most images and can be ordered from The Pepin Press/Agile Rabbit Editions.

If you have bought this book, the images on the CD can be used free of charge for most applications, including all private and non-commercial endeavours, web design and small-scale commercial use (for example, brochures with a print run of fewer than 5000 copies in which fewer than 5 pictures are used). Permission must be sought for large-scale commercial use, and especially for use in other publications. Further digital distribution in any form is prohibited. If in doubt, please contact us. Our permissions policy is very reasonable and fees charged, if any, tend to be minimal.

For inquiries about permissions and fees, please contact:
mail@pepinpress.com
Fax +31 20 4201152

「折り方のアイディア」では、趣味からプロの仕事に至るまで幅広く使用できる、カードや封筒のデザインアイディアを紹介します。それぞれのデザインにはテンプレートが付いており、それを利用してカードや封筒に模様を加えることができます。デザインはPDF形式で付録のCDに収録されています。

PDFファイルは、Acrobat Readerを使用して簡単に開くことができます。デザインに文字などを追加して印刷する場合は、ワープロソフトなどを使用して書類を作成し、そこにデザインを画像としてインポートします。デザインをインポートしたら、文字、画像、模様などを追加します。また、より高度なDTPソフトを使用して、PDFファイルを画像として取り込んだり、ベクトル編集ソフトでファイルを開き、独自にデザインを編集することもできます。

本書に写真で紹介している絵柄や模様（およびその他の追加画像）も付録のCDに収録されていますので、ご自由にお使いいただけます。これらの画像は、The Pepin Press社のさまざまな出版物より引用されています。詳細は、弊社ウェブサイト「www.pepinpress.com」にアクセスしてください。

紙と封筒のサイズ

本書で紹介されているデザインは、2種類の形式で提供されており、CD内のそれぞれ異なるフォルダーに入っています。

FI-Aフォルダーに入っているデザインは、本書に印刷されたイメージと同様の画像です。この形式のファイルは、グラフィックデザインや大型プリンターで出力する場合に適しています。ほとんどの画像は、A3またはタブロイドサイズで、一部それ以上のサイズの画像も含まれています。大きいサイズの出力は、出力センターなどの店舗でも扱っています。

FI-Bフォルダーに入っているデザインは、一般的なプリンターで印刷できるよう編集されています。大きなサイズのデザインは前もって分割されており、A4またはUS Letterサイズの用紙に出力することができます。分割した画像にはのりしろが含まれているので、簡単につなぎ合わせることができます。つなぎ合わせ方は、ページ14から15を参照してください。

本書で紹介しているほとんどのカードは、普通サイズの封筒に収まるようデザインされています。一部のカードには、専用の封筒が付いています。

デザインは自由に縮小し、小さい用紙に印刷できますが、出来上がるカード/封筒も同様に縮小されますのでご注意ください。

デザインテンプレートの使用方法

ここで紹介しているデザインを利用して、さまざまな独自のカードや封筒を作ることができます。

例1

デザインをお好みの用紙に印刷することで、簡単にオリジナルのカードや封筒が出来上がります。この場合、用紙の裏面にデザインを印刷することをお勧めします（10ページ参照）。デザインを切り抜き、折りたたんだら、糊付けします。11ページの写真は、367ページで紹介したデザインを和風の絵柄の用紙に印刷して作った封筒です。

例2

より個性的な作品を作るには、普通用紙またはブランクのカードにデザインを印刷し、手作業で飾りを施します。ブランクのカードまたは厚手の用紙を使用する場合は、折り曲げる個所に事前に折り目を入れておくことをお勧めします。折り曲げる線に沿って、ナイフの背を使って筋をいれます。このときに、線が曲がらないよう定規を使用してください。折り目の筋は、デザインの表側（折り目の山となる側）に入れてください。折り目の付け方は12ページの写真を参照してください。この例では、本書で紹介してい

るカードに最適な220 gsm（US 80 lb）の用紙を使用しています。

印刷したデザインは、鉛筆、マーカー、グリッター、シールなど、お好みの素材で飾り付けてください。

例3

パソコンを使って模様などを追加することもできます。カードや封筒をセットにして複数作る場合はこの方法が便利です。お使いのソフトによってデザインテンプレートの活用方法が異なります。14ページに、デザインテンプレートに絵柄や文字を追加する方法を紹介します。

デザインに絵柄や文字を追加し、お好みの用紙に印刷します。CDのFI-Bフォルダーにある分割されたデザインを使用する場合は、のりしろで部品を接着する必要があります。14と15ページを参照してください。

CD-ROM及びイメージの著作権について

付録のCDに納められた画像は、グラフィックデザインの参考にしたり、インスピレーションを得るための材料としてご使用ください。CDの各ファイル名は、本書のページ番号に対応しています。このCDは本書の附録であり、CD-ROMのみの販売はいたしておりません。Pepin Press/Agile RabbitのCD収録のファイルは、ほとんどのアプリケーションに対応できるサイズです。より大きなサイズのファイルをご希望の方は、The Pepin Press/Agile Rabbit Editions宛てにご連絡ください。

本書をご購入された場合は、CDに収録された画像を無料でご利用いただけます。個人的および非営利目的での使用、ウェブデザインや小規模な商業目的（たとえば、印刷部数5000冊以下で掲載画像5点以下のパンフレット）などでご利用ください。他の出版物でのご利用など、大規模な商業目的での利用をご希望の際は、弊社の許可が必要です。画像のデジタル形式での配付は、いかなる場合でも禁止されております。判断が困難な場合は、ご相談ください。著作権料が必要となる場合でも最小限の料金でご提供させていただきます。

使用許可と著作権料については下記にお問い合わせください。
mail@pepinpress.com
ファックス：31 20 4201152

Idées de pliage rassemble de nombreuses idées pour la création de cartes et d'enveloppes. Le but de ce recueil est de servir d'inspiration aux passionnés tout comme aux créateurs en tous genres. Chaque dessin est accompagné d'un modèle permettant de personnaliser la carte ou l'enveloppe traitée. Tous ces dessins se trouvent également sur le CD inclus, au format PDF.

Acrobat Reader constitue le logiciel le plus simple à utiliser pour les ouvrir et les imprimer. Pour agrémenter un dessin avant de l'imprimer, vous pouvez, par exemple, l'importer dans un document sous forme d'image à l'aide d'un logiciel de traitement de texte. Vous pouvez ensuite y ajouter du texte, des images ou des motifs à votre guise. Les créateurs peuvent également importer les fichiers PDF sous forme d'images dans des logiciels de mise en page avancée ou bien ouvrir les fichiers directement dans un logiciel vectoriel, ce qui leur permet de s'en inspirer pour créer leurs propres variations.

Les décorations et les motifs des photographies présentées dans ce livre, entre autres, sont également à votre disposition sur le CD. Ces images sont tirées d'une sélection de livres publiés par The Pepin Press. Pour en savoir plus, veuillez consulter notre site Web à l'adresse www.pepinpress.com.

Formats de papier et d'enveloppes

La plupart des illustrations de ce livre figurent sur le CD en deux formats. Elles ont été regroupées en deux dossiers placés sur le CD.

Les modèles du dossier FI-A sont identiques à ceux du livre. Ils sont s'adressent parfaitement aux infographistes et à ceux disposant d'une imprimante grand format. La plupart d'entre eux tiennent sur un format condensé ou A3 mais certains sont encore plus grands. Les formats plus grands peuvent être tirés chez la plupart des imprimeurs.

Les modèles du dossier FI-B, quant à eux, sont adaptés pour une impression standard. Les grands dessins du livre sont ici divisés en pièces plus petites qui sont arrangées de manière à les imprimer sur du papier au format standard (A4 ou US Letter). Les différentes pièces comportent des languettes à coller afin d'assembler les éléments en toute simplicité. Voir l'exemple d'assemblage de ces modèles aux pages 14 et 15.

La plupart des cartes de ont été conçues pour tenir sur des enveloppes internationales standard. D'autres ont été élaborées pour un type d'enveloppes différent.

Tous les dessins peuvent bien entendu être réduits pour du papier aux dimensions inférieures. Il convient cependant de noter que le format de la carte ou de l'enveloppe s'en trouvera alors réduit en conséquence.

Utilisation des modèles

Il existe une foule de possibilités pour créer vos propres cartes et enveloppes d'après les dessins proposés.

Exemple 1

Le meilleur moyen de personnaliser un modèle est de l'imprimer sur papier fantaisie et de l'assembler. Dans le cadre de cette technique, il est recommandé d'imprimer au dos du papier (page 10). Après avoir coupé le dessin, il suffit de le plier et de le coller. La photographie de la page 11 illustre le résultat du dessin d'enveloppe de la page 367 imprimé sur papier avec une belle estampe japonaise.

Exemple 2

Il est possible de confectionner d'autres cartes personnalisées en imprimant un dessin sur du papier vierge ou du papier cartonné, puis en le décorant à la main. Si vous utilisez du papier cartonné ou du papier plus épais, le pliage est plus aisé et plus net si vous travaillez le papier au préalable. Une technique simple consiste à passer le côté non tranchant d'un couteau de cuisine le long de la ligne de pliage à l'aide d'une règle. Le procédé peut paraître étrange mais le pli doit être réalisé sur le côté du papier qui se trouvera à l'extérieur du pliage. Les photographies des page 12 illustrent le procédé. Le papier utilisé dans cet exemple est le papier 220 g, qui offre un poids s'adaptant particulièrement bien aux dessins des cartes de ce livre.

Une fois le dessin imprimé, vous pouvez faire appel à pratiquement tous les outils possibles afin de décorer votre carte ou votre enveloppe : crayons, marqueurs, peinture, paillettes, autocollants, etc. Les possibilités sont infinies.

Exemple 3

Vous pouvez également réaliser tout ou partie du garnissage directement sur votre ordinateur. Cela s'avère pratique si vous voulez produire des cartes ou des enveloppes en série. La meilleure façon de manipuler un modèle dépend alors du logiciel que vous utilisez. L'exemple de la page 14 présente certaines des quelques méthodes possibles pour ajouter des décorations et du texte aux modèles.

Une fois le dessin terminé, vous pouvez l'imprimer sur le papier de votre choix. Si le dessin doit être assemblé (modèles du dossier FI-B sur le CD), vous

devez coller les morceaux ensemble par leurs languettes, comme illustré aux pages 14 et 15.

CD et droits d'auteur des illustrations

Les dessins présents dans cet ouvrage figurent sur le CD fourni et peuvent servir de source d'inspiration ou de ressource graphique. Le nom des fichiers du CD correspond au numéro de la page correspondante dans le recueil. Le CD est fourni gratuitement avec ce livre et ne peut être vendu séparément. Les fichiers des CD de The Pepin Press/Agile Rabbit sont d'une résolution suffisamment grande pour la plupart des applications. Cependant, des fichiers contenant des images dans une résolution supérieure pour la plupart d'entre elles sont disponibles et peuvent être commandés auprès des éditions The Pepin Press/Agile Rabbit.

Si vous êtes l'acquéreur de ce livre, les images du CD vous sont exploitables gratuitement dans la plupart des applications, y compris tout usage privé et non commercial, tout usage dans la conception de sites Web et usage commercial à petite échelle (des brochures imprimées à moins de 5 000 exemplaires dans lesquelles figurent moins de cinq images, par exemple). Tout usage commercial à grande échelle, particulièrement au sein d'autres publications, exige une autorisation spéciale. Toute redistribution sous quelque forme numérique que ce soit est interdite. En cas de doute, veuillez nous contacter. Notre politique d'autorisation d'auteur est très raisonnable et le montant des droits, le cas échéant, est généralement minime.

Pour en savoir plus sur les autorisations et les droits d'auteur, veuillez contacter :
mail@pepinpress.com
Fax +31 20 4201152

Esto libro presenta una amplia selección de ideas para diseñar tarjetas y sobres, con el objetivo de que pueda servir de fuente de inspiración para aficionados y diseñadores de todos los niveles. Además, para cada diseño hay una plantilla, que puede utilizarse para personalizar la tarjeta o el sobre. Todos los diseños están incluidos como archivos PDF en el CD adjunto.

El programa con el que resulta más sencillo abrir e imprimir un archivo PDF es Acrobat Reader. De todos modos, si desea decorar un diseño antes de imprimirlo, puede importarlo como imagen en otro documento mediante una aplicación de procesamiento de textos, por ejemplo. Una vez que haya colocado el diseño, podrá añadir texto, imágenes o dibujos a su gusto. Los diseñadores también pueden importar los archivos PDF como imágenes en avanzados programas de edición o abrirlos directamente en aplicaciones de edición vectorial, que permiten introducir las variaciones deseadas.

Los ornamentos y los dibujos que aparecen en las fotografías de este volumen (además de muchas otras) también están incluidos en el CD. Estas imágenes son una selección de las publicadas en diferentes libros de The Pepin Press. Para obtener más información, consulte nuestro sitio web en www.pepinpress.com.

Tamaños del papel y los sobres

La mayor parte de los diseños que forman parte de este libro aparecen en dos formatos en el CD, clasificados en dos carpetas distintas.

Las plantillas de la carpeta FI-A son tal y como aparecen en el libro. Están pensadas especialmente para diseñadores gráficos y usuarios de impresoras de gran formato. La mayoría puede imprimirse en papel tamaño A3 o tabloide o incluso en otros de mayores dimensiones. Los tamaños más grandes pueden imprimirse en copisterías.

Las plantillas de la carpeta FI-B están adaptadas para aquellos que solo tienen acceso a las impresoras convencionales. En este caso, se han dividido los diseños grandes en partes más pequeñas y se han colocado de tal manera que puedan imprimirse en papel estándar (A4 o carta). Además, se han incorporado lengüetas adhesivas para poder unir fácilmente las partes separadas. Consulte las páginas 14 y 15 para ver ejemplos de montaje de estas plantillas.

La mayor parte de tarjetas de esta colección están diseñadas para encajar en los sobres de tamaños internacionales estándar. Y algunas tarjetas tienen sobres con diseños a juego.

Evidentemente, todos los diseños pueden reducirse si deben caber en un papel más pequeño, pero hay que tener en cuenta que también se reducirá el tamaño final de la tarjeta o el sobre.

Cómo utilizar las plantillas de diseño

Estos diseños pueden utilizarse de mil y una maneras para crear tarjetas y sobres únicos.

Ejemplo 1

La forma más sencilla de personalizar un diseño es imprimirlo en papel de fantasía y montarlo. Si se utiliza esta técnica, es preferible imprimir en el reverso del papel (página 10). Después de recortarlo, ya solo hace falta plegarlo y pegarlo. En la fotografía de la página 11 puede apreciarse el resultado tras imprimir el diseño del sobre de la página 367 en un papel con una bella estampa japonesa.

Ejemplo 2

Si lo que le interesa es crear tarjetas más personalizadas, puede imprimir un diseño en un papel normal o para tarjetas y luego decorarlo a mano. Si utiliza papel para tarjetas u otros más gruesos, los pliegues quedarán más pulidos si marca los marca primero. Una forma sencilla de hacerlo es reseguir la línea de pliegue con la parte no afilada de un cuchillo de cocina, con la ayuda de una regla para mantener la línea recta. Aunque parezca extraño, la marca debe realizarse en la cara del papel que terminará en la parte exterior del pliegue. En las fotografías de la páginas 12 podrá ver cómo se hace. El papel empleado en este ejemplo es 220 g, un gramaje que funciona bien con los diseños de tarjetas incluidos en este volumen.

Y con el diseño impreso en las manos, podrá utilizar prácticamente cualquier cosa para decorar la tarjeta o el sobre: lápices, rotuladores, pintura, purpurina, adhesivos, etc. Las posibilidades son infinitas.

Ejemplo 3

Los elementos de decoración también pueden introducirse, total o parcialmente, desde el ordenador. Esta opción es especialmente recomendable si desea crear una serie de tarjetas o sobres. La mejor forma de trabajar con una plantilla de diseño desde el ordenador depende del programa que utilice. El ejemplo de la página 14 presenta distintas maneras de añadir decoraciones y texto a las plantillas de diseño.

Cuando haya terminado con el diseño, puede imprimirlo en el papel que prefiera. Si hay que montar el diseño (plantillas de la carpeta FI-B del CD), deberá unir las distintas partes con las lengüetas adhesivas, tal y como se indica en las páginas 14 y 15.

Derechos de las imágenes del CD

Las imágenes del libro están incluidas en el CD adjunto y pueden utilizarse como fuente de inspiración o como recurso gráfico. Los nombres de los archivos contenidos en el CD se corresponden con los números de página del libro. El CD se suministra de forma gratuita con el libro. Queda prohibida su venta por separado. Los archivos incluidos en los CD de Pepin Press/Agile Rabbit tienen una resolución suficiente para usarlas con la mayoría de aplicaciones. Sin embargo, si lo precisa, puede encargar archivos con mayor definición a The Pepin Press/Agile Rabbit Editions.

Si ha adquirido este libro, puede utilizar las imágenes del CD de forma gratuita para la mayoría de usos, como fines privados y no comerciales, el diseño de páginas web y aplicaciones comerciales de poca envergadura (por ejemplo, folletos con unas tiradas inferiores a las 5.000 copias en los que se utilizan menos de cinco imágenes). En cambio, hay que solicitar una autorización para su uso con fines comerciales de amplia difusión y, sobre todo, para su aparición en otras publicaciones. Queda totalmente prohibida la distribución digital en otros medios. En caso de duda, póngase en contacto con nosotros. Nuestra política de permisos es razonable y las tarifas aplicadas tienden a ser mínimas.

Para solicitar información sobre autorizaciones y tarifas, póngase en contacto con:
mail@pepinpress.com
Fax +31 20 4201152

Piegare con arte è una raccolta di idee per la creazione di biglietti e buste da utilizzare come fonte di ispirazione per hobbisti e disegnatori a tutti i livelli. Ogni disegno è accomopagnato da un modello che può essere utilizzato per personalizzare un biglietto o una busta. I disegni sono contenuti in formato PDF nel CD accluso.

Il programma più facile da utilizzare per aprire e stampare un file PDF è Acrobat Reader. Se desiderate decorare un disegno prima di stamparlo, potete importarlo come immagine all'interno di un altro documento utilizzando, ad esempio, un programma di elaborazione testi. Una volta realizzata tale operazione, potete aggiungere testo, immagini o motivi a vostro piacimento al disegno. Inoltre, i disegnatori possono importare i file PDF come immagini in programmi avanzati di impaginazione o aprire i file direttamente con programmi per la manipolazione del formato vettoriale, potendo così apportare delle modifiche personali.

Le decorazioni e i motivi delle fotografie contenute nel libro (e altri ancora) sono disponibili anche sul CD, perché possiate utilizzarli. Le immagini sono state scelte da una selezione di libri pubblicati da The Pepin Press. Per ulteriori informazioni, visitate il nostro sito web su www. pepinpress.com

Dimensioni delle buste e dei fogli

La maggior parte dei disegni contenuti nel libro appare in due formati sul CD. Le immagini sono state quindi disposte in due cartelle separate, a seconda del formato.

I modelli nella cartella FI-A sono esattamente così come appaiono nel libro. Sono l'ideale per disegnatori grafici e per chi ha accesso a stampanti per grandi formati. La maggior parte di tali modelli sono adatti al formato A3 o Tabloid. I fogli con formato maggiore possono essere stampati nella maggior parte delle copisterie.

I modelli nella cartella FI-B sono stati adattati per chi ha accesso solamente ad una stampante standard. A tale fine, i disegni di grandi dimensioni contenuti nel libro sono stati divisi in piccole parti e disposti in modo che sia possibile stamparli su un foglio standard (sia A4 che US Letter). Sono state aggiunte delle linguette per consentire una facile unione delle parti: consultate le pagine 14 e 15 per ottenere degli esempi di come unire tali modelli.

La maggior parte dei biglietti contenuti in questa raccolta è adatta ai formati internazionali delle buste. Alcuni biglietti sono stati creati con delle buste corrispondenti.

Ovviamente, è possibile ridurre le dimensioni dei disegni per adattarli a fogli più piccoli; in questo modo, però, anche le dimensioni del biglietto o della busta finali risulteranno ridotte.

Utilizzare i modelli

Esiste un'inifintà di modi in cui potete utilizzare i modelli contenuti nel libro per la creazione dei vostri propri biglietti e buste.

Esempio 1

Il modo migliore di personalizzare un disegno è stamparlo su un foglio a fantasia e montarlo. Quando si utilizza questa tecnica, è meglio stampare sul retro del foglio (pagina 10). Una volta ritagliato il disegno, è sufficiente piegarlo e incollarlo. La fotografia a pagina 11 mostra il risultato ottenuto dalla stampa del disegno per buste di pagina 367 su una carta con splendide decorazioni giapponesi.

Esempio 2

È possible creare altri biglietti personalizzati stampando un disegno su un foglio bianco o cartonato e decorandolo quindi a mano. Se utilizzate fogli cartonati o pesanti, facendo pressione sulla linea di piegatura formerete un "solco" che faciliterà la realizzazione delle pieghe. Un modo semplice per farlo consiste nel passare il lato non tagliente (il retro) di un coltello da cucina lungo la linea ideale della piega, utilizzando un righello per fare in modo che la linea risulti dritta. Potrebbe sembrare strano, ma la piegatura deve essere fatta sul lato del foglio che si troverà sul lato esterno della busta. Le fotografie a pagina 12 mostrano il modo in cui procedere. La carta utilizzata in questo esempio è da 220 g, grammatura ideale per i disegni contenuti nel libro.

Una volta stampati i disegni, è possibile utilizzare praticamente qualsiasi materiale per decorare il biglietto o la busta: matite, pennarelli, tempere, brillantini, adesivi... Le possibilità sono infinite.

Esempio 3

Inoltre, potete realizzare alcune o tutte le decorazioni sul computer. Questa opzione è molto utile per produrre una serie di biglietti o di buste. Il modo migliore di lavorare un modello sul computer dipende dal programma che utilizzate. L'esempio di pagina 14 mostra alcuni dei modi in cui è possibile aggiungere decorazioni e testo ai modelli.

Una volta completato il disegno, potete stamparlo sulla carta di vostra scelta. Se il disegno deve essere montato (modelli nella cartella FI-B del CD), le varie parti devono essere incollate utilizzando le apposite linguette, come mostrato a pagina 14 e 15.

CD e diritti di immagine

Le immagini contenute in questo libro sono salvate
sul CD accluso e possono essere utilizzate come fonte di ispirazione o risorsa grafica. I nomi dei file sul
CD corrispondono ai numeri di pagina indicati nel
libro. Il CD viene fornito gratuitamente con il libro
e non è vendibile separatamente. I file sui CD della
Pepin Press/Agile Rabbit sono di dimensione adatta per la maggior parte delle applicazioni. In ogni
caso, per la maggior parte delle immagini sono disponibili file più grandi che possono essere ordinati
alla Pepin Press/Agile Rabbit Editions.

Se avete comprato questo libro, potrete utilizzare le immagini sul CD senza costi aggiuntivi per la
maggior parte delle applicazioni possibili, compresi
tutti gli usi privati e a fini non commerciali, l'uso nel
design di pagine web e a fini commerciali su piccola
scala (ad esempio, opuscoli con una tiratura inferio-
re alle 5.000 copie in cui vengono utilizzate meno di
5 immagini). Per gli usi commerciali su larga scala, e
specialmente per l'uso in altre pubblicazioni, è ne-
cessario ottenere un'autorizzazione. È proibita la di-
stribuzione digitale ulteriore, in qulasiasi forma. In
caso di dubbi, siete pregati di contattarci. La nostra
gestione delle autorizzazioni è estremamente ra-
gionevole e le tariffe addizionali applicate, qualora
ricorrano, sono minime.

Per ulteriori domande riguardo le autorizzazioni e
le tariffe, vi preghiamo di contattarci ai seguenti
recapiti:
mail@pepinpress.com
Fax +31 20 4201152

Faltideen präsentiert eine Zusammenstellung von Designvorlagen für Karten und Umschläge, die als Inspirationsquelle für Designer gedacht sind - vom Hobbybastler bis zum Profi. Zu jeder dieser Designideen gehören gebrauchsfertige Schablonen, mit der sich die einzelnen Entwürfe individuell gestalten lassen und die zusätzlich (als PDF-Datei) auf einer CD dem Buch beigelegt sind.

Am einfachsten lassen sich die PDF-Dateien mit Hilfe des Programms Acrobat Reader öffnen und ausdrucken. Wenn Sie eine Vorlage aber schon vor dem Ausdrucken mit einem Dekor versehen wollen, können Sie das Design auch als Bild in ein anderes Dokument importieren (z.B. mit Hilfe eines Textverarbeitungsprogramms), dort frei platzieren und mit zusätzlichem Text, Bildern oder Mustern versehen. Ebenso gut lassen sich die PDF-Dateien in professionelle Layoutprogramme exportieren bzw. direkt in einer vektorbasierten Software öffnen und zu neuen, individuellen Mustern editieren.

Die Ornamente und Muster, die auf den Fotos in diesem Buch abgebildet sind, befinden sich (zusammen mit vielen weiteren Designs) auch auf der beigelegten CD und können frei verwendet werden. Sie wurden aus verschiedenen Titeln zusammenge-

stellt, die alle bei The Pepin Press erschienen sind. Weitere Informationen finden Sie auf unserer Website www.pepinpress.com.

Papier- und Umschlaggrößen

Der Großteil der in diesem Buch vorgestellten Designvorlagen ist auf der CD in zwei Formaten abgespeichert, wobei die unterschiedlichen Formate in separaten Ordnern abgelegt wurden.

Die Schablonen im Ordner FI-A entsprechen in Größe und Form exakt den Vorlagen im Buch; sie eignen sich ideal für Grafikdesigner und alle anderen Anwender, die Zugang zu einem Großformatdrucker haben. Die meisten passen auf Papierbögen im DIN A3- oder Tabloid-Format, doch einige sind sogar noch etwas größer. Drucker für solche "Übergrößen" finden Sie in vielen Copy-Shops.

Die Schablonen im Ordner FI-B sind für die Nutzung mit Standarddruckern angepasst. Zu diesem Zweck wurden die größeren Schablonen aus diesem Buch in kleinere Abschnitte unterteilt und so arrangiert, dass sie sich auf Papier im herkömmlichen DIN A4- bzw. US Letter-Format ausdrucken lassen. Diese Designs sind mit zusätzlichen Kleberändern versehen, so dass die Einzelteile leicht zusammengefügt werden können. Auf den Seiten 14 und 15 finden Sie ein Beispiel für die Montage einer solchen Schablone.

Die meisten Karten in dieser Kollektion sind so entworfen, dass sie in international übliche Umschlaggrößen passen; bei anderen Karten wurde der Entwurf für den dazu passenden Umschlag gleich hinzugefügt.

Selbstverständlich lassen sich alle Designs auch verkleinern und auf kleinerem Papierformat ausdrukken, doch dadurch verringert sich natürlich auch die Größe des fertigen Karten- bzw. Umschlagentwurfs.

Nutzung der Designvorlagen

Mit Hilfe der Designs in diesem Buch können Sie problemlos Ihre ganz persönlichen Karten und Umschläge gestalten.

Beispiel 1

Am einfachsten lässt sich eine Designvorlage individuell gestalten, indem Sie sie z.B. auf Künstlerpapier drucken und zusammensetzen. In diesem Fall sollten Sie am besten die Rückseite des Papiers bedrucken (siehe Seite 10). Nach dem Ausschneiden des Designs müssen Sie es nur noch falten und zusammenkleben. Das Foto auf Seite 11 zeigt Ihnen, wie die Designvorlage des Umschlags von Seite 367

aussieht, nachdem sie auf Papier mit einem wunderbaren japanischen Motiv ausgedruckt wurde.

Beispiel 2

Karten lassen sich individuell gestalten, indem Sie die Designvorlage auf schlichtes weißes Papier oder Cardstock (Scrapbook-Karton) drucken und danach von Hand verzieren. Karton oder Papiere mit einem höheren Gewicht lassen sich leichter und sauberer falten, wenn sie zuvor gefalzt wurden. Zu diesem Zweck legen Sie am besten ein Lineal an die zu faltende Linie und ziehen dann mit dem stumpfen Rücken eines Küchenmessers diese Linie nach. Auch wenn dies im ersten Moment seltsam erscheint: Die Falzlinien müssen auf der Seite des Papiers oder Kartons gezogen werden, die später die Außenseite der Karte bildet. Die Fotos auf den Seite 12 zeigen Ihnen die einzelnen Arbeitsschritte. Das Papier, das in diesem Beispiel verwendet wurde, hat ein Gewicht von 220 g/m2 und ist damit perfekt für die Kartenentwürfe in diesem Buch geeignet.

Haben Sie Ihre Karten oder Ihre Umschläge einmal ausgedruckt, können Sie sie ganz nach Wunsch verzieren, mit Stiften, Markern, Farbe, Glitter, Aufklebern ... die Möglichkeiten sind endlos.

Beispiel 3

Natürlich können Sie die Designvorlagen auch komplett mit Hilfe Ihres Computers individuell gestalten. Diese Vorgehensweise eignet sich vor allem dann, wenn Sie ganze Sätze von Karten oder Umschlägen anfertigen wollen. Die Arbeit mit Designschablonen auf dem PC hängt natürlich von den Programmen ab, die Sie benutzen. Auf Seite 14 finden Sie einige Beispiele dafür, wie Designvorlagen mit Dekors und Text ergänzt und gestaltet werden können.

Nach der Fertigstellung können Sie Ihren Entwurf auf einem Papier Ihrer Wahl ausdrucken. Falls Ihr Design aus einzelnen Teilen besteht (z.B. aus den Schablonen im Ordner FI-B auf der beiliegenden CD) und zusammengesetzt werden muss, können Sie die Einzelteile an den Kleberändern miteinander verkleben - siehe dazu die Seiten 14 und 15.

CD und Bildrechte

Alle Abbildungen in diesem Buch sind auf der beigelegten CD gespeichert und können als Anregung oder Ausgangsmaterial für grafische Zwecke genutzt werden. Die Namen der Bilddateien auf der CD entsprechen den Seitenzahlen dieses Buchs. Die CD wird kostenlos mit dem Buch geliefert und ist nicht separat verkäuflich. Alle Bilddateien auf den CDs von The Pepin Press/Agile Rabbit sind so groß dimensioniert, dass sie für die meisten Applikationen ausreichen; zusätzlich können jedoch größere Dateien der meisten Bilder bei The Pepin Press/Agile Rabbit Editions bestellt werden.

Als Käufer dieses Buchs dürfen Sie die Bilder auf der CD kostenfrei für die meisten Applikationen nutzen; dies gilt u.a. für sämtliche private und nichtkommerzielle Anwendungen, zum Zweck des Webdesigns sowie für kommerzielle Zwecke in kleinem Rahmen (z.B. Broschüren mit einer Druckauflage von bis zu 4.999 Exemplaren bei Nutzung von maximal 4 Bildern). Für eine kommerzielle Nutzung im größeren Rahmen sowie bei der Veröffentlichung in anderen Publikationen muss unbedingt die vorherige Genehmigung von The Pepin Press/Agile Rabbit Editions eingeholt werden. Jede weitere Art der digitalen Verbreitung (in jedweder Form) ist untersagt. In Zweifelsfällen bitten wir Sie, uns zu kontaktieren: Im Normalfall erteilen wir solche Genehmigungen recht großzügig und erheben - wenn überhaupt - nur geringe Gebühren.

Für Fragen zu Genehmigungen und Gebühren wenden Sie sich bitte an:
mail@pepinpress.com
Fax +31 20 4201152

Simple Folds

簡単な折り
Pliages simples
Pliegues simples
Cartotecnica semplice
Einfache Faltideen

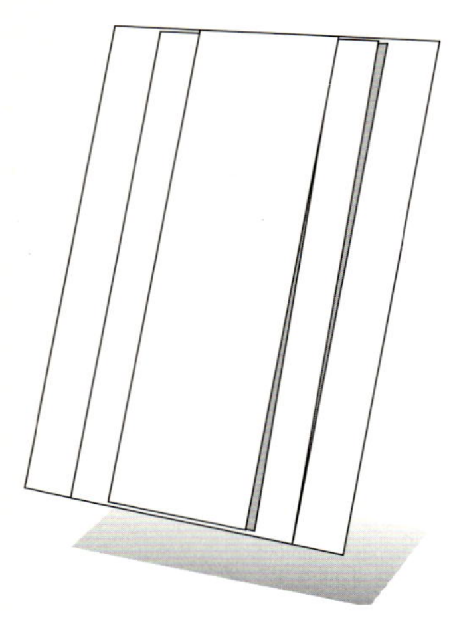

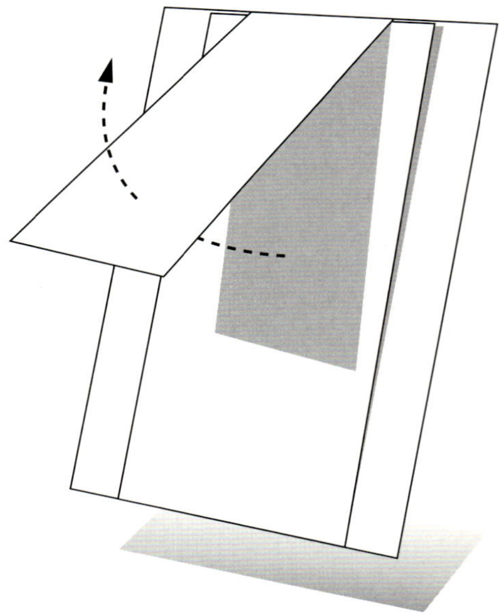

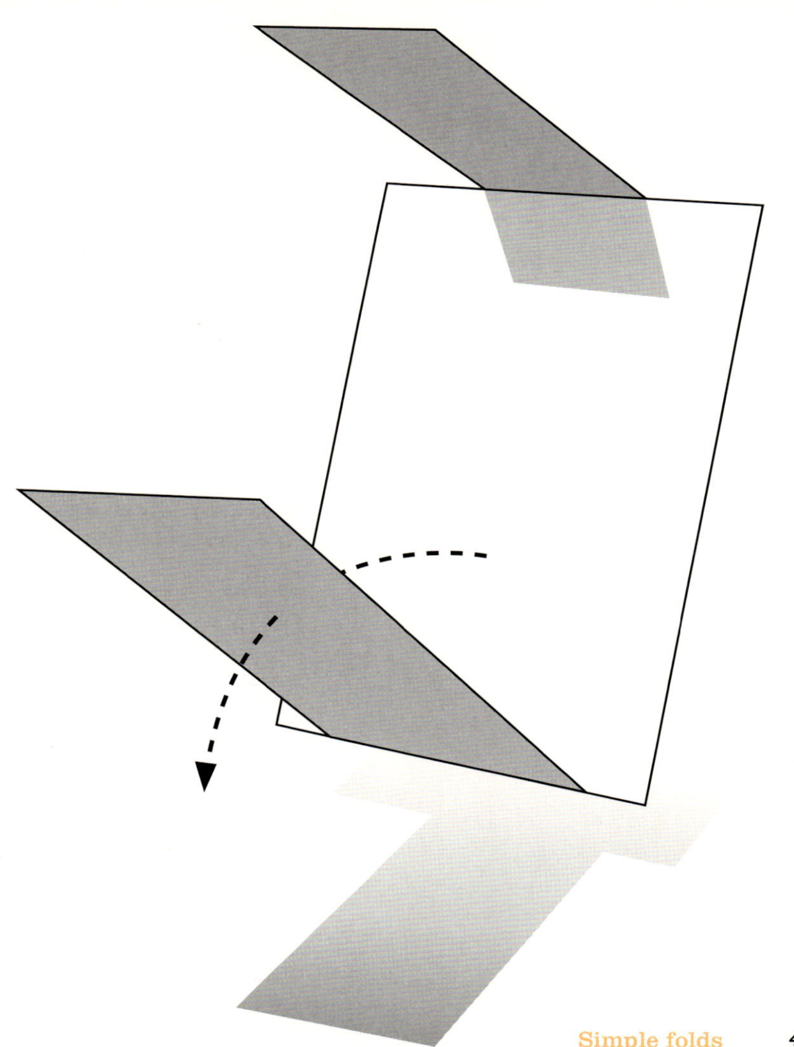

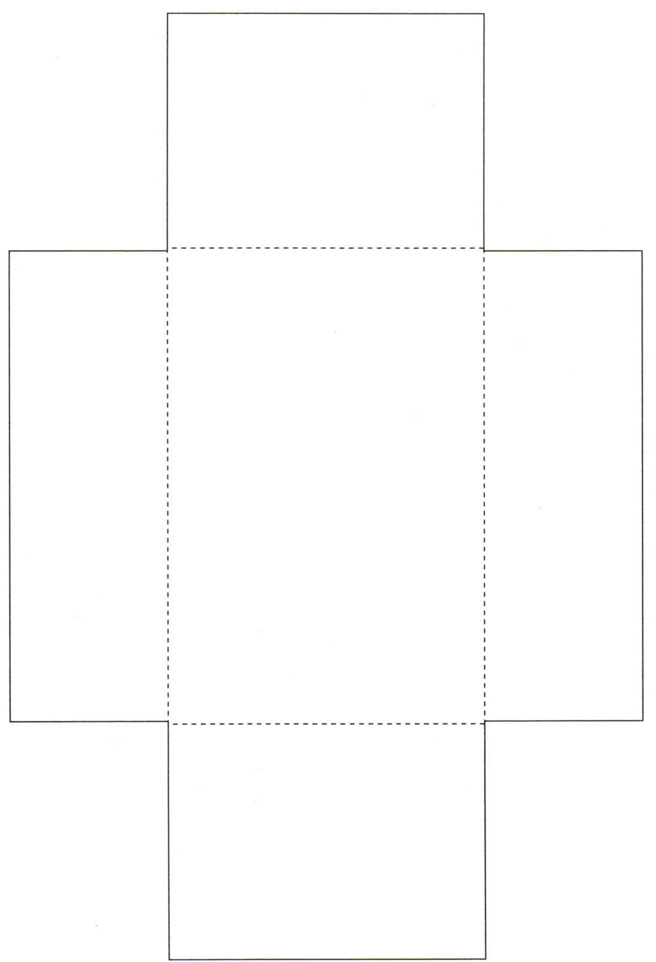

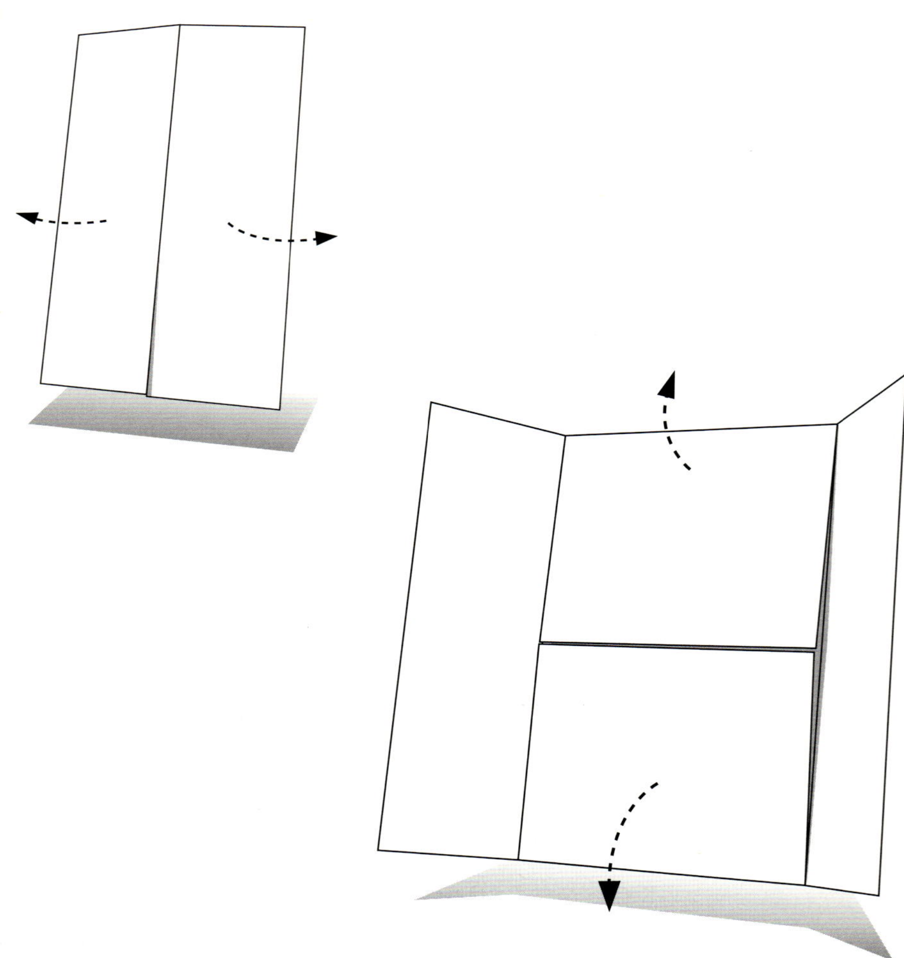

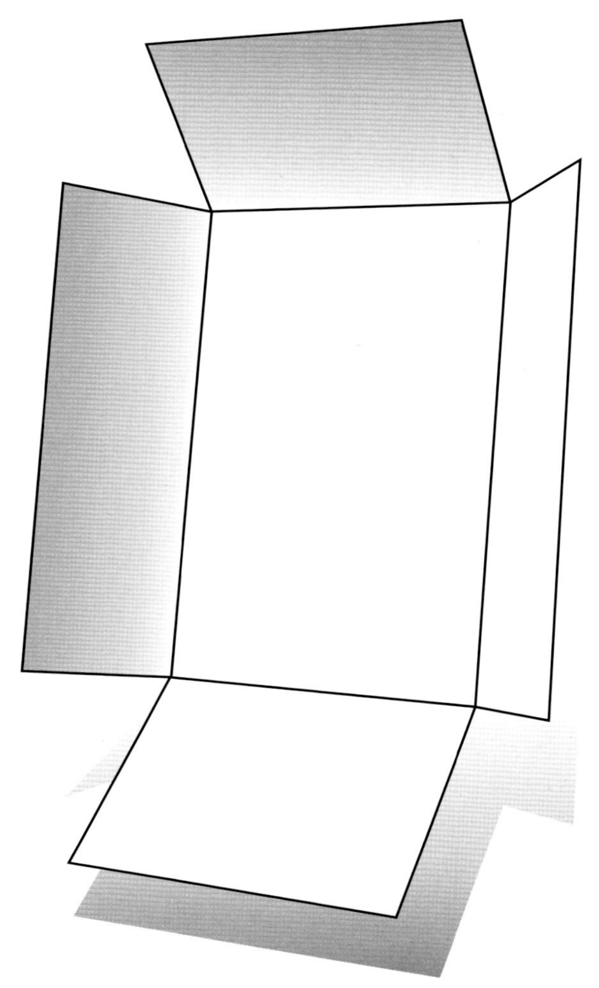

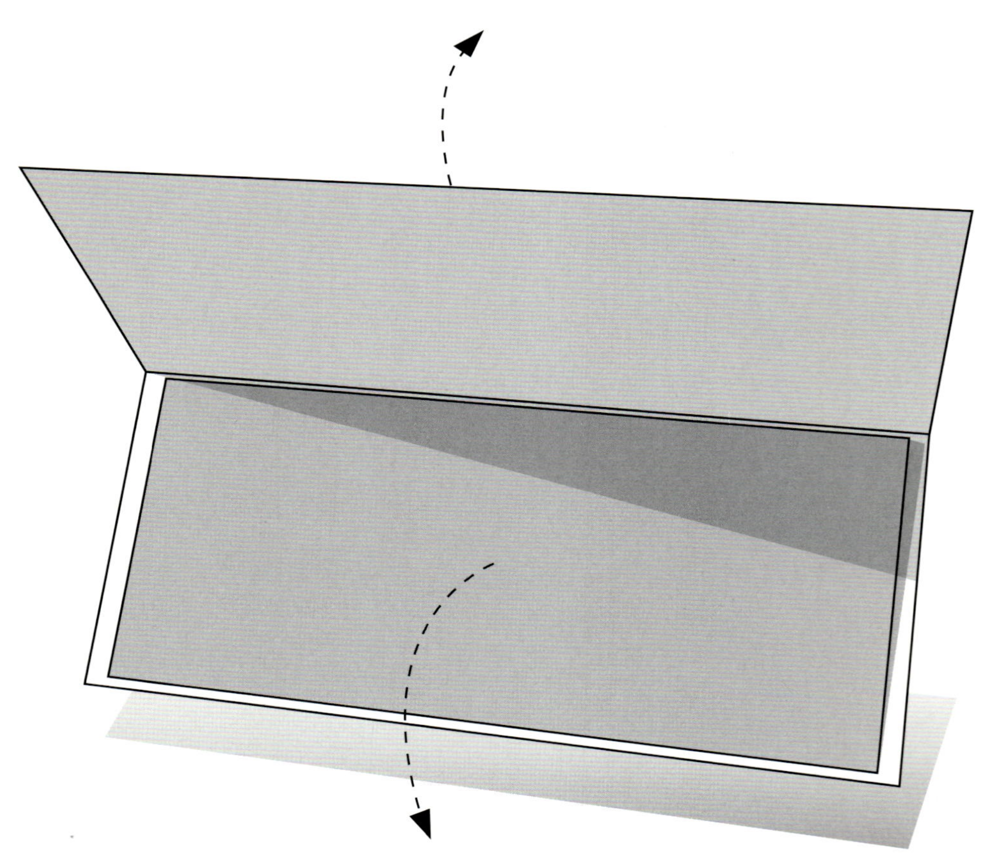

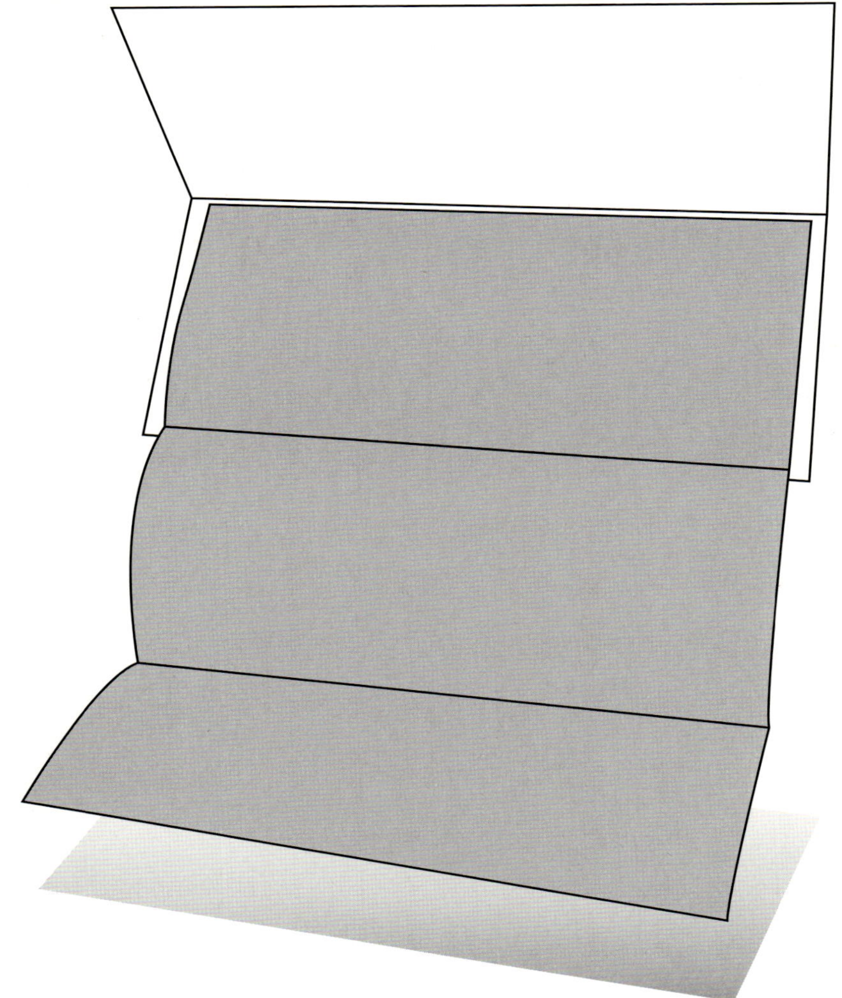

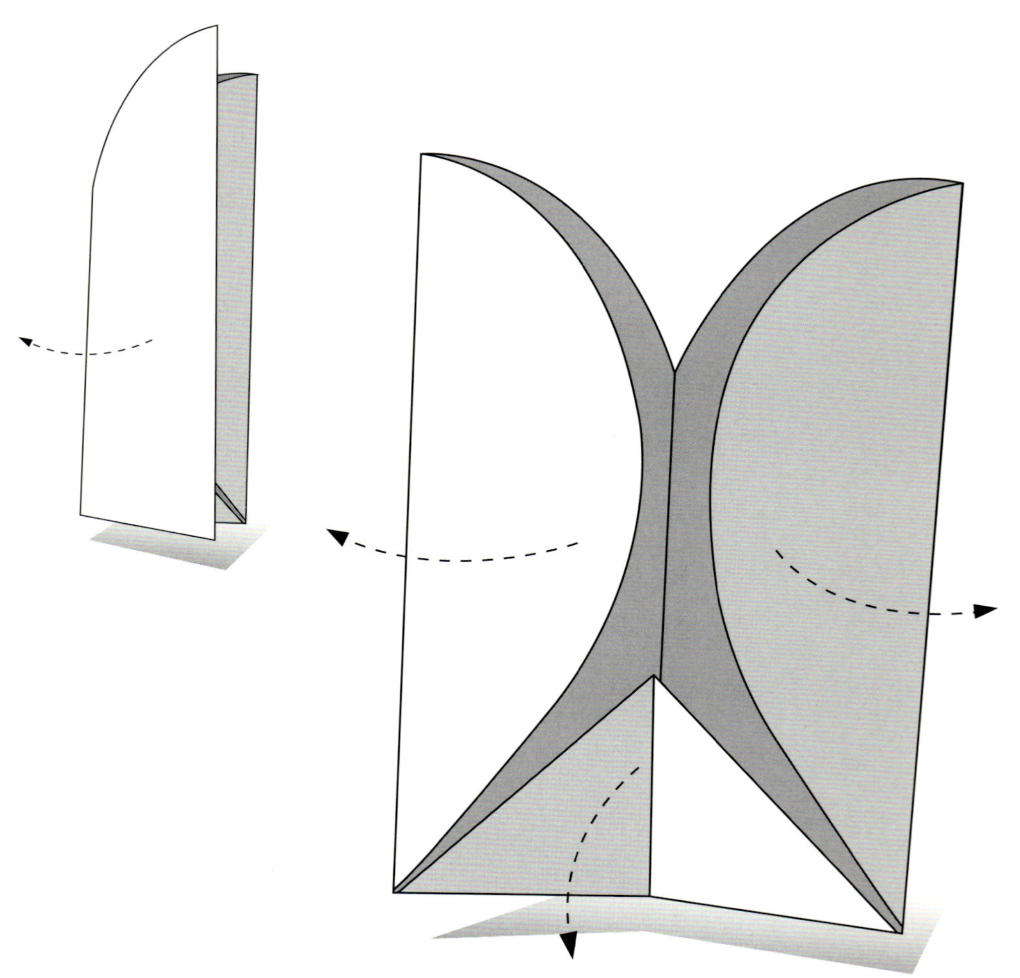

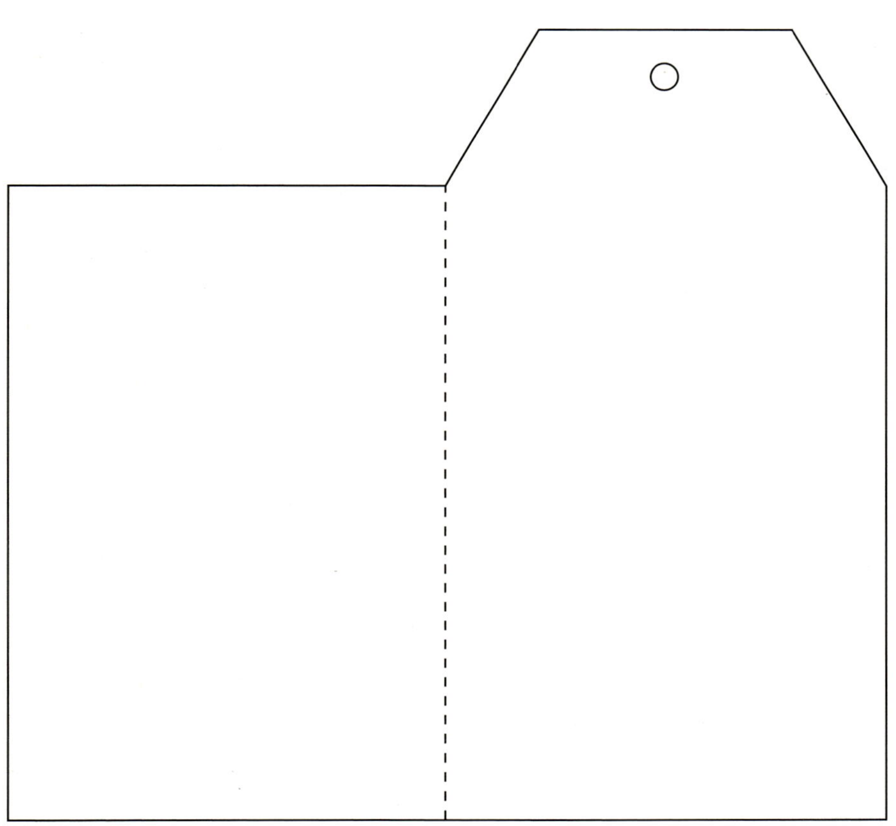

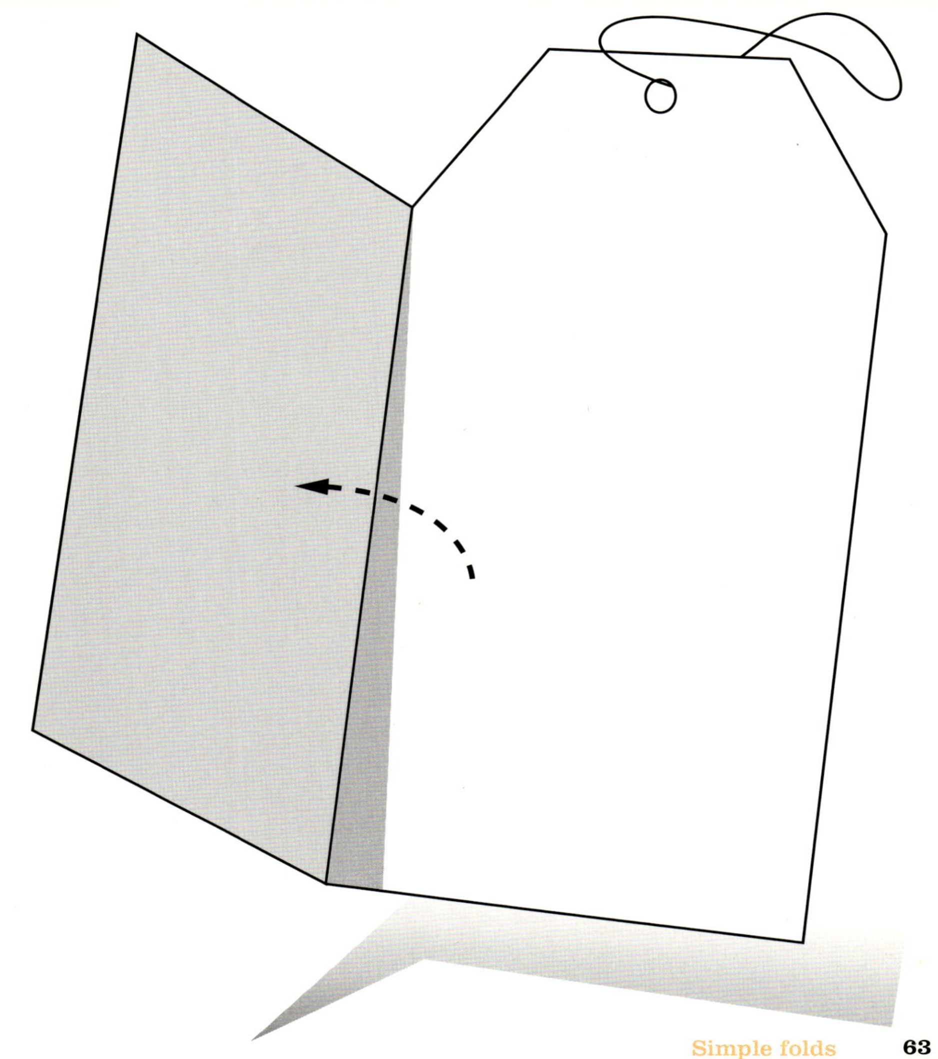

CLASSIFIED
Classified

It's a
Surprise Party!

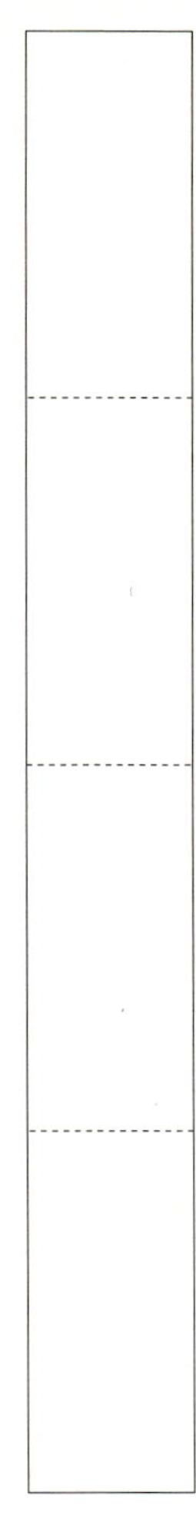

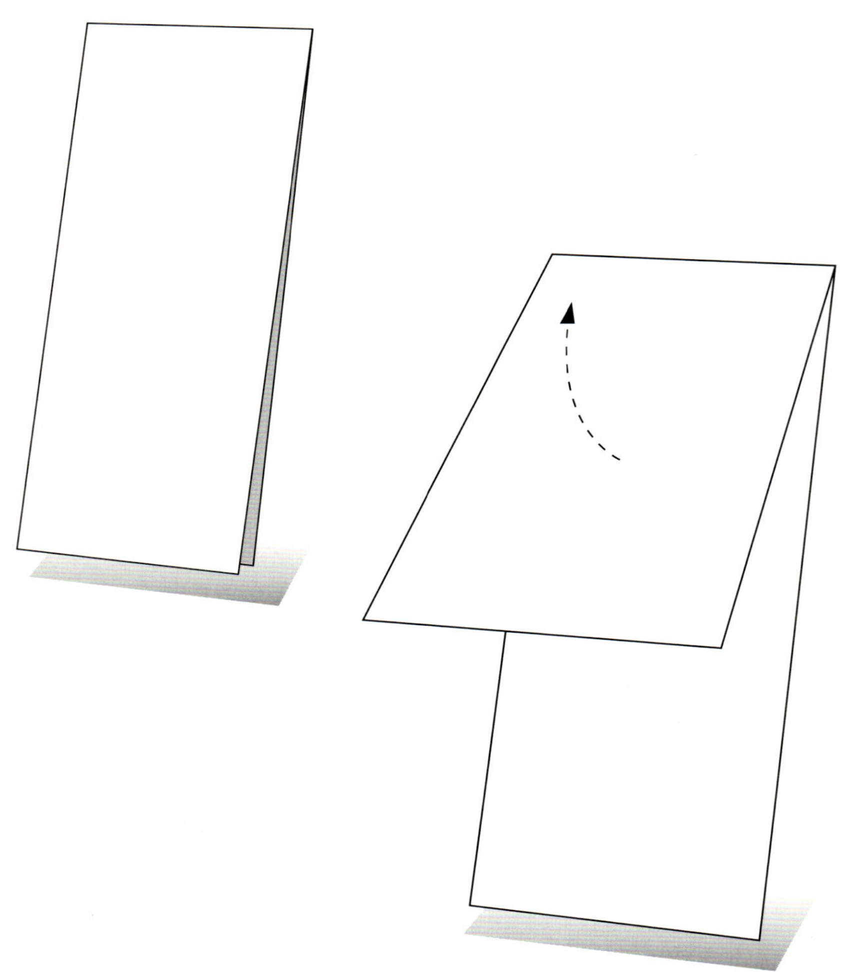

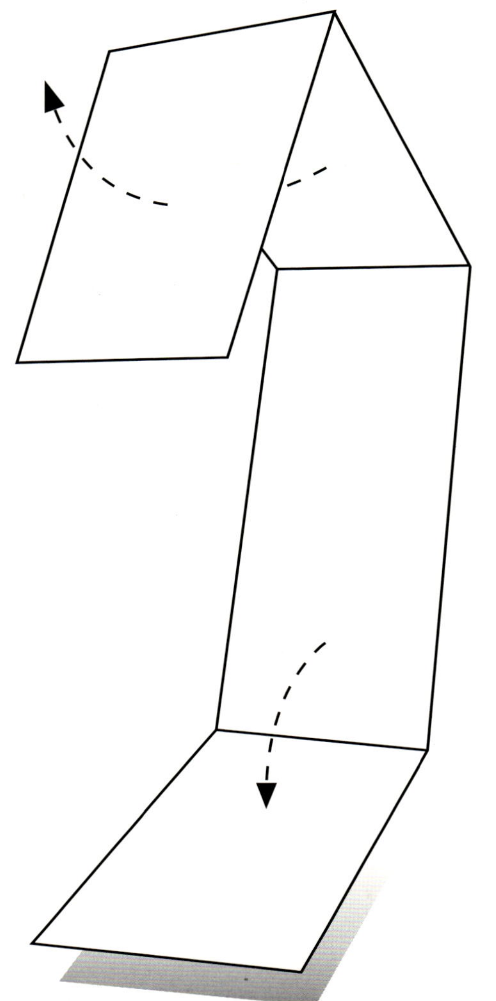

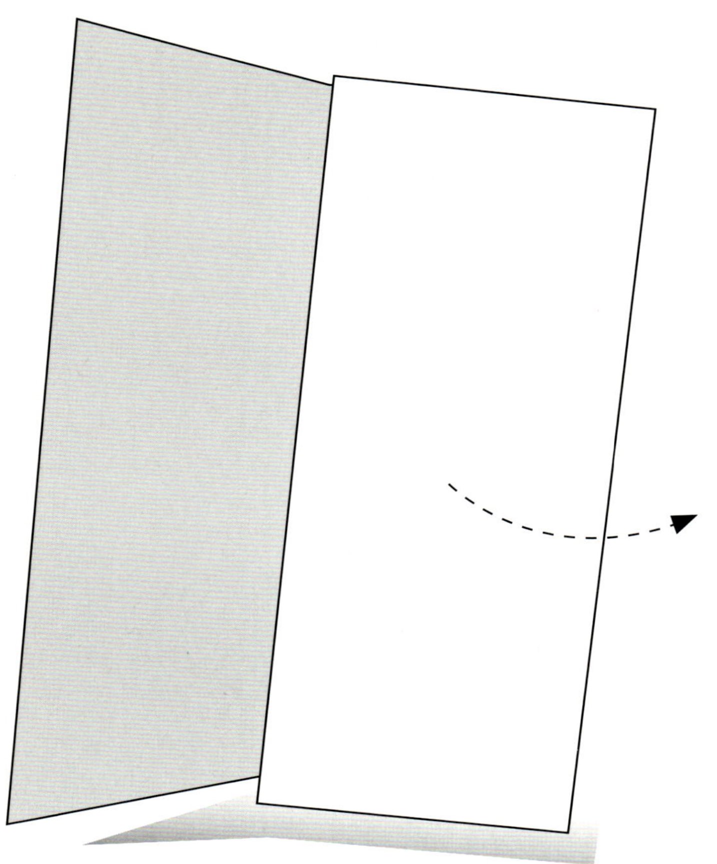

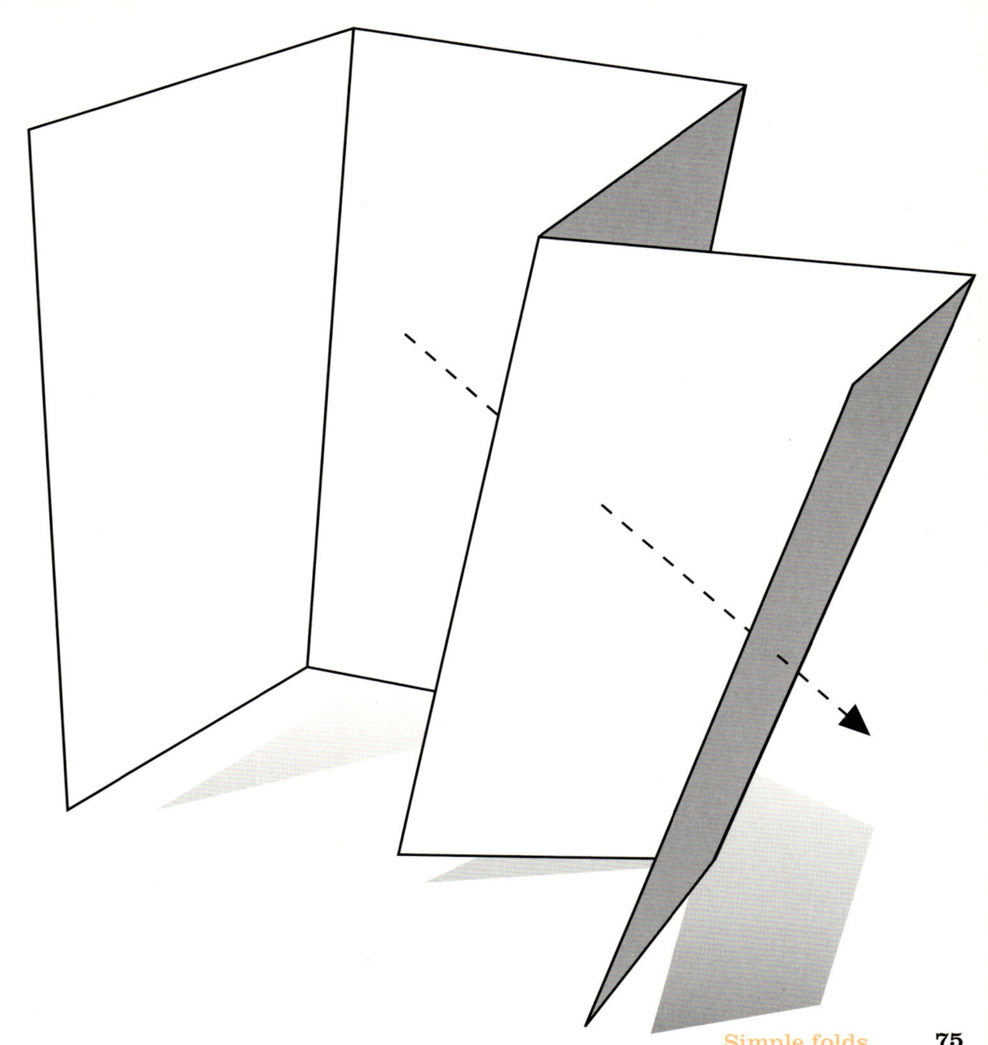

LOOK!

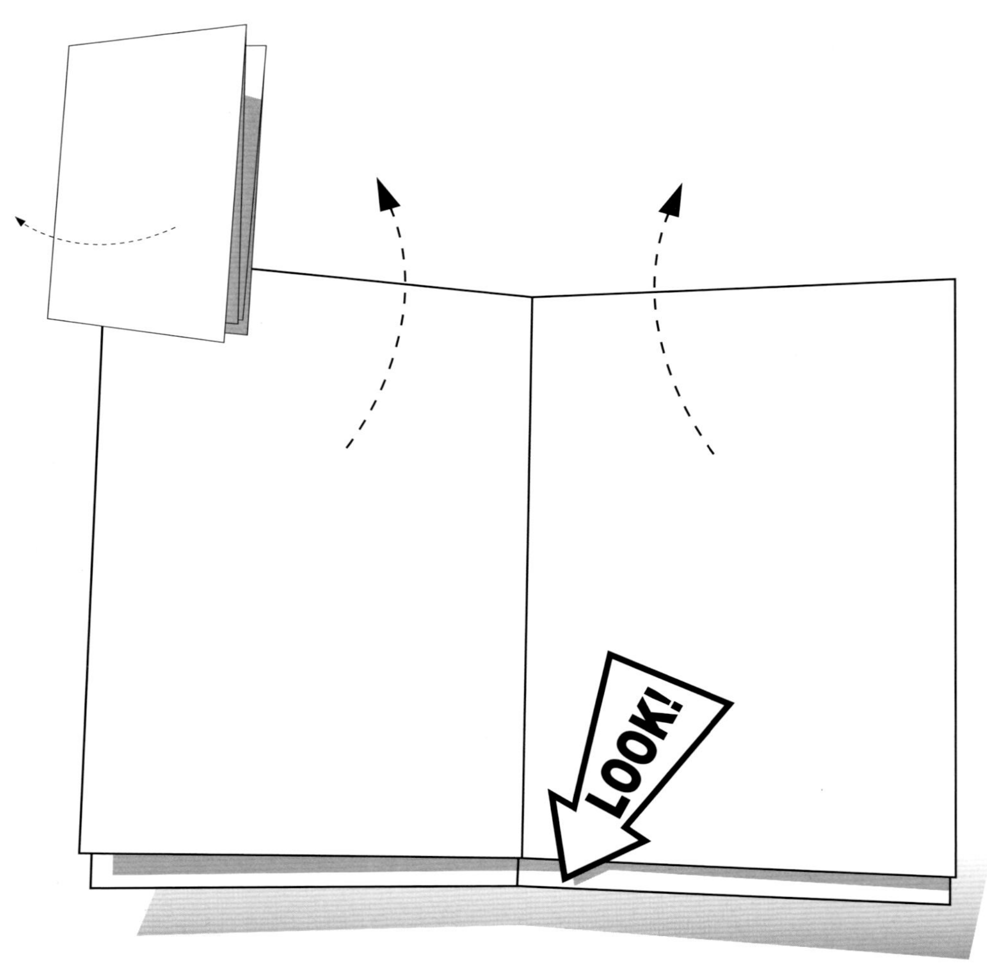

LOOK!

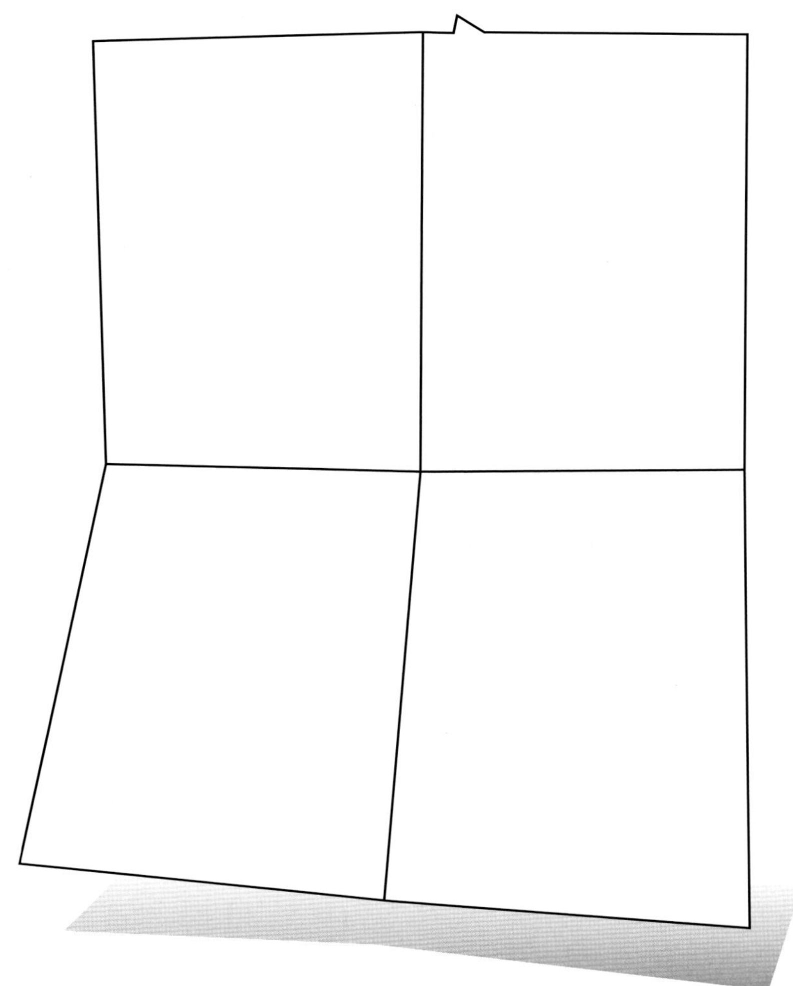

Cards

カード
Cartes
Cartas
Biglietti
Karten

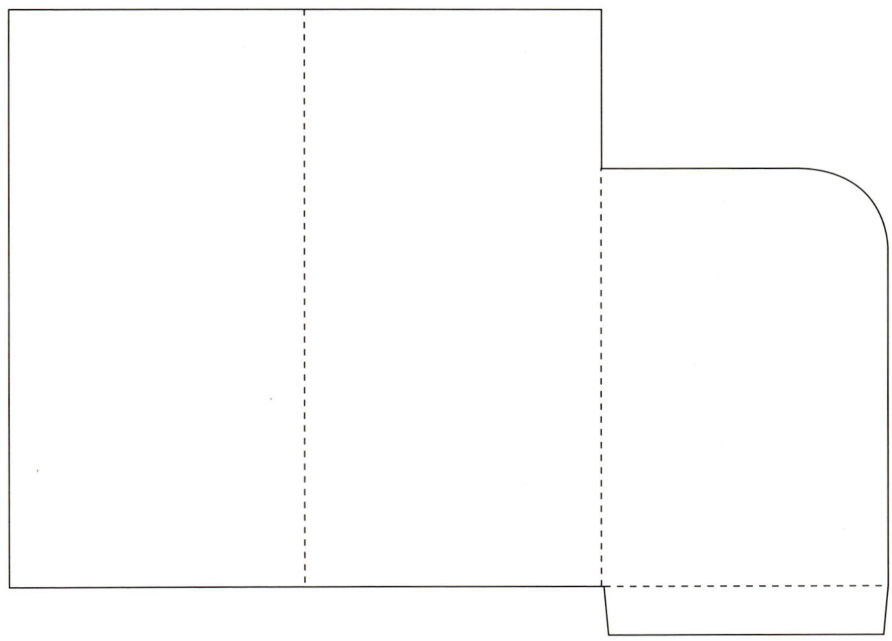

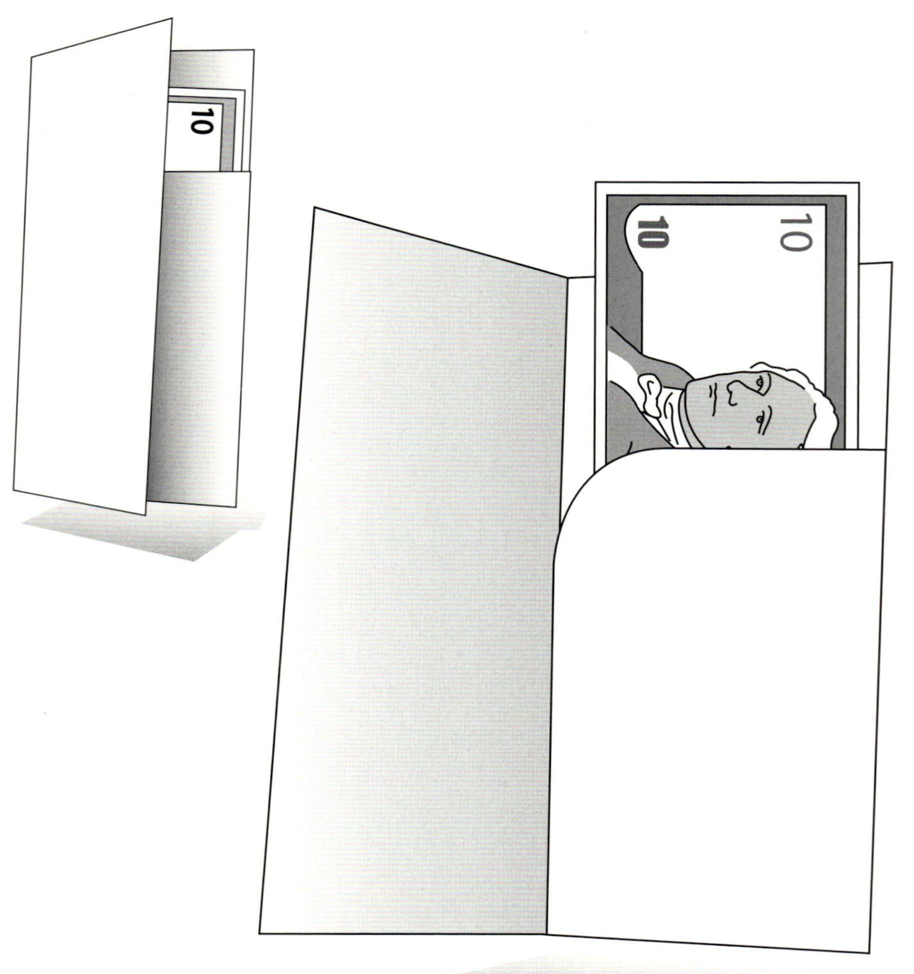

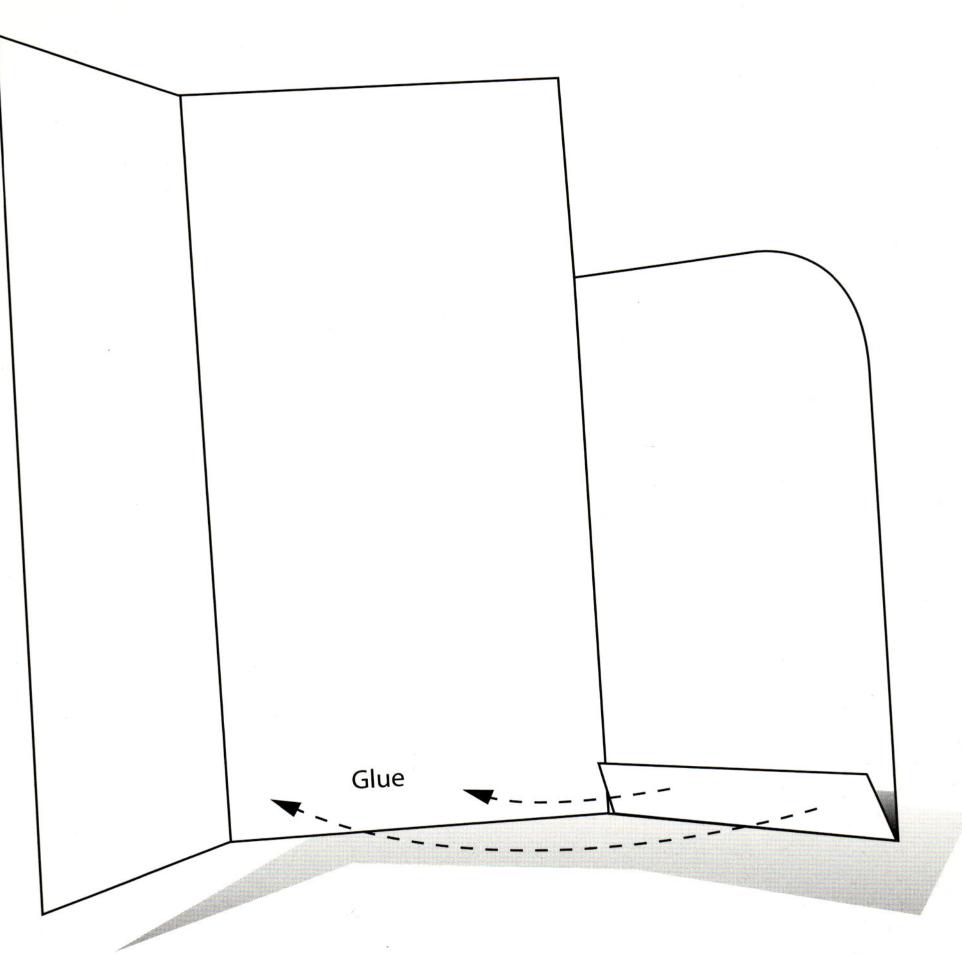

Glue

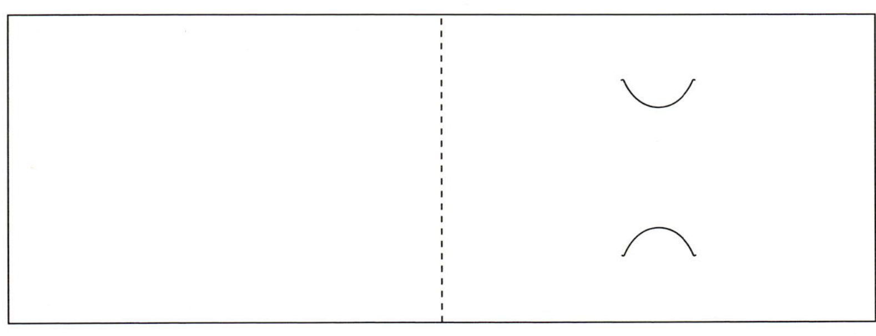

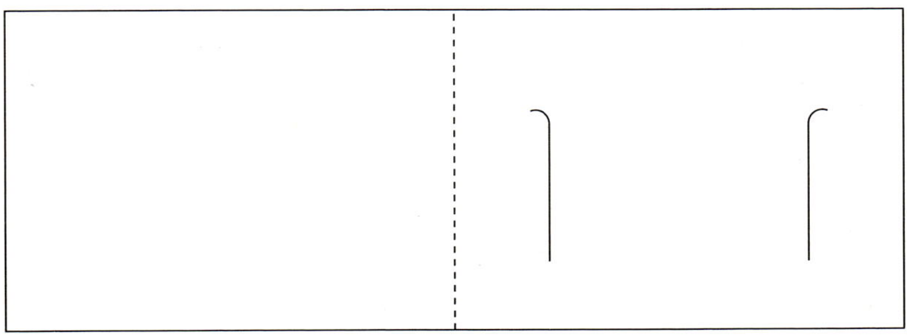

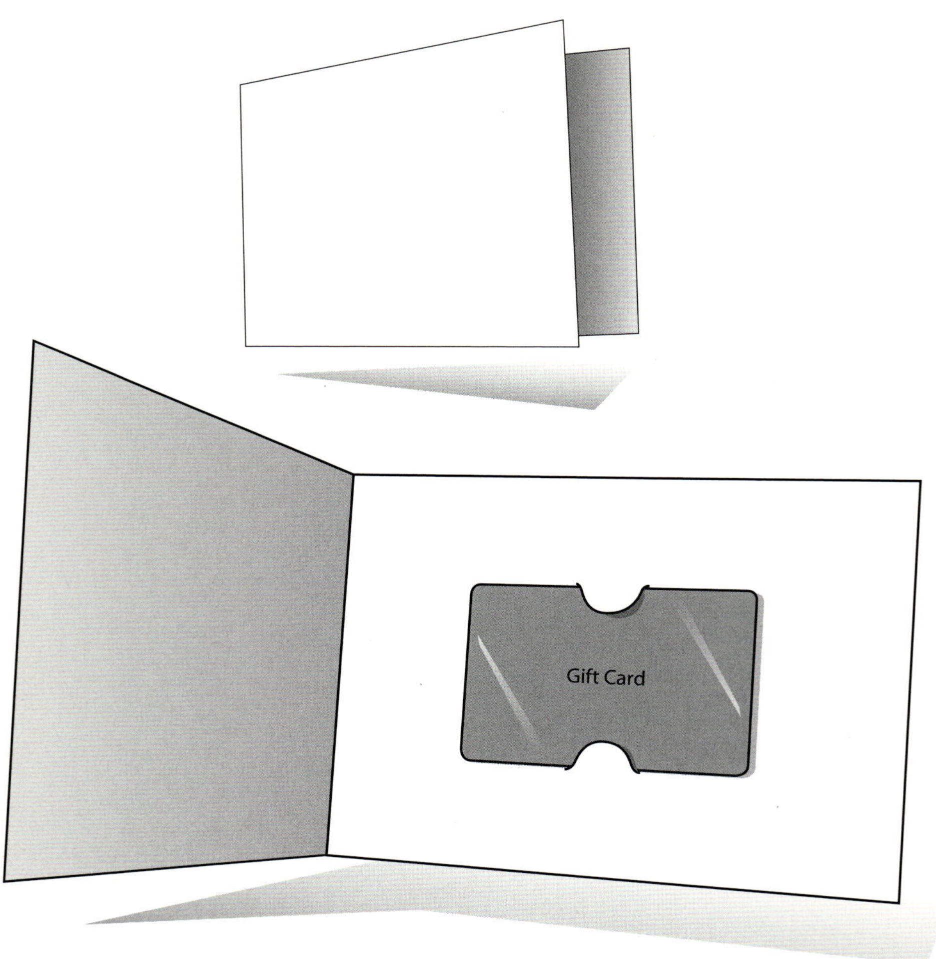
Gift Card

Gift Card

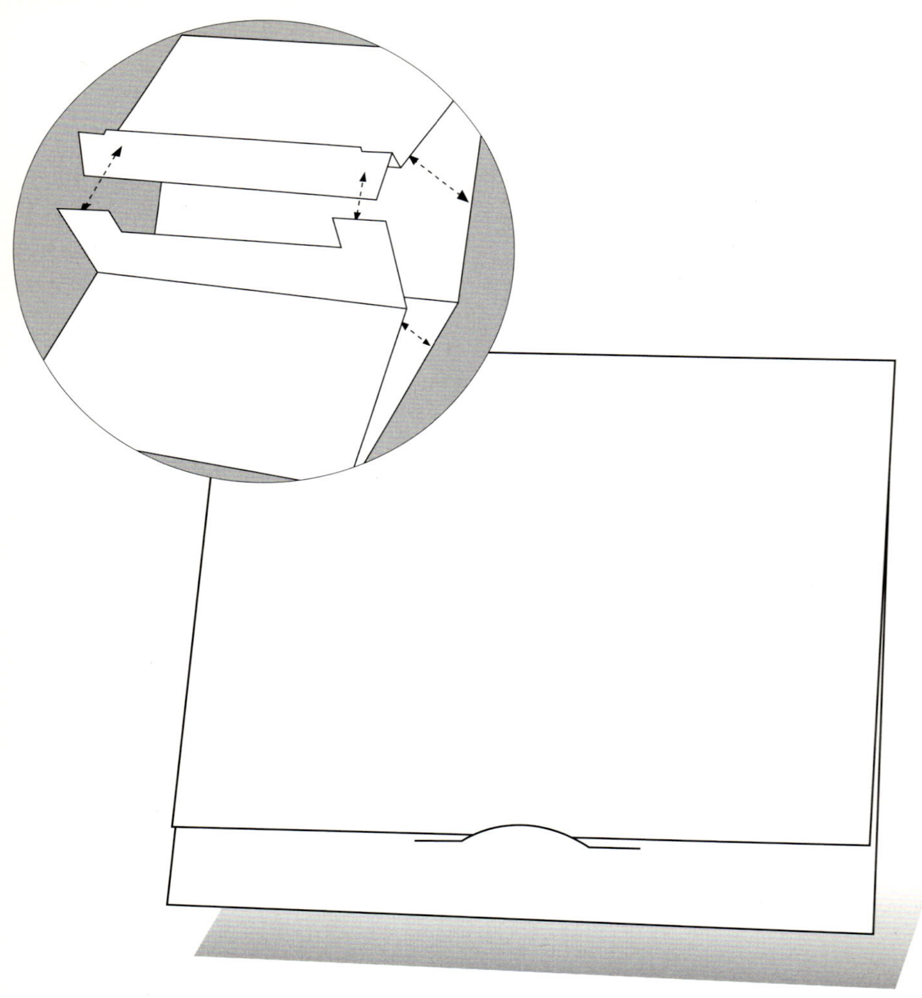

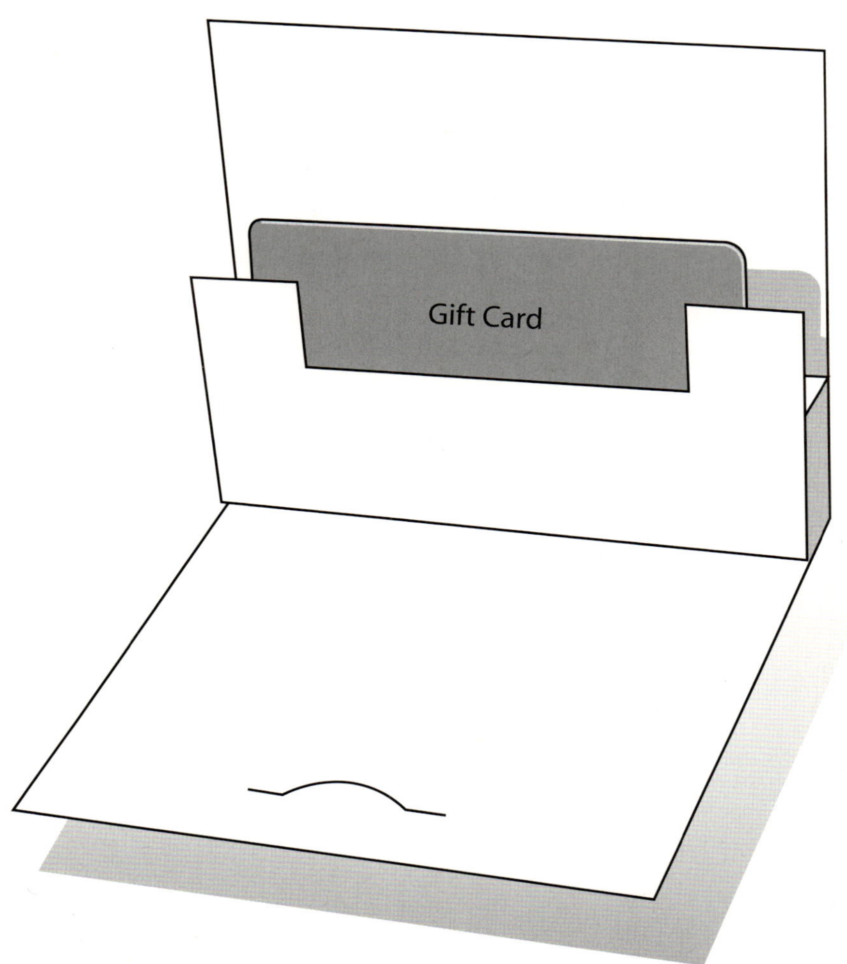

Gift Card

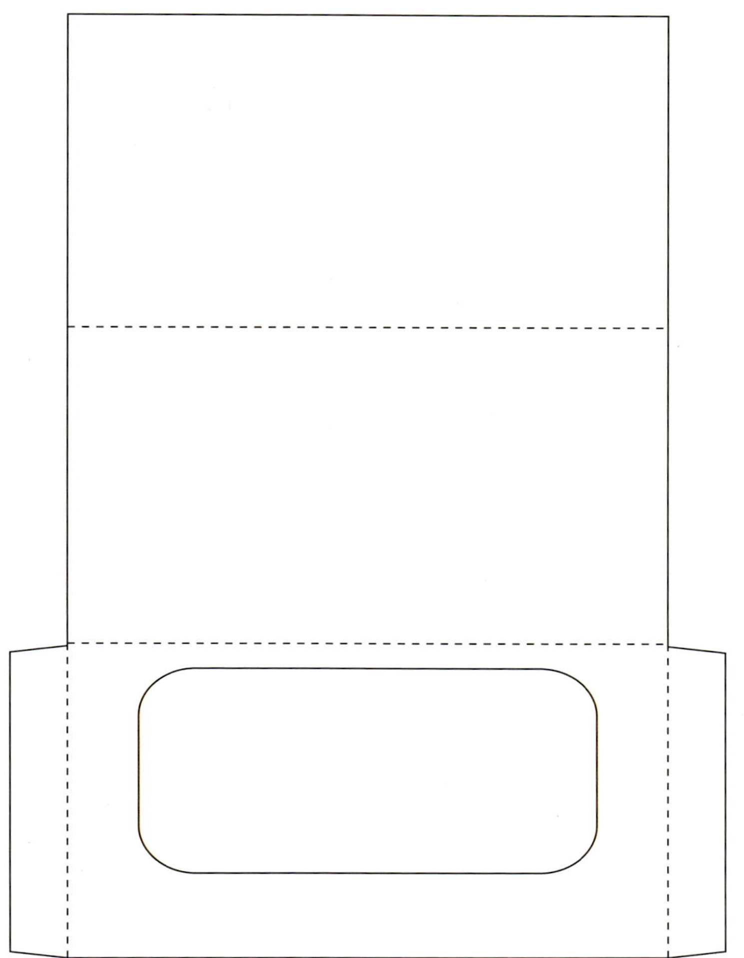

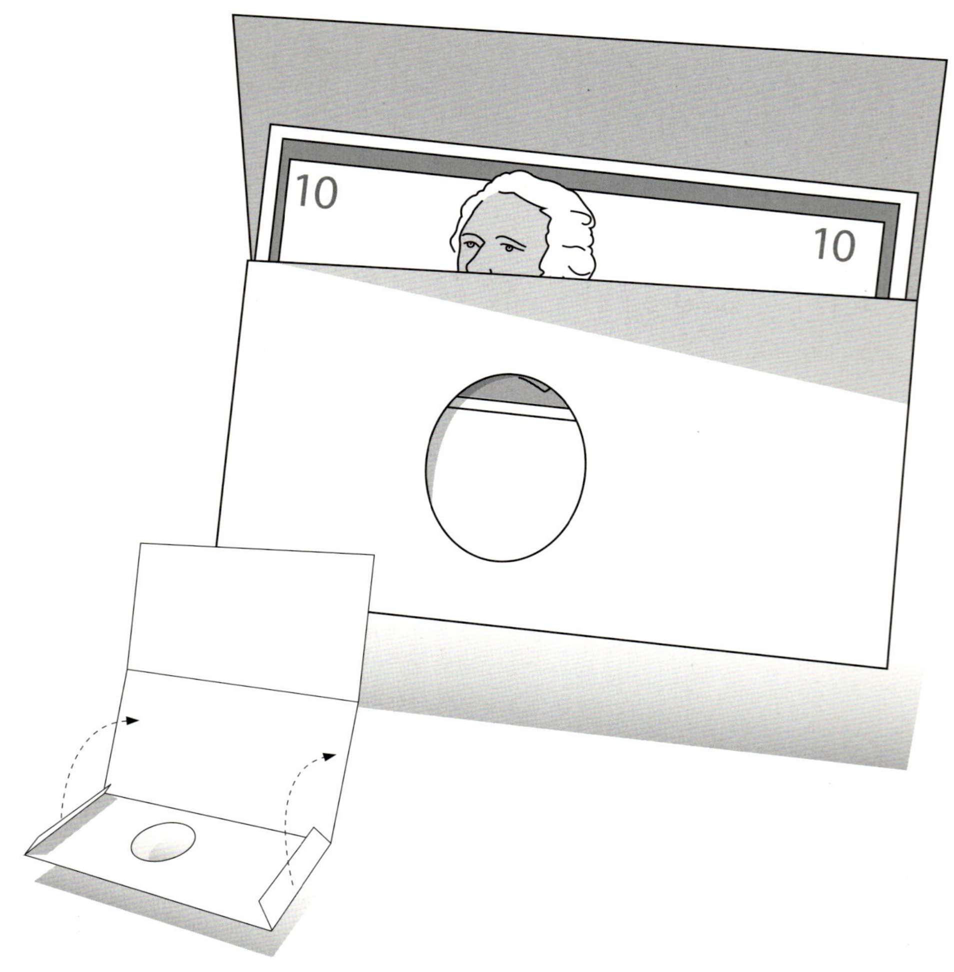

 Cards

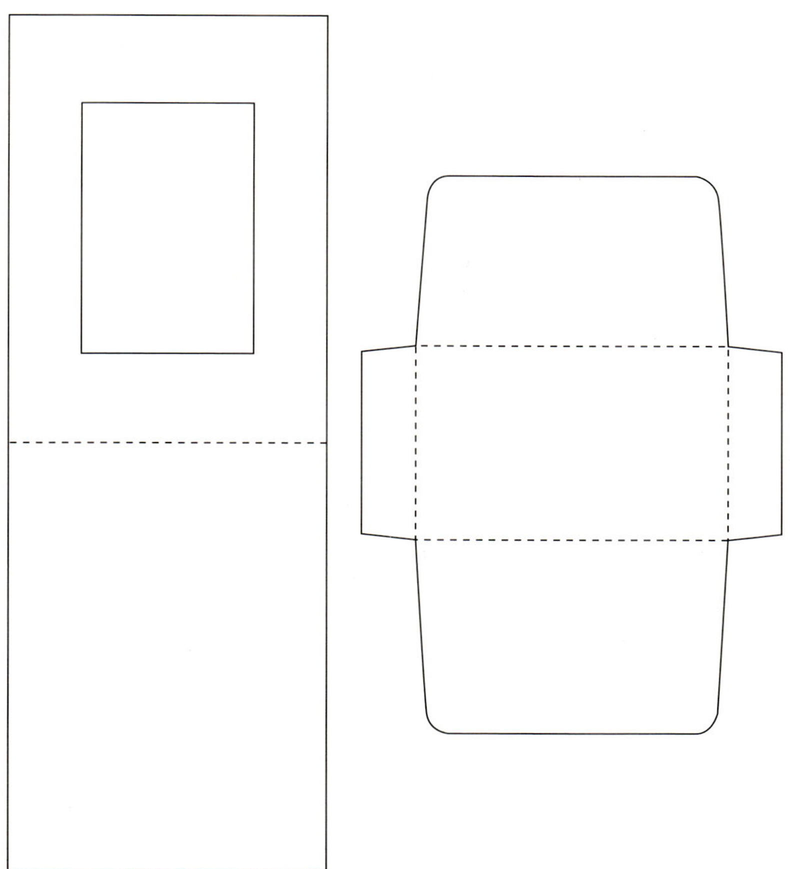

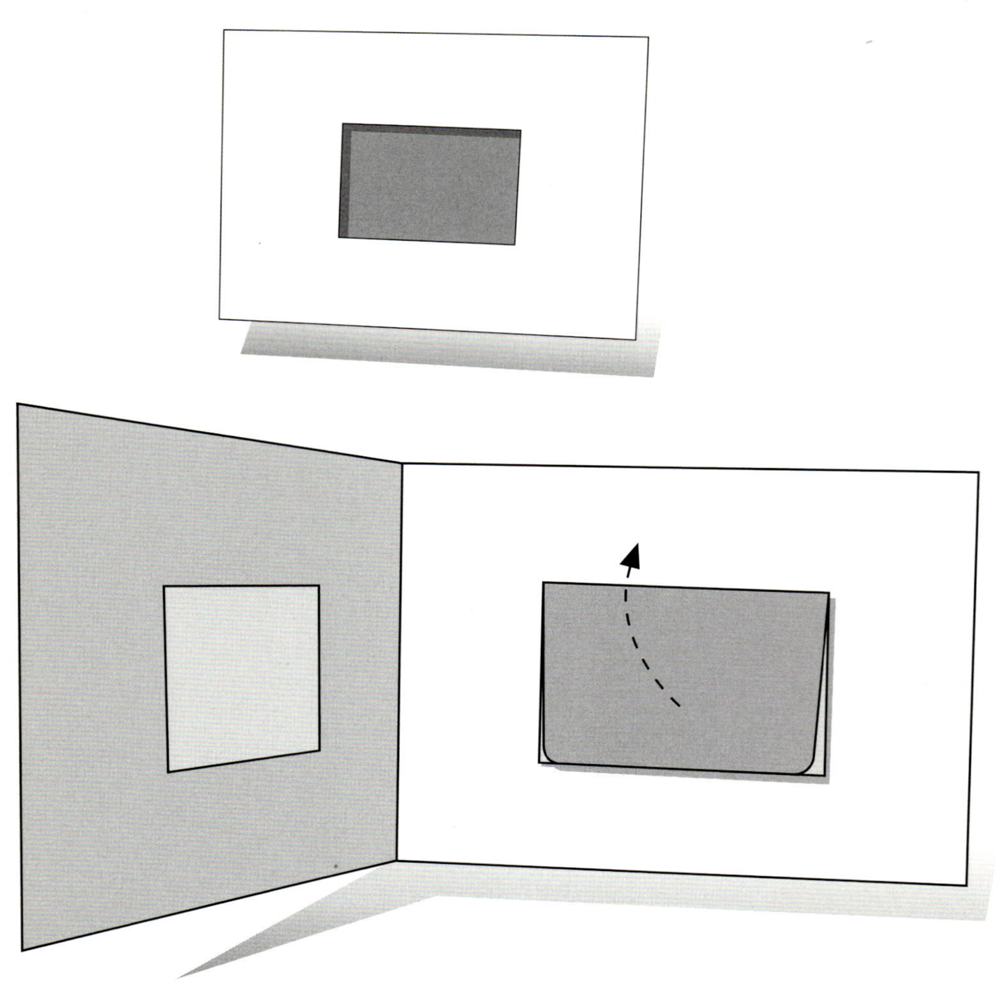

100 Cards

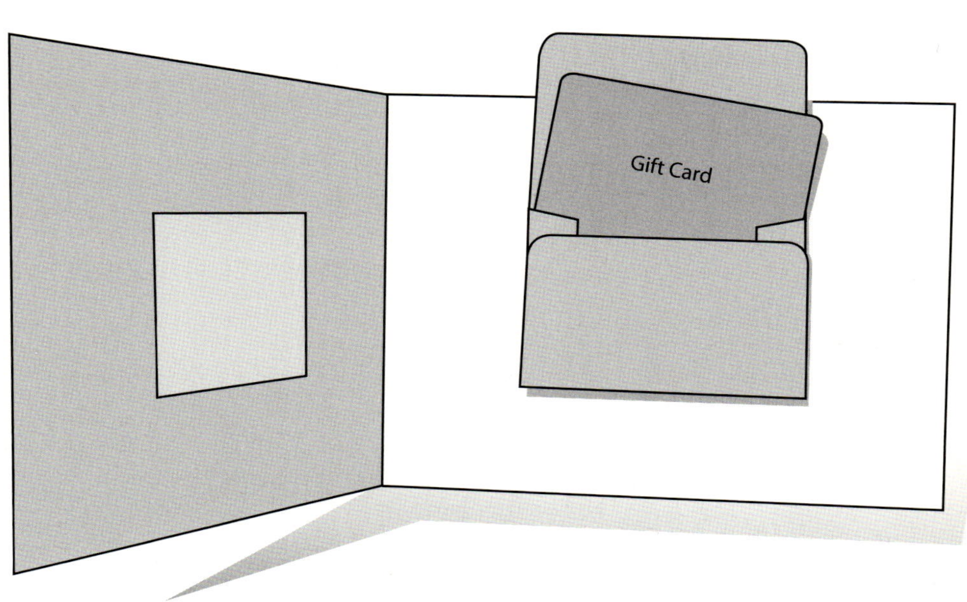
Gift Card

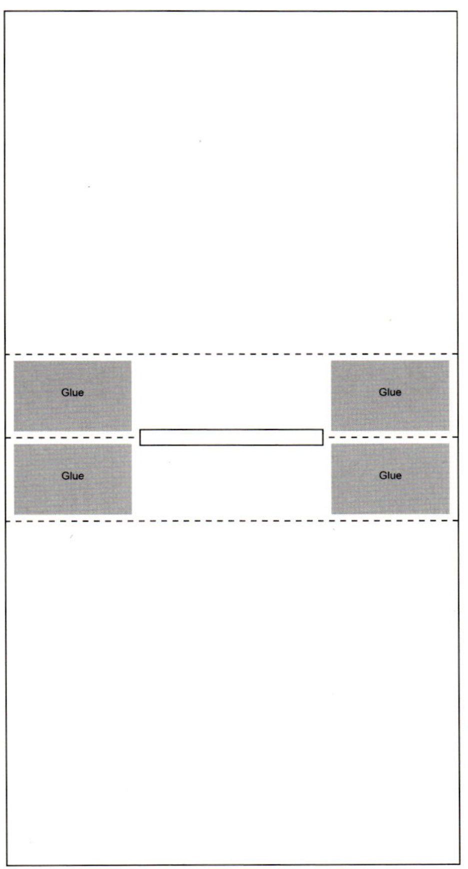
Glue
Glue
Glue
Glue

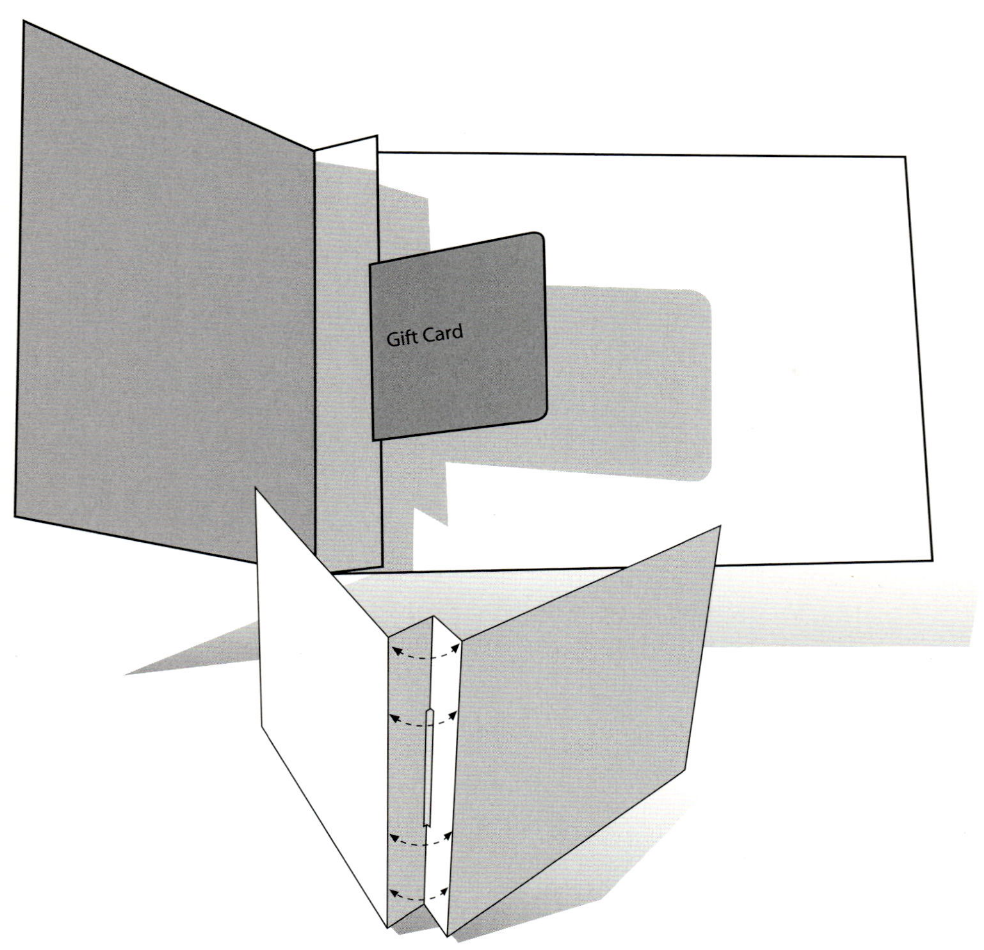

Gift Card

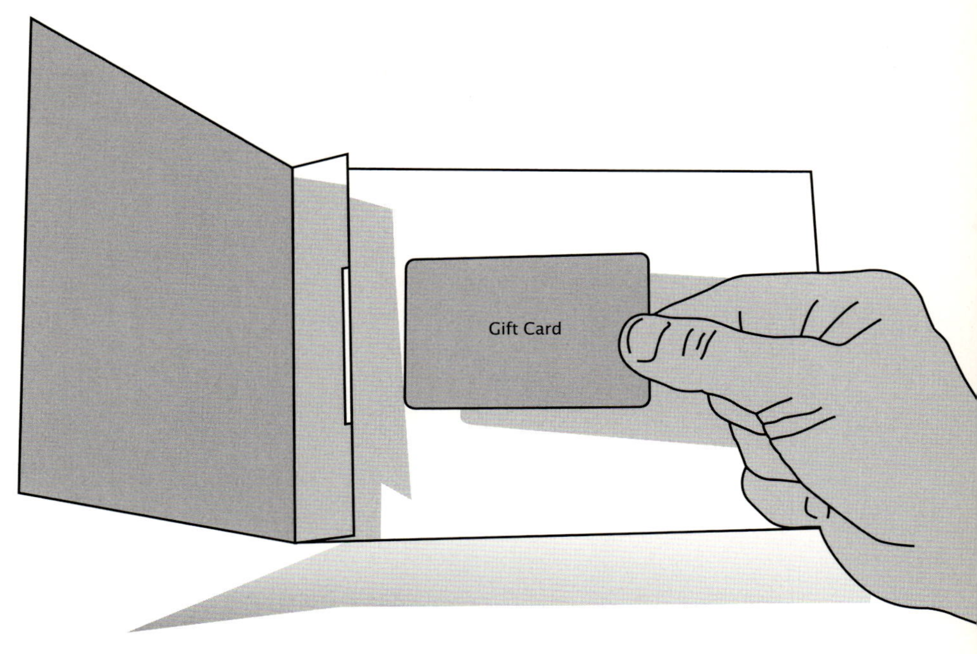

Gift Card

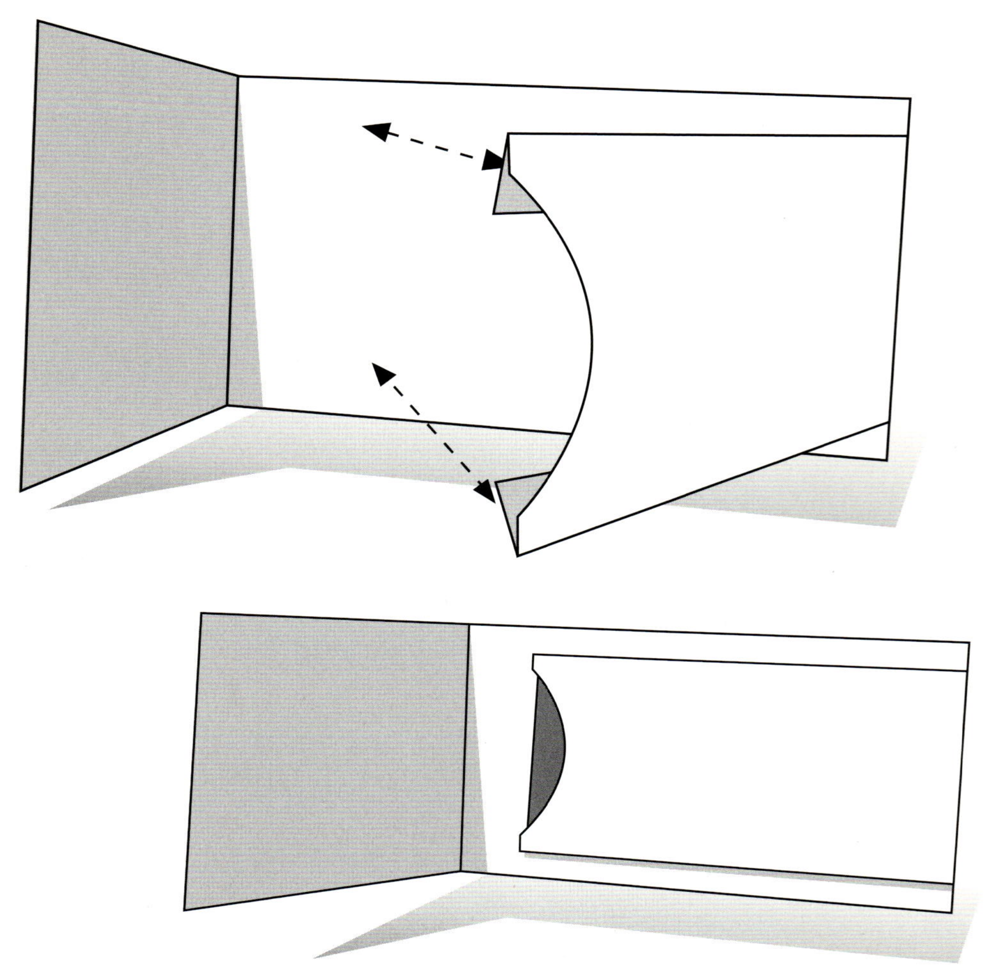

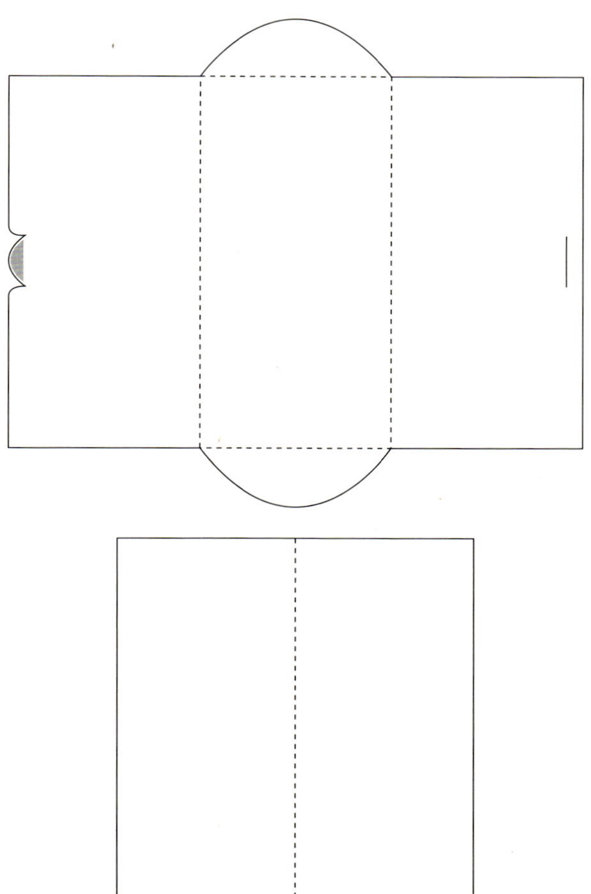

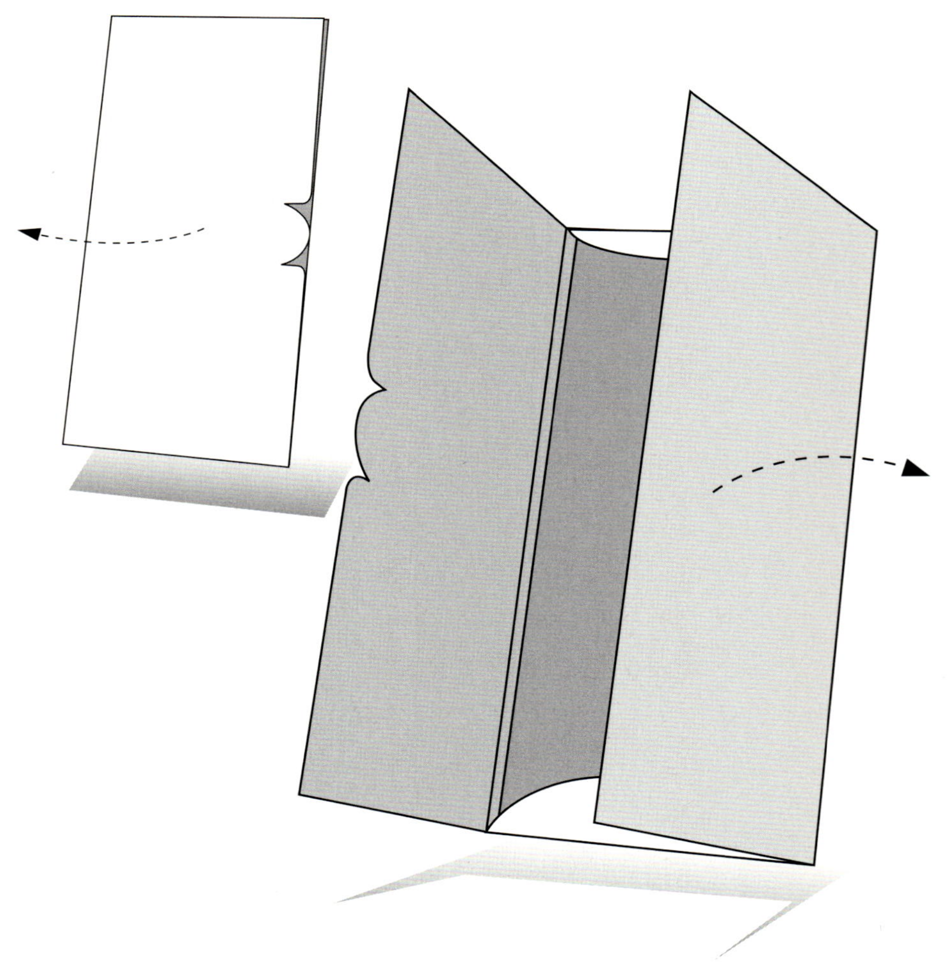

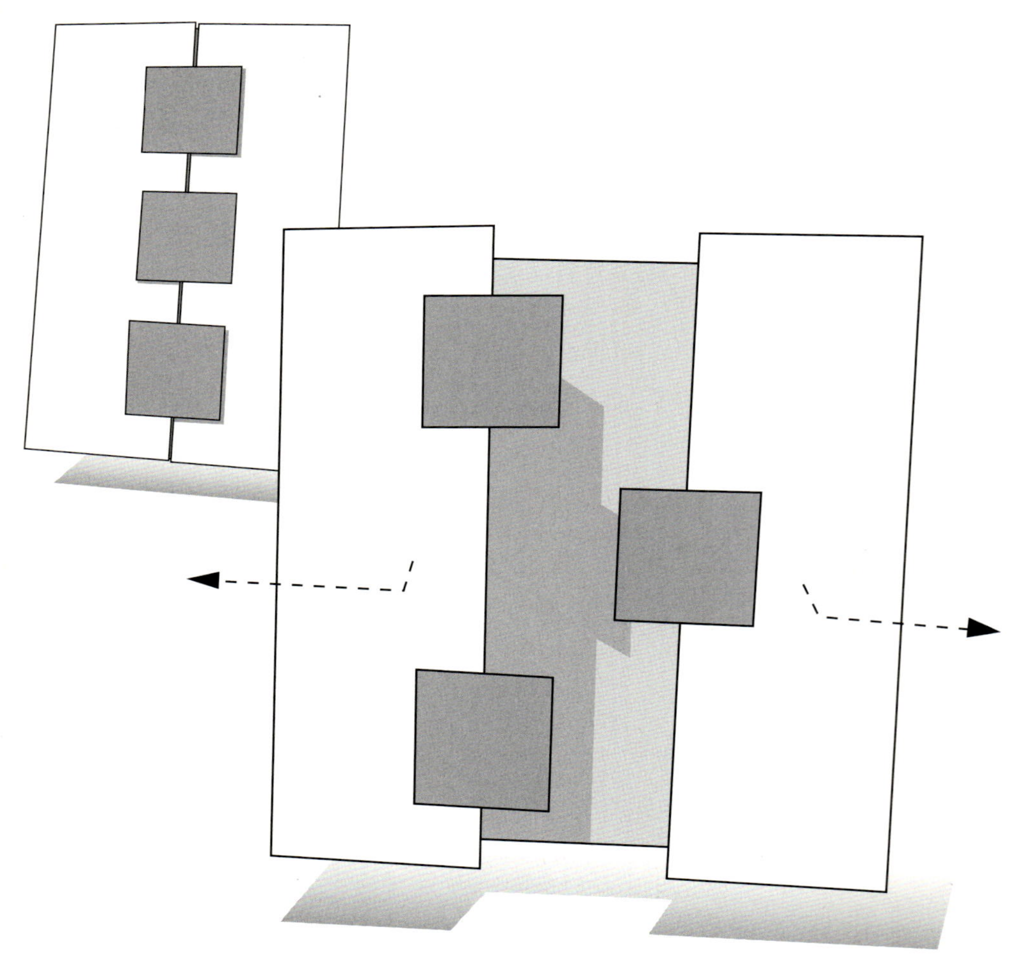

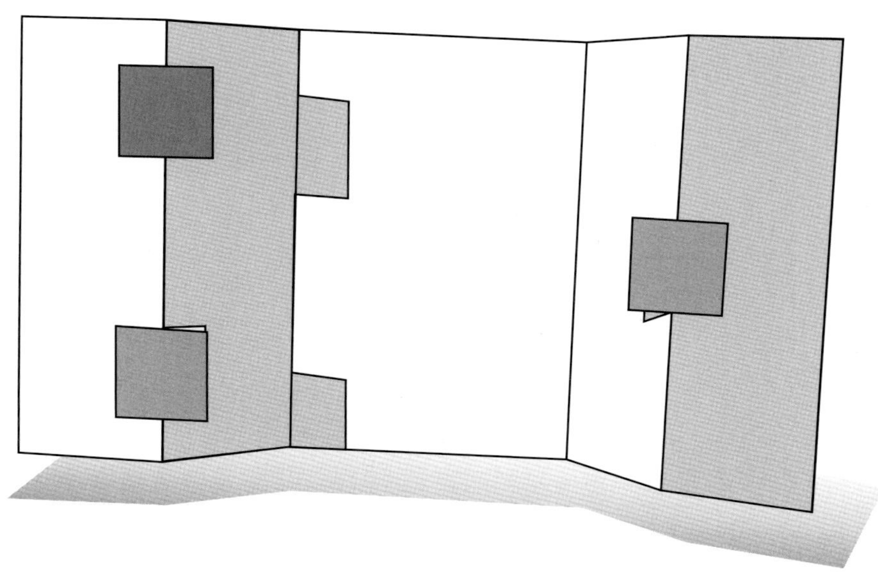

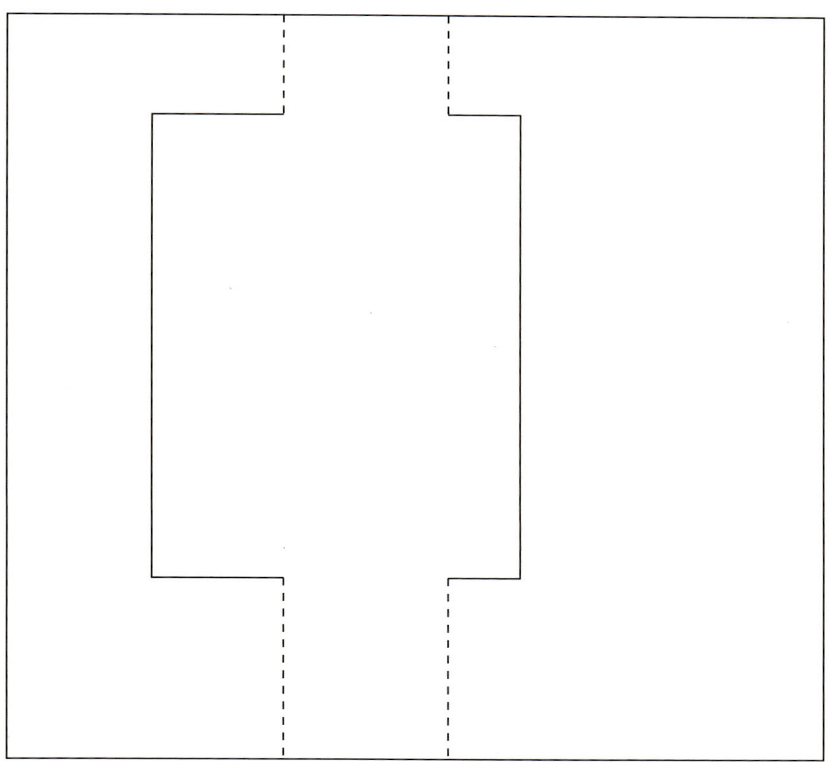

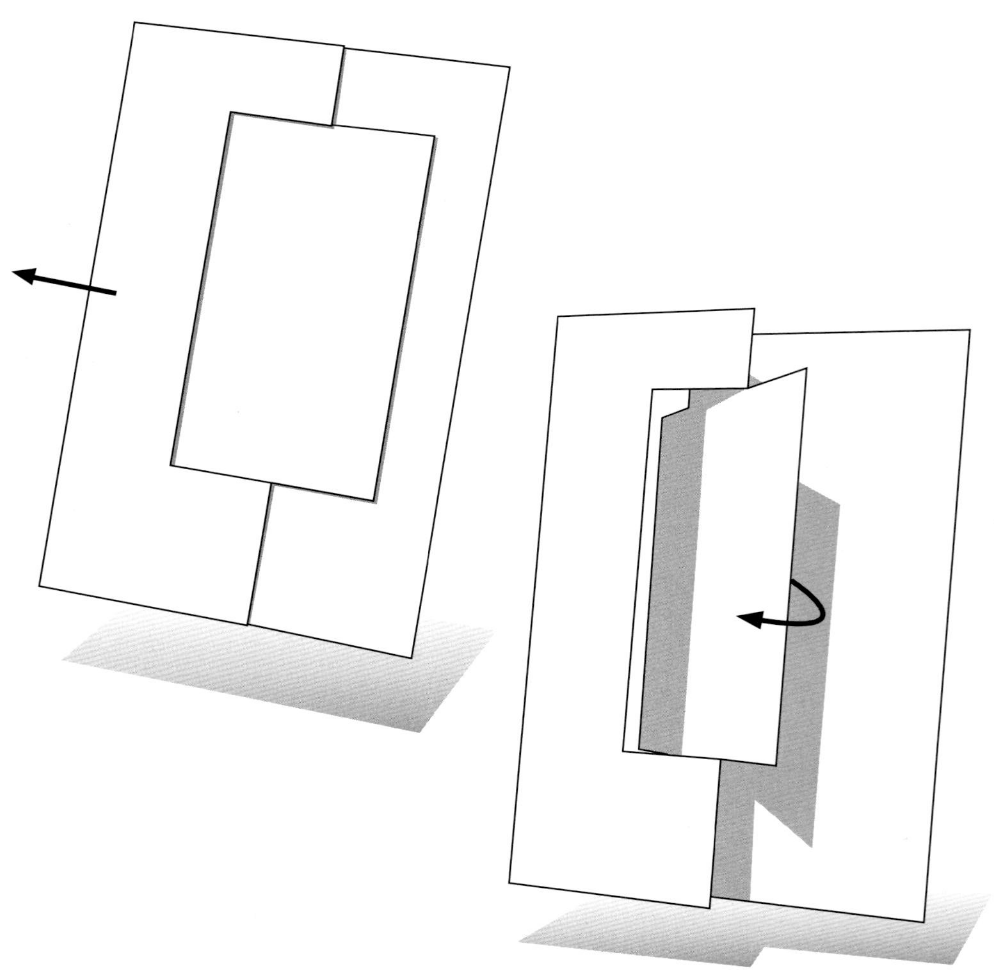

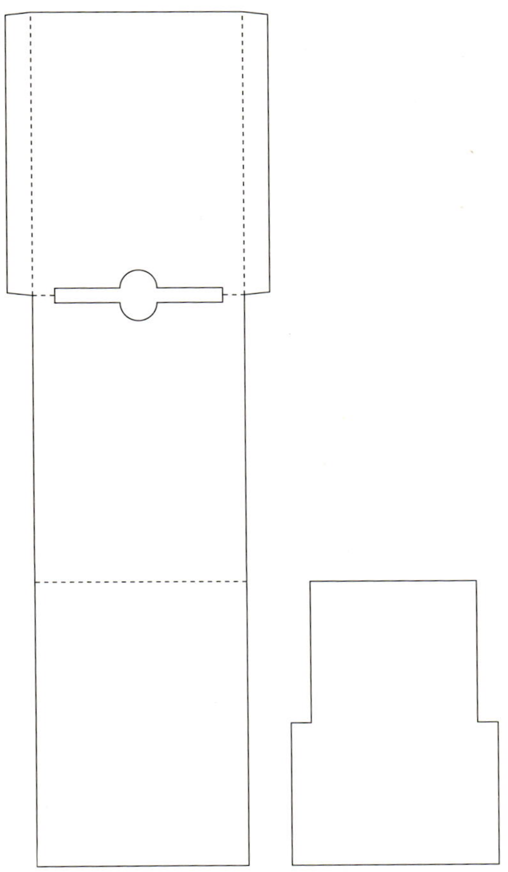

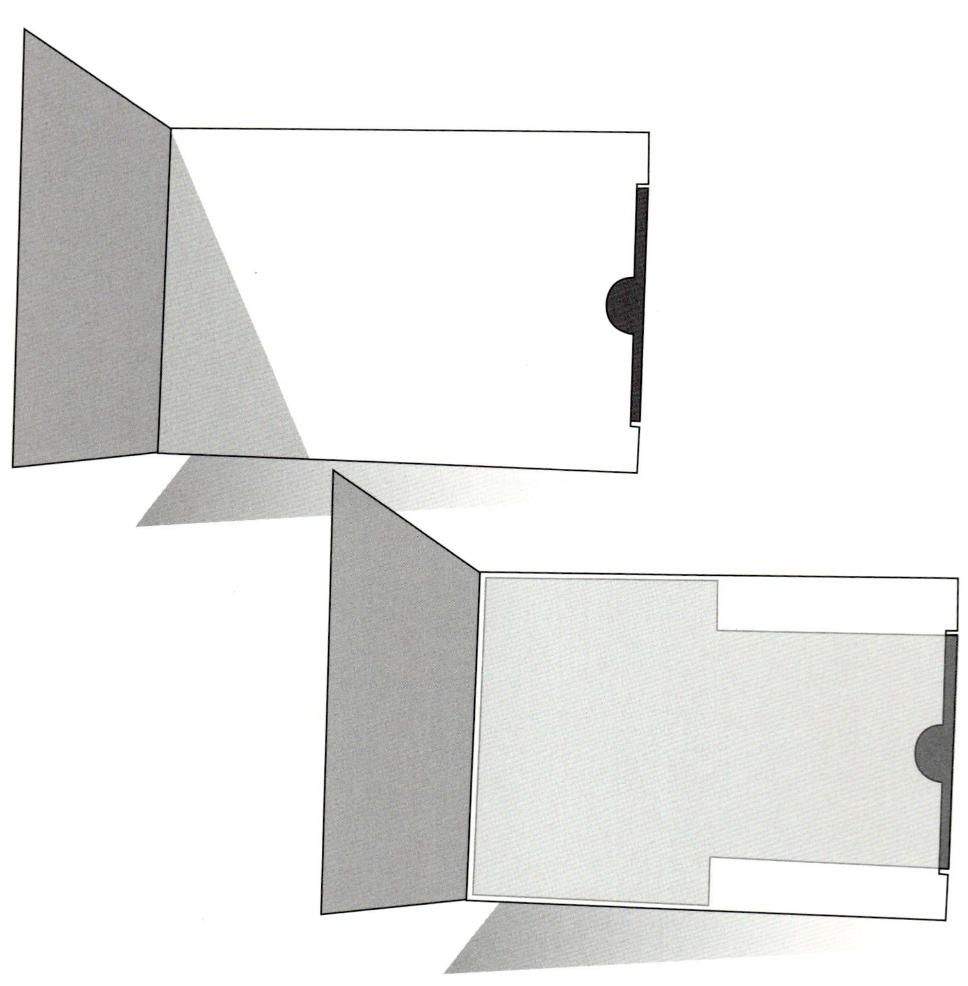

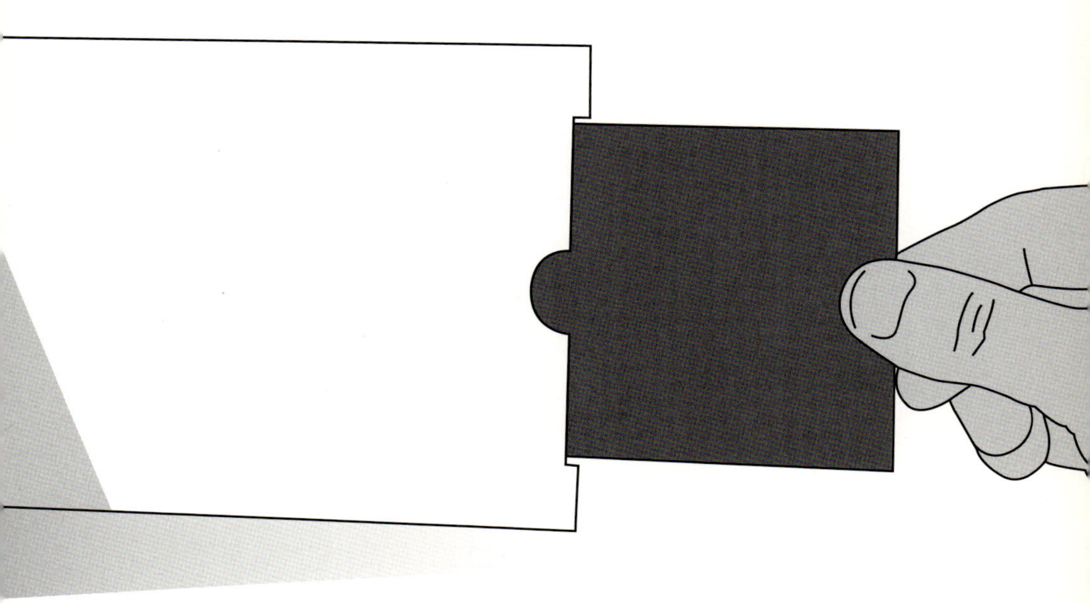

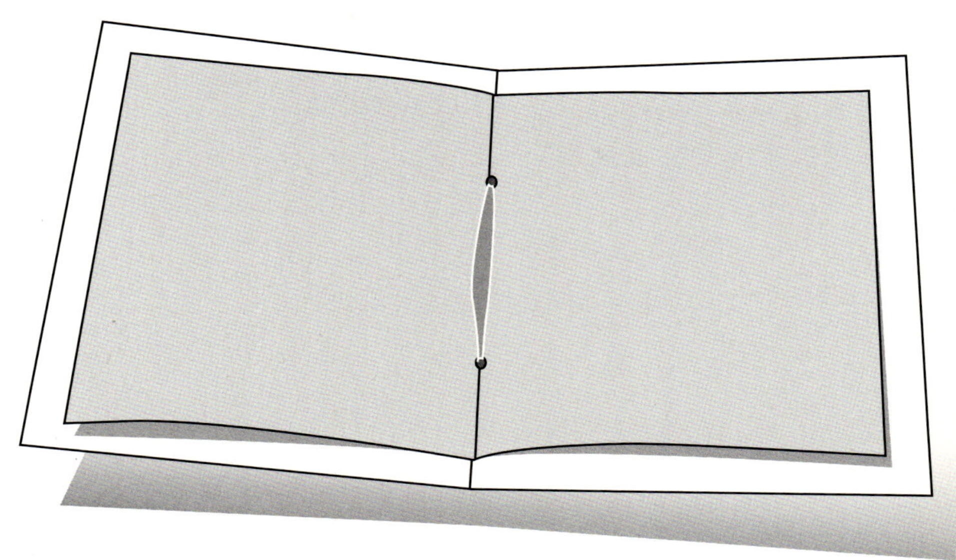

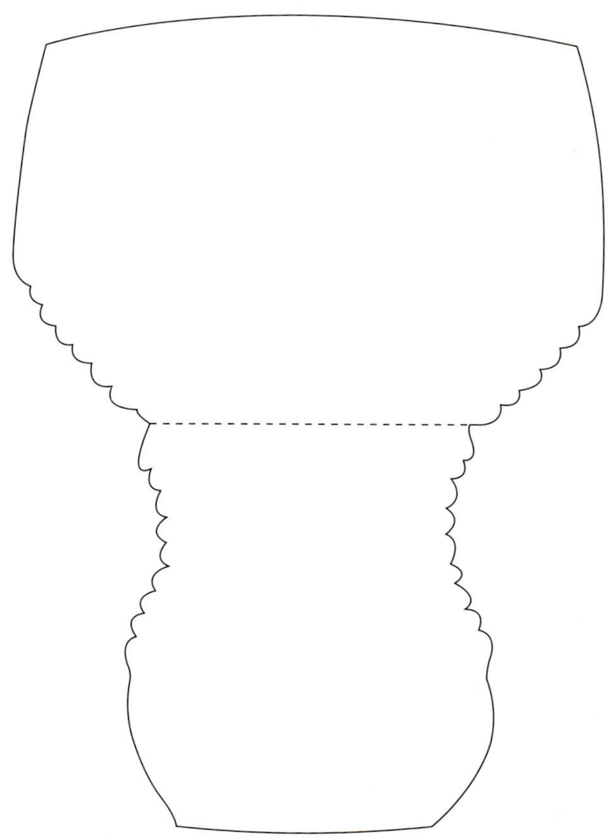

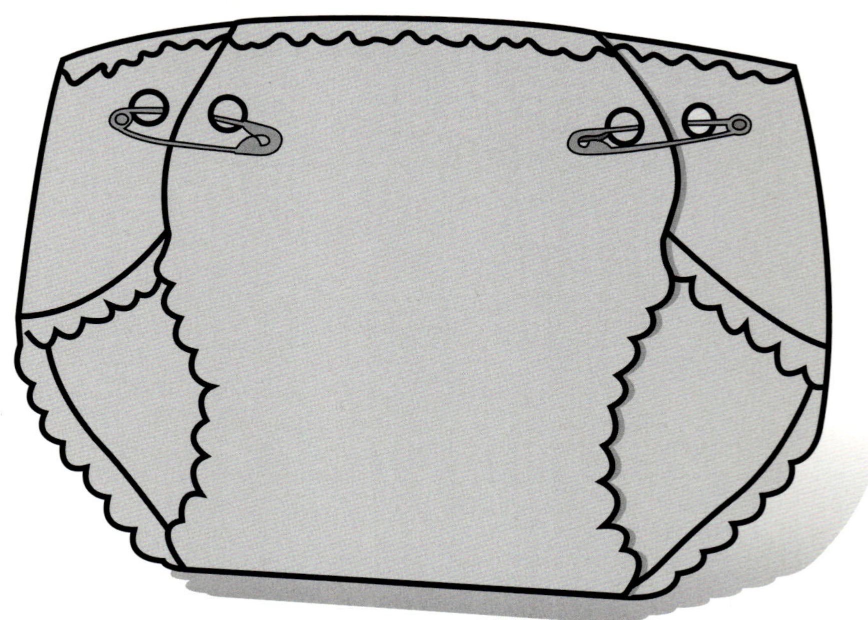

    Cards

It's a boy!
Name
D.O.B.
Weight
Length
Eyes

Frames and Windows

フレーム、窓
Cadres et fenêtres
Marcos y ventanas
Cornici e finestre
Fenster und Rahmen

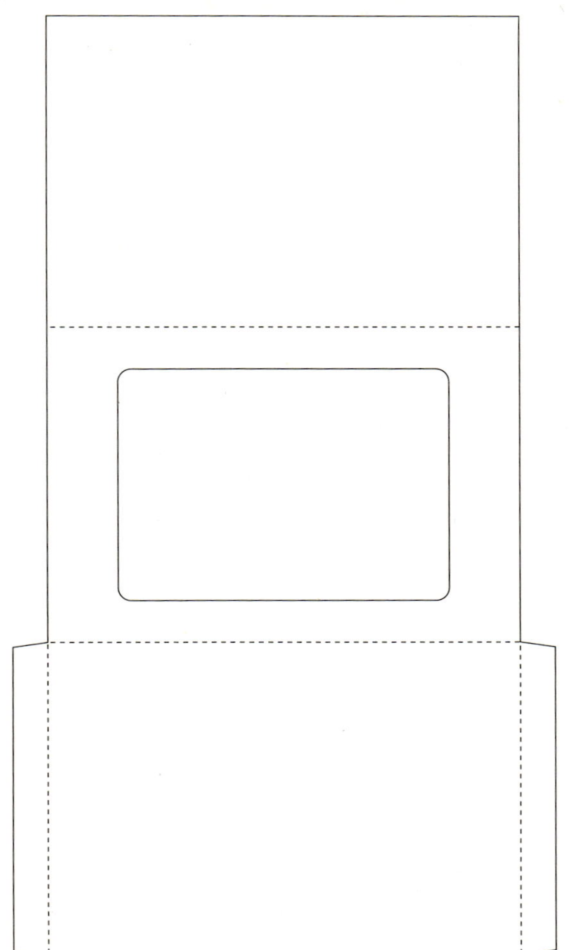

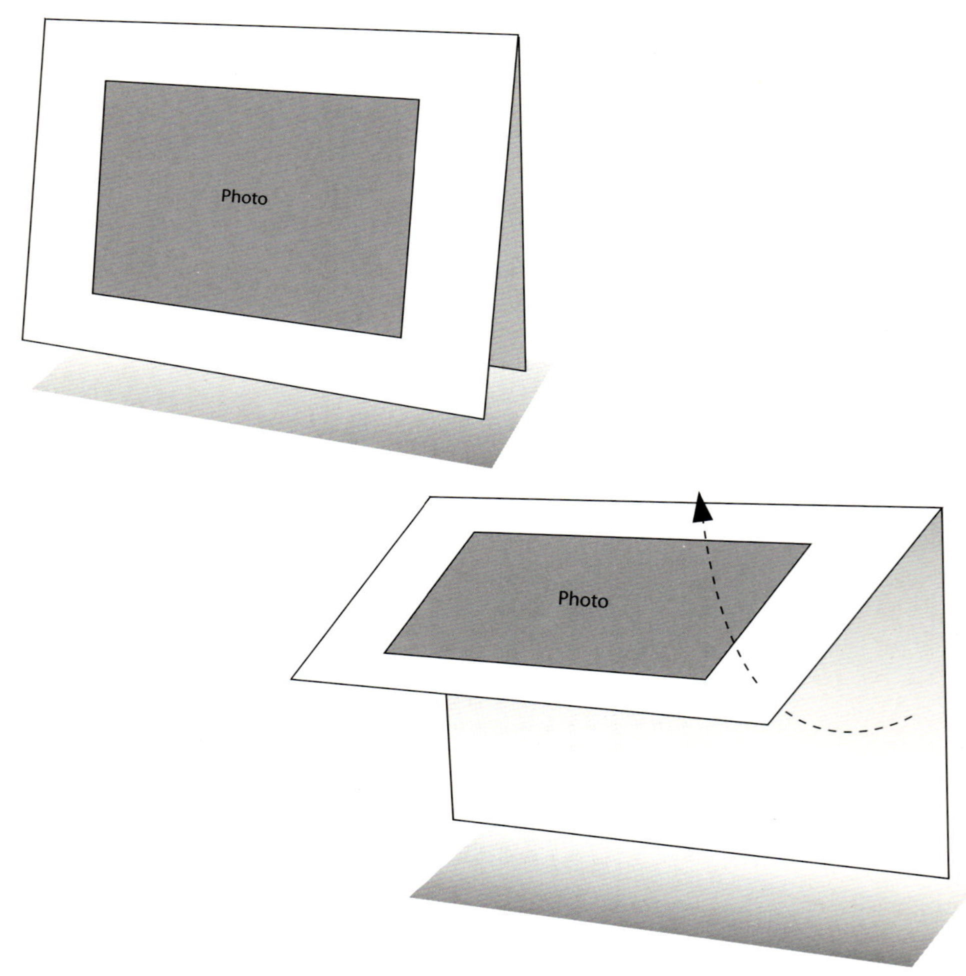
Photo
Photo

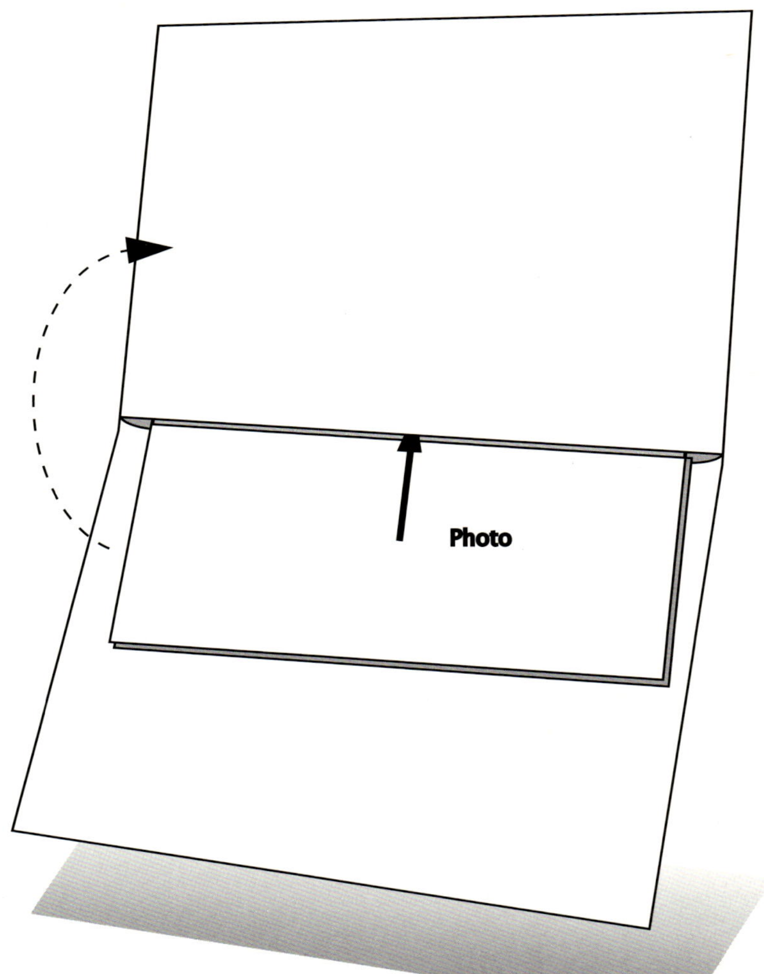

Photo

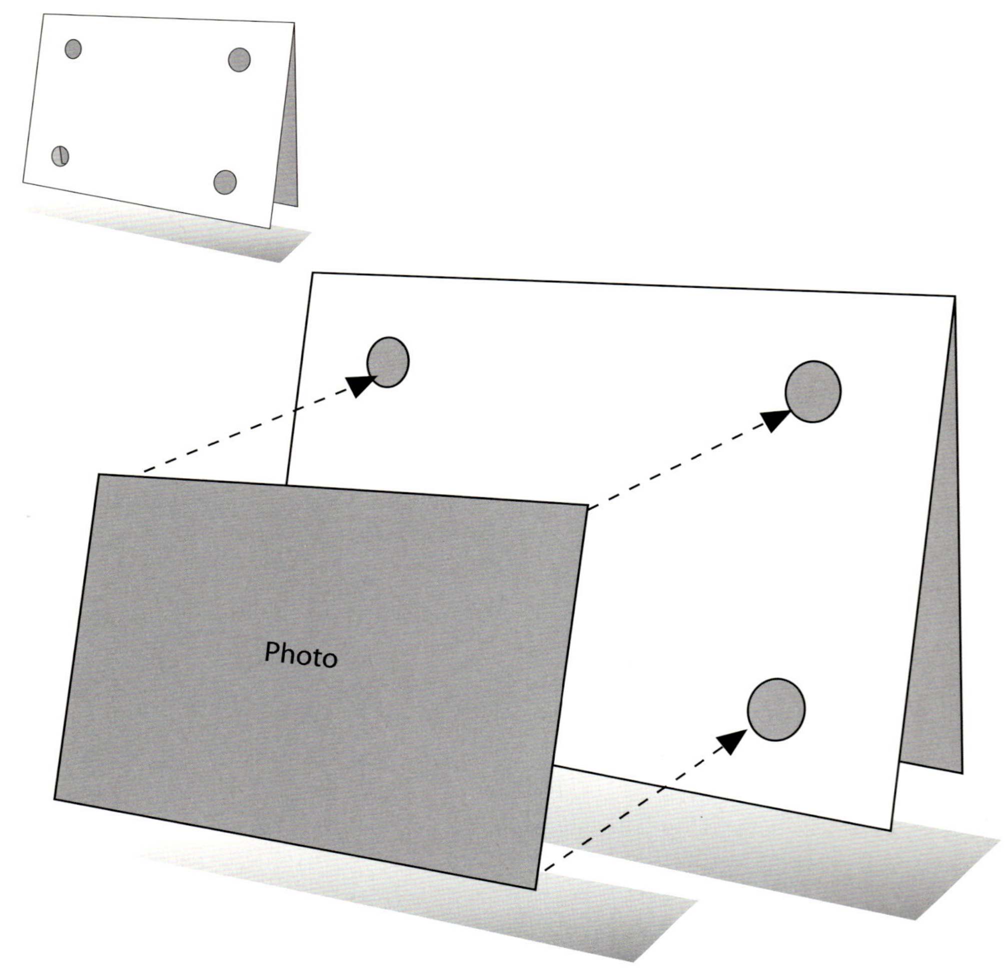

Photo

Photo

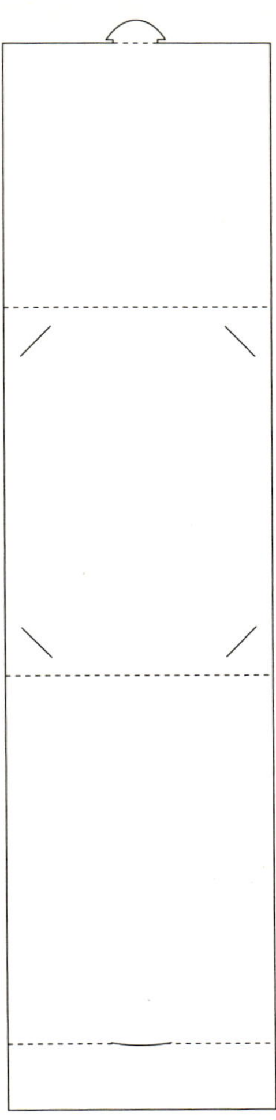

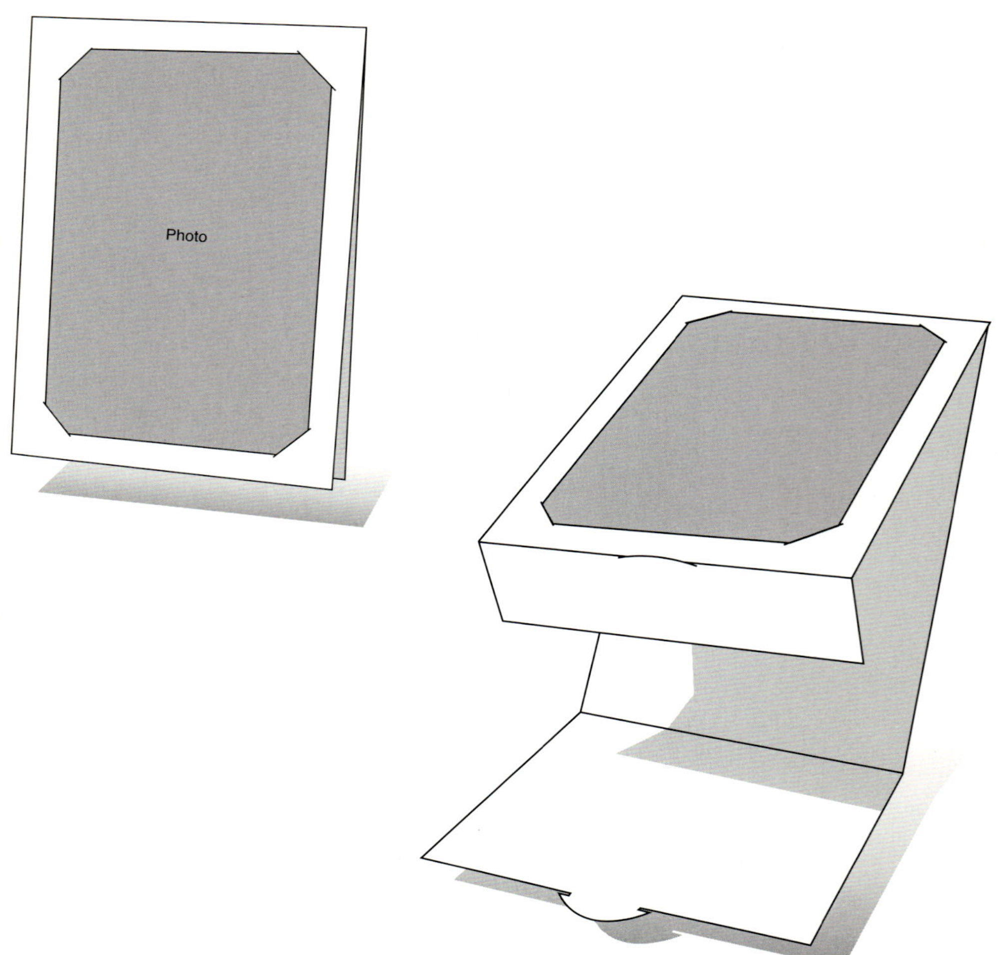

   Frames and Windows

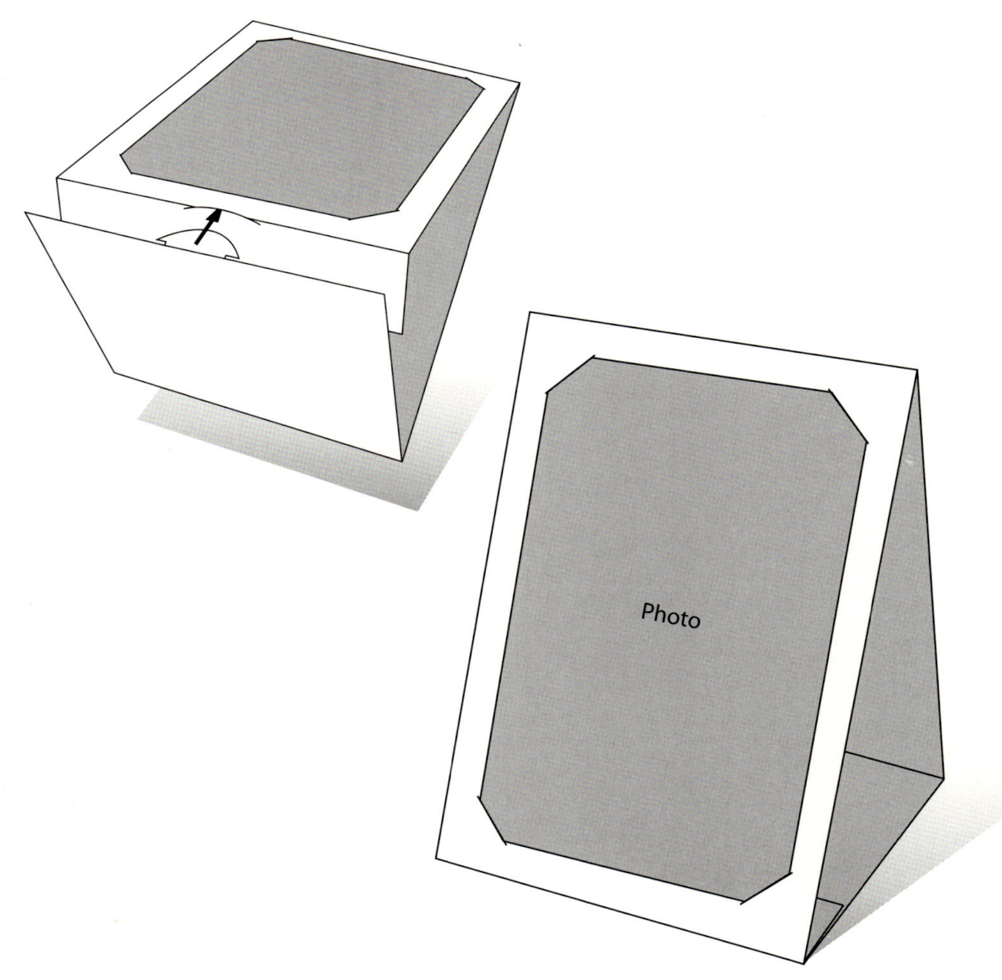
Photo

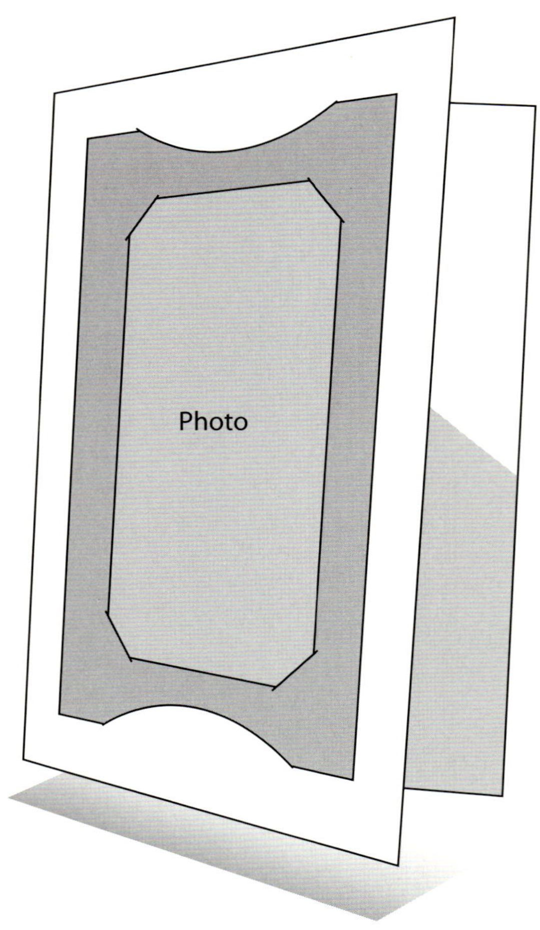

 Frames and Windows

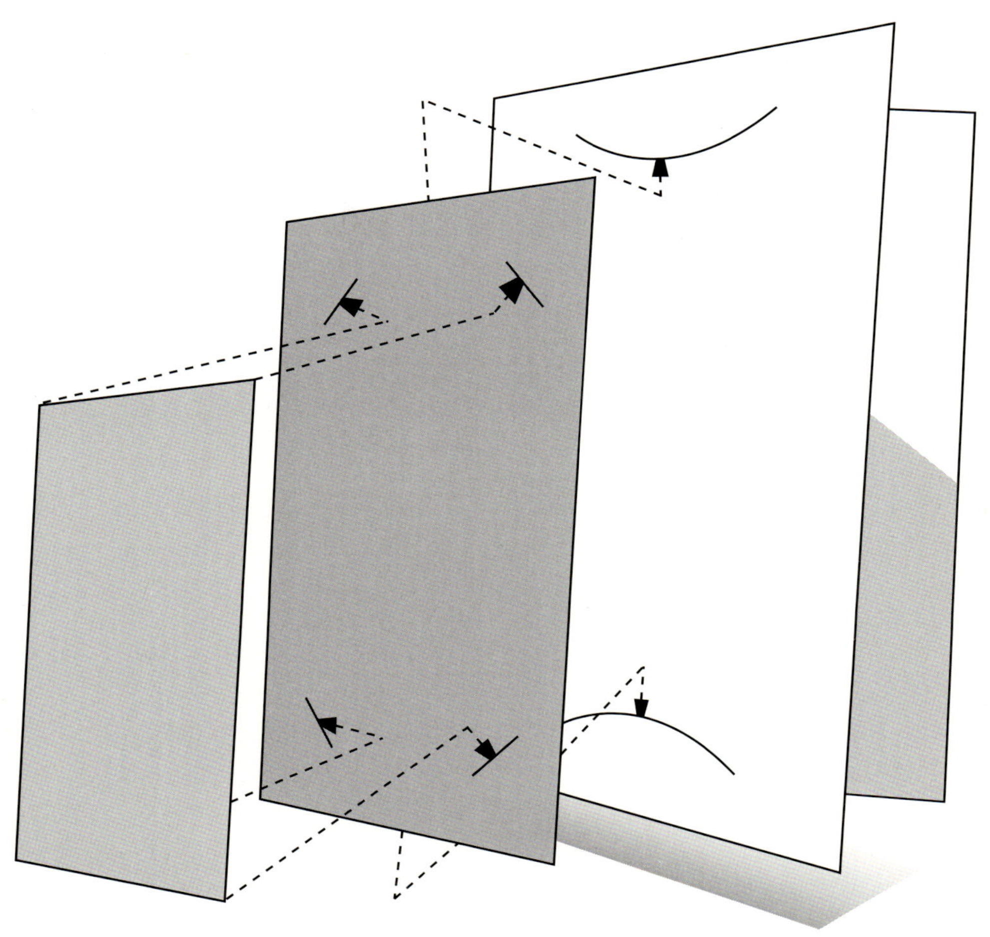

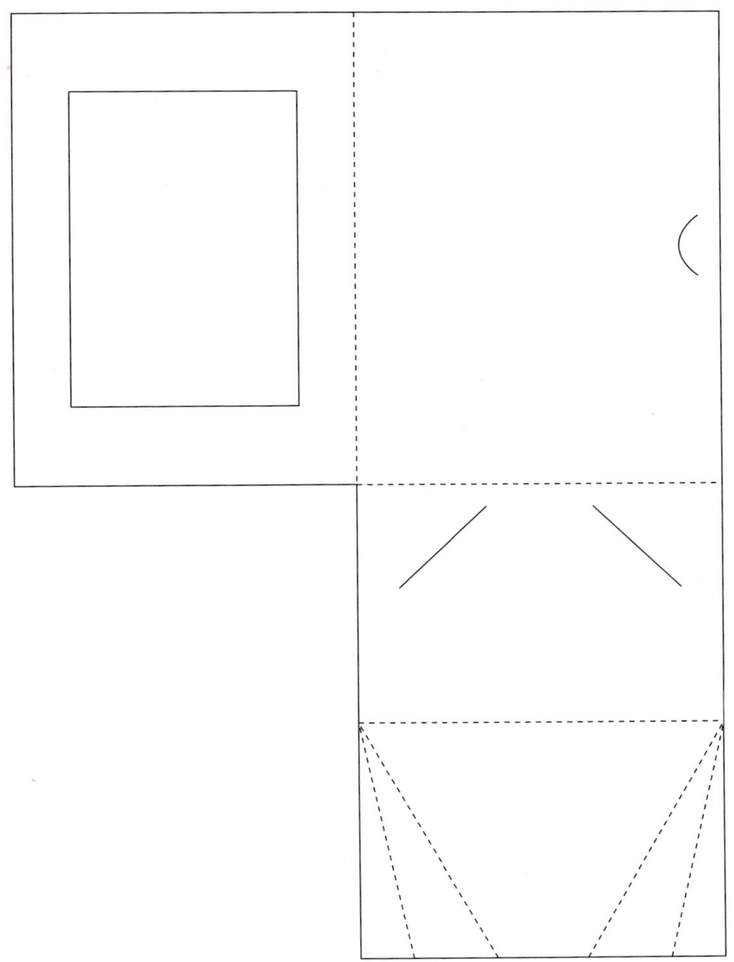

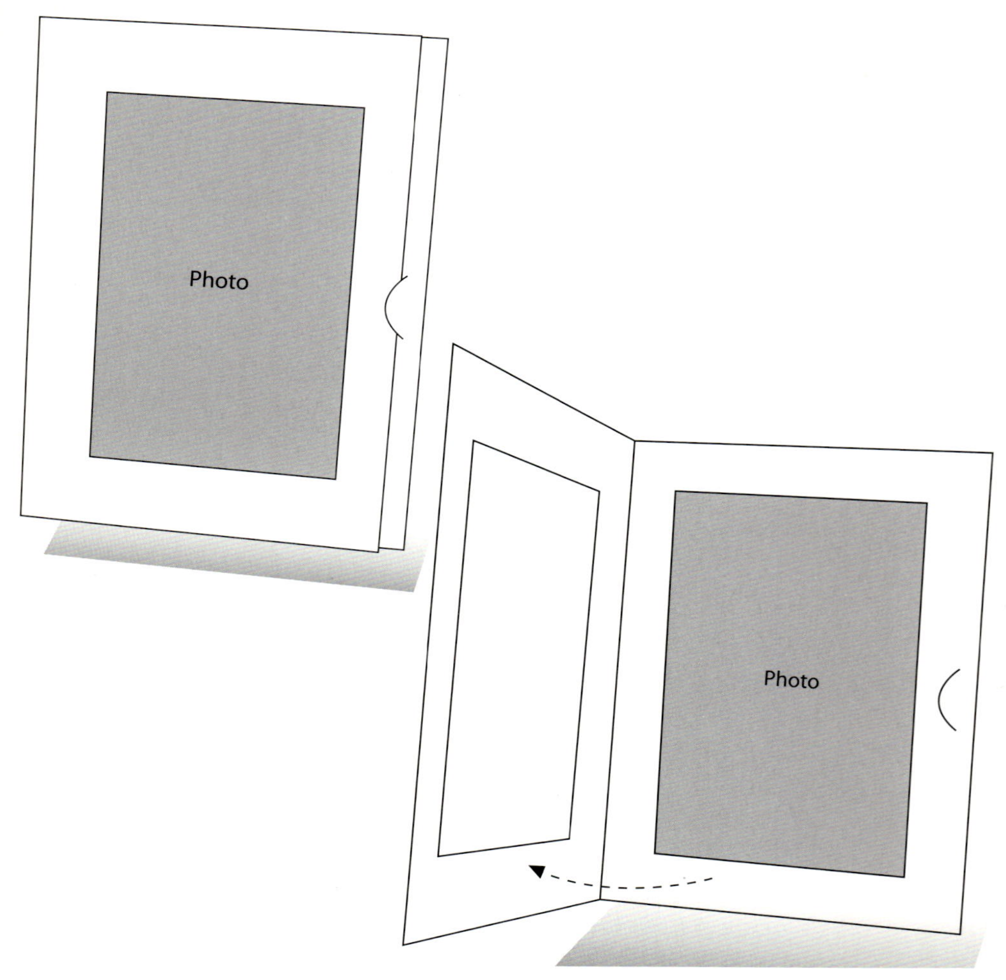

Photo
Photo

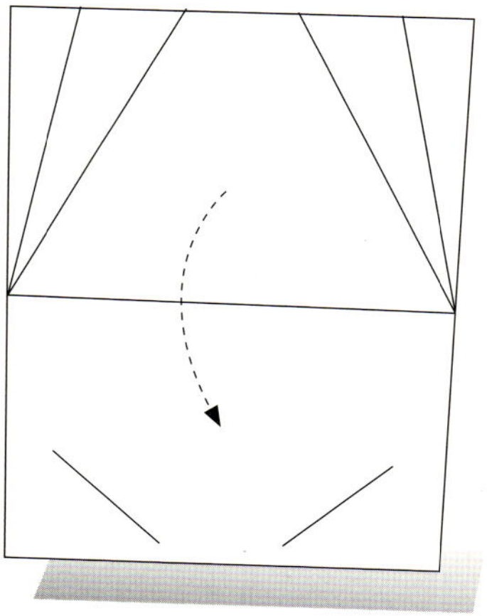

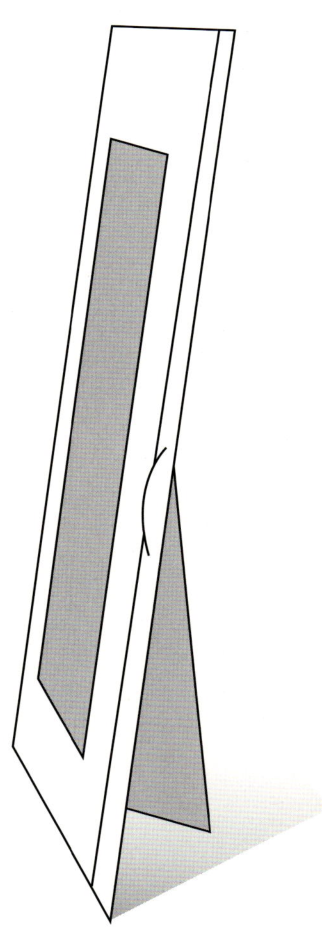

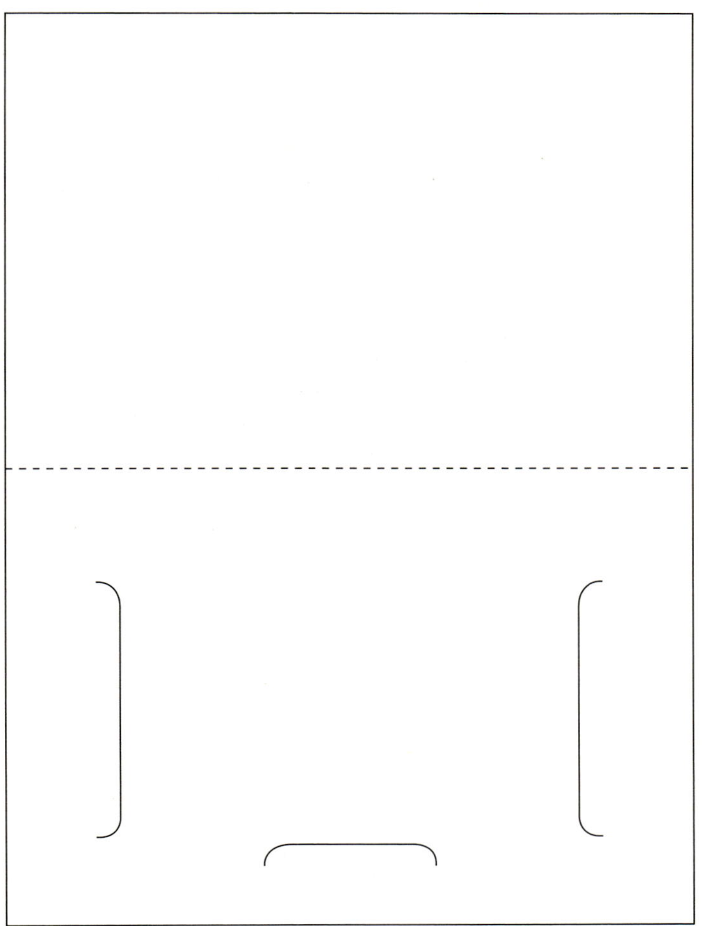

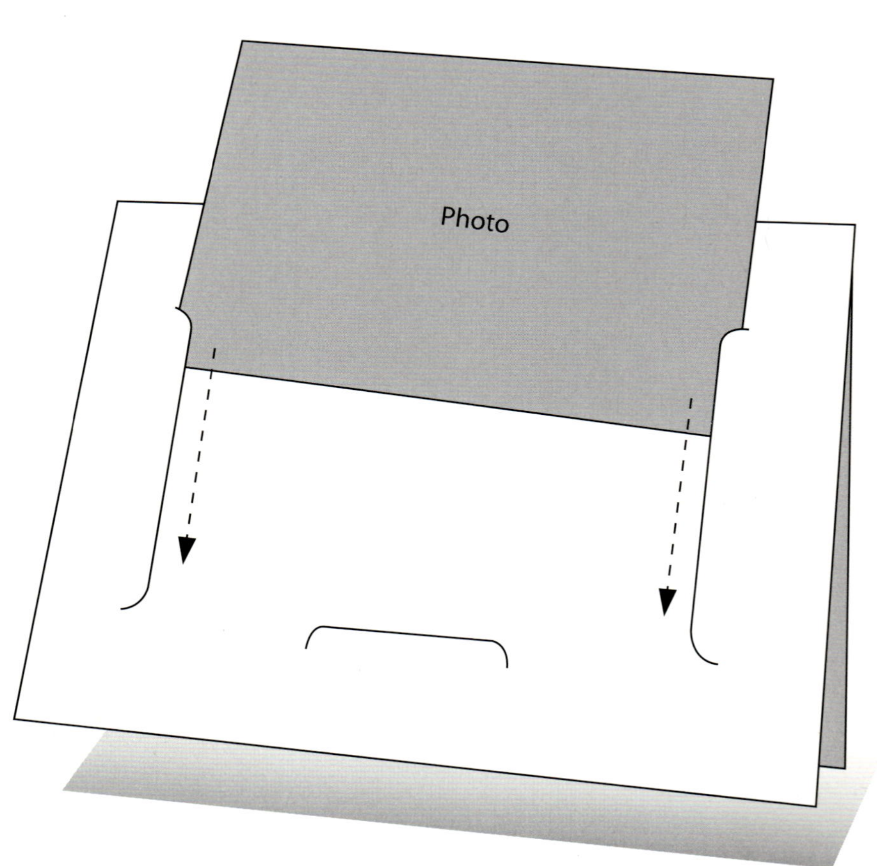

Photo

Photo

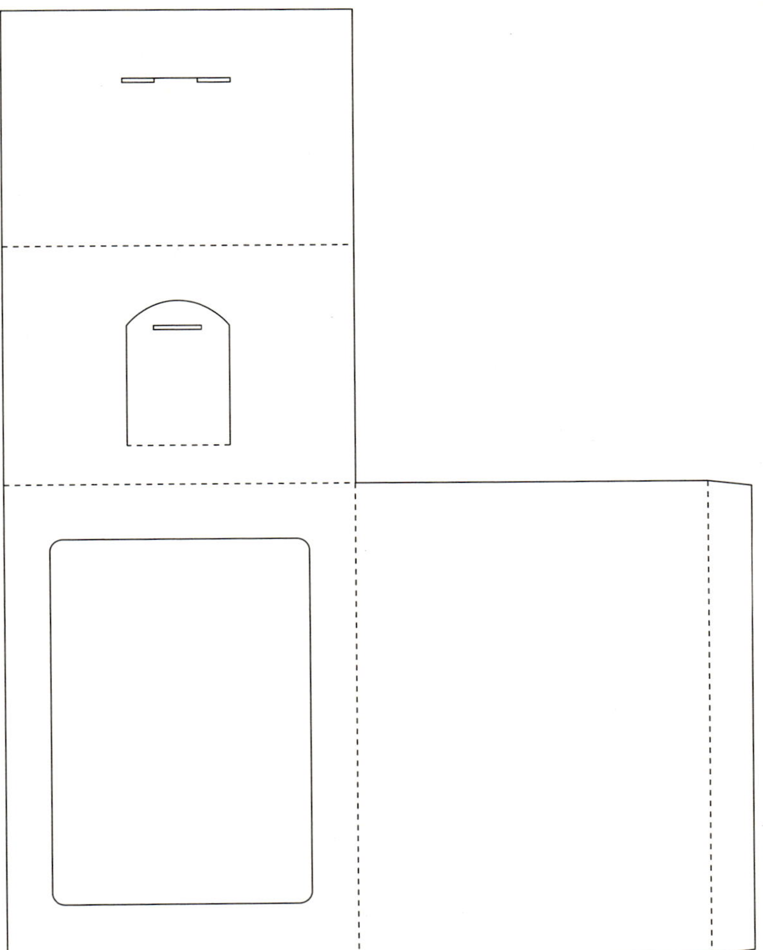

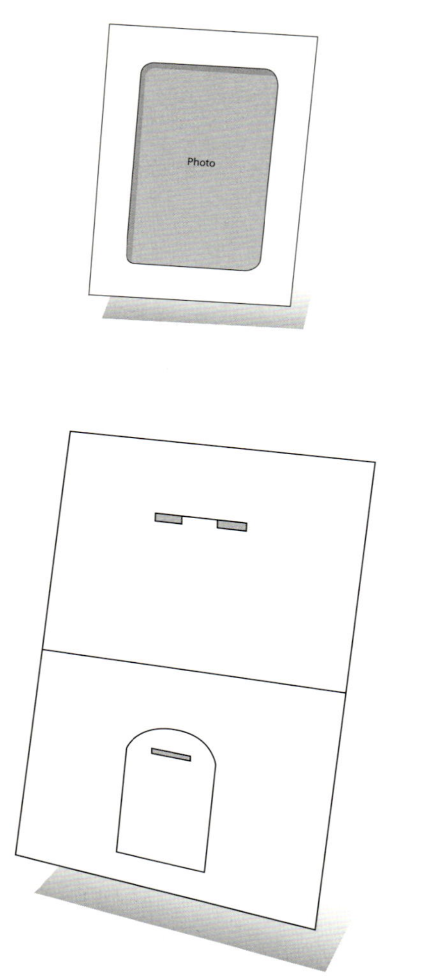

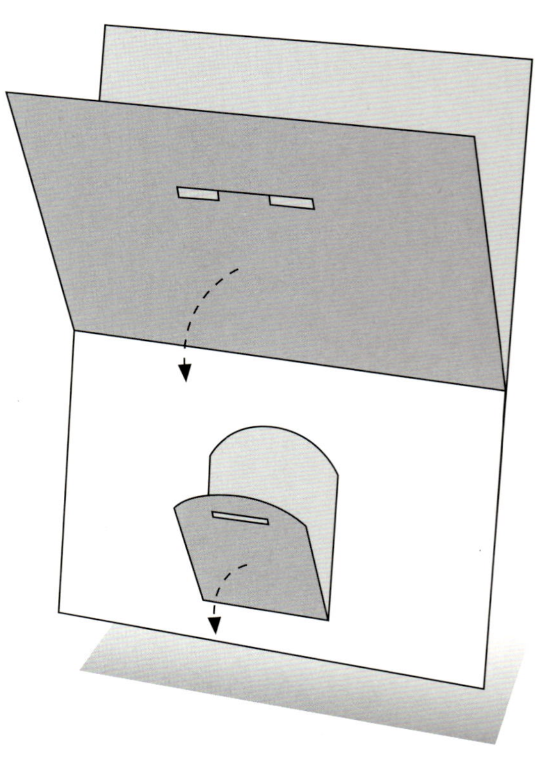

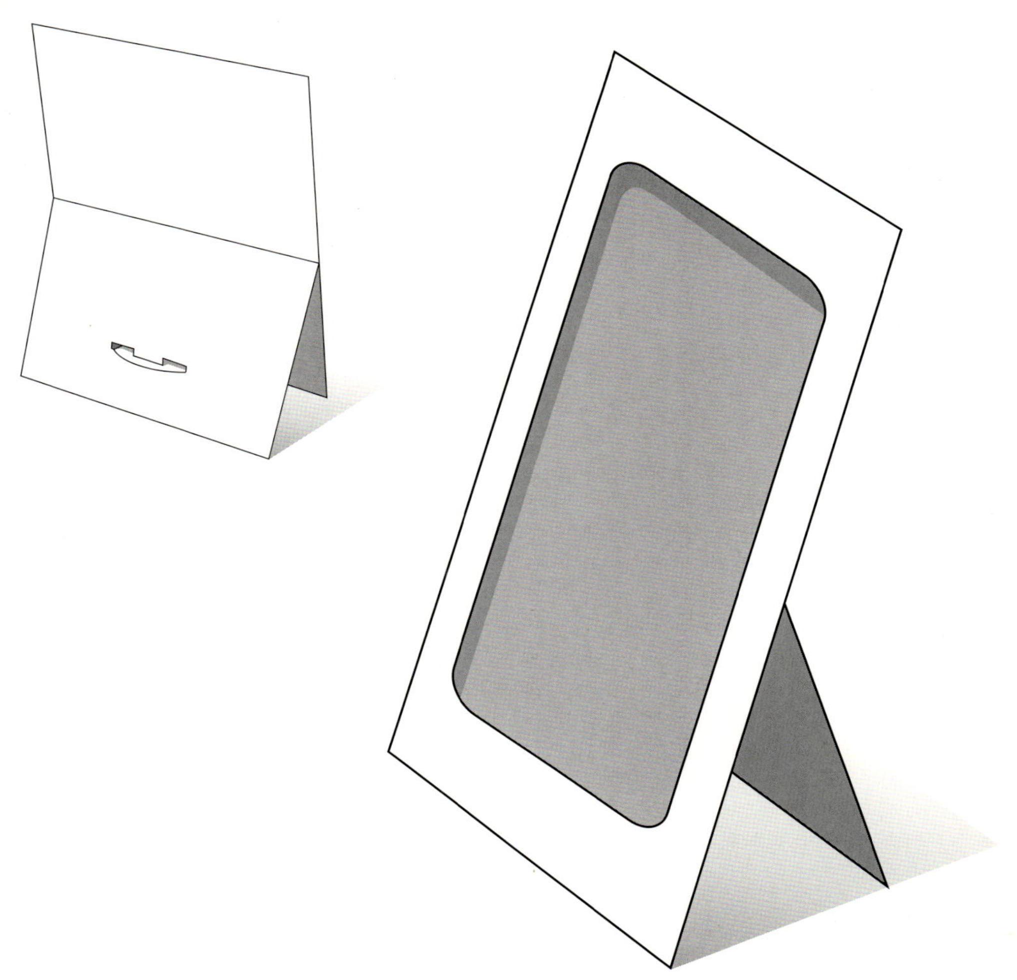

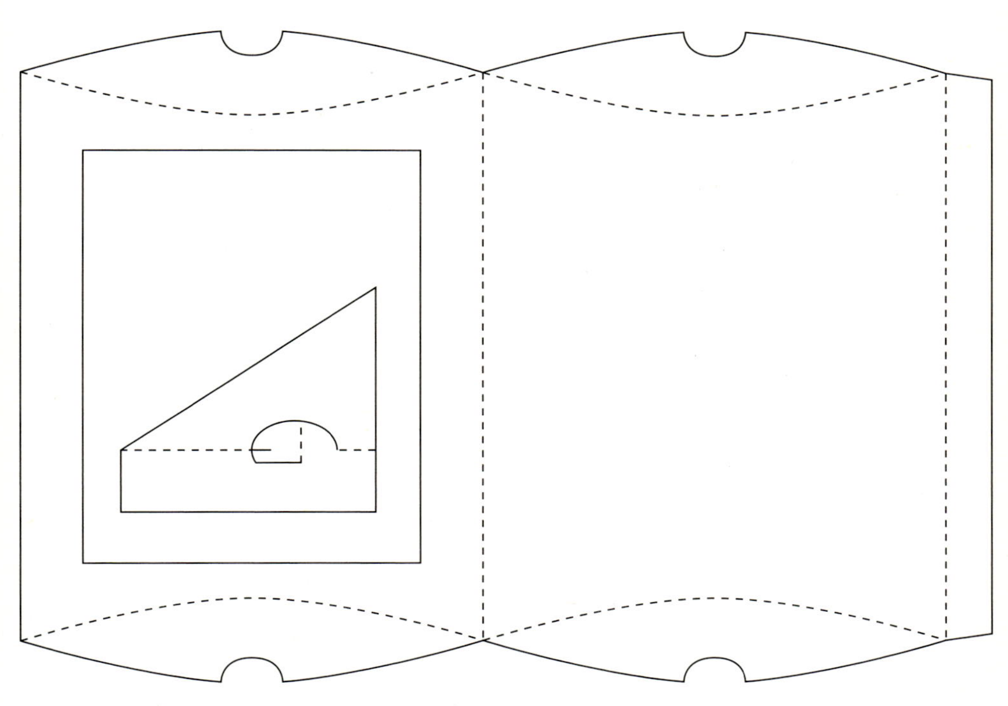

Photo

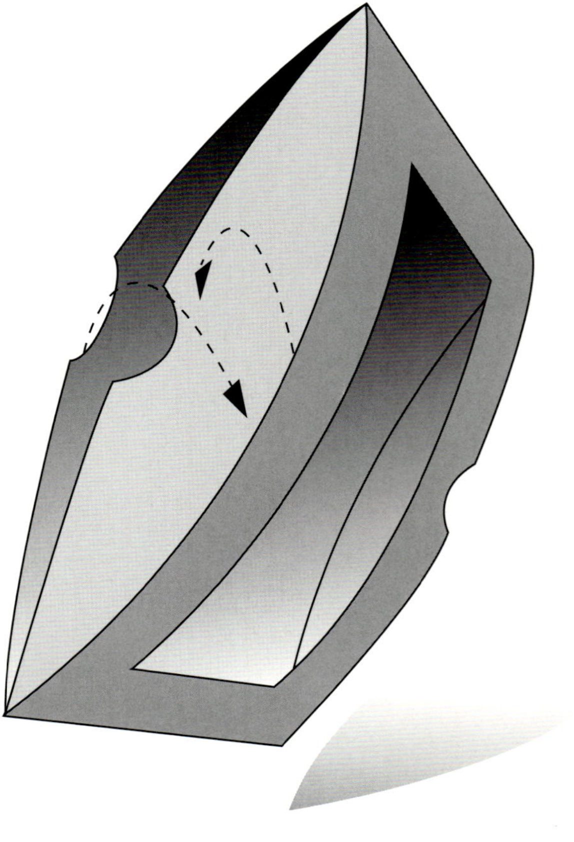

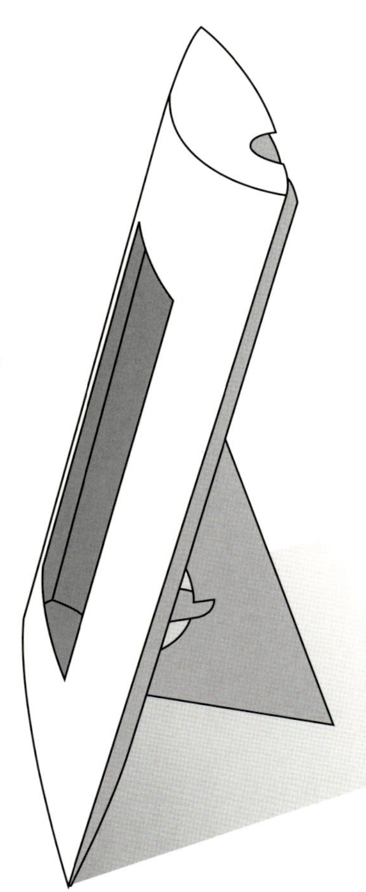

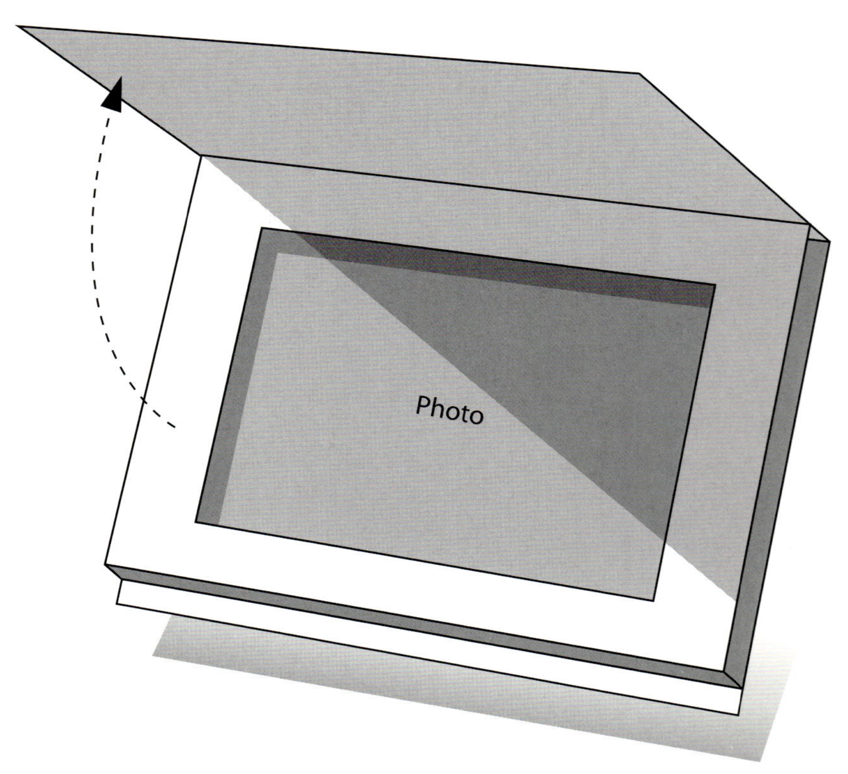
Photo

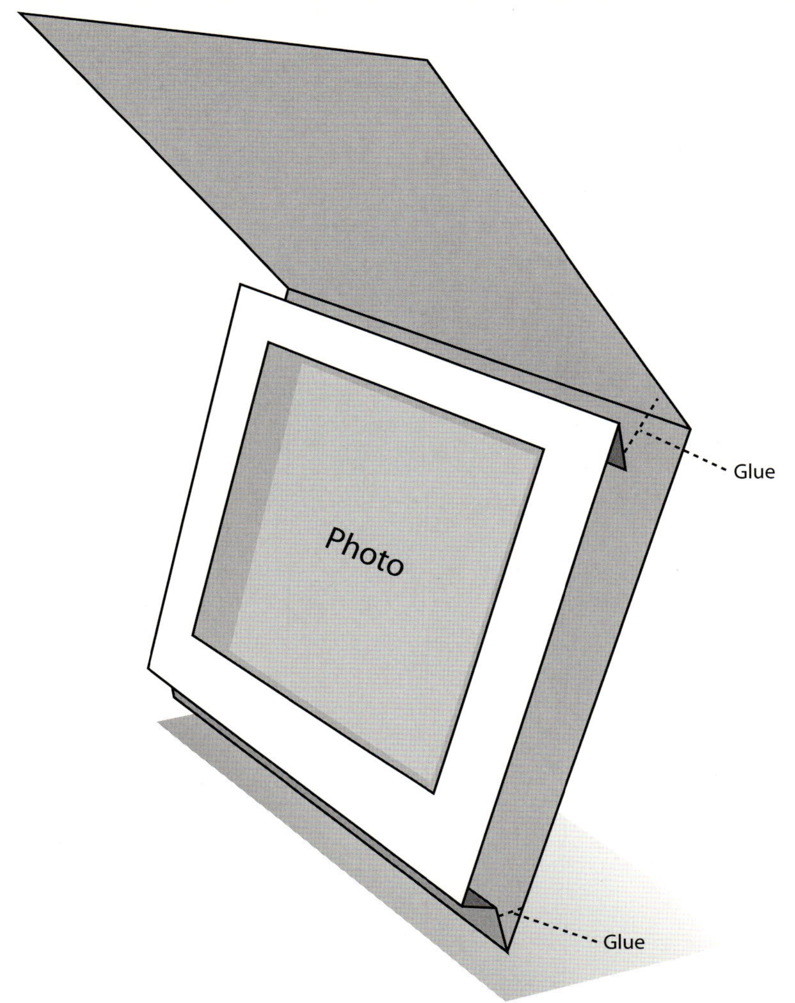
Glue
Photo
Glue

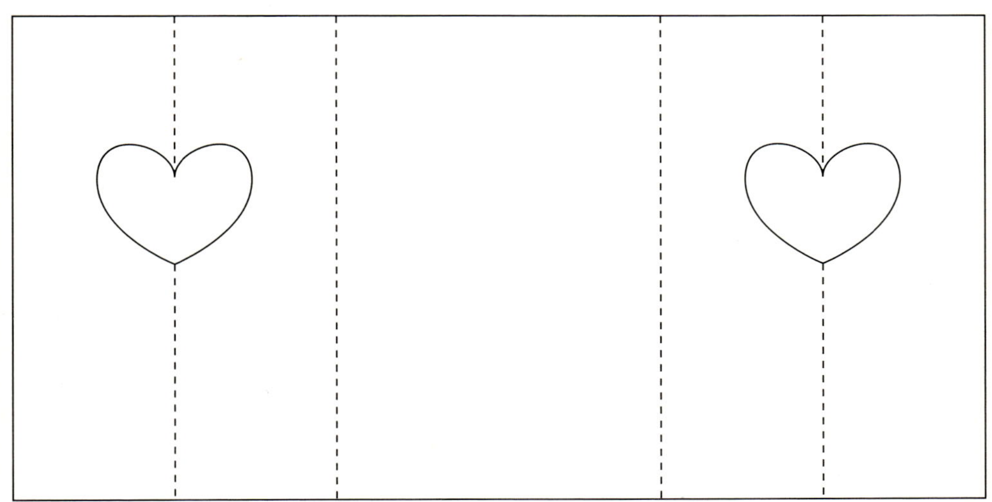

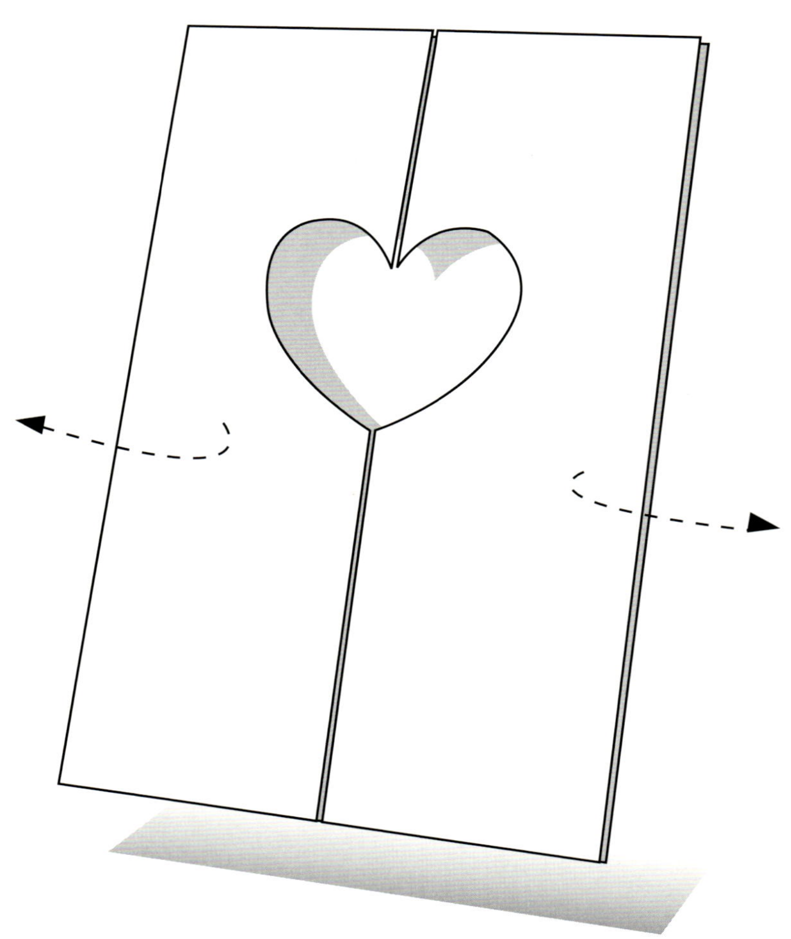

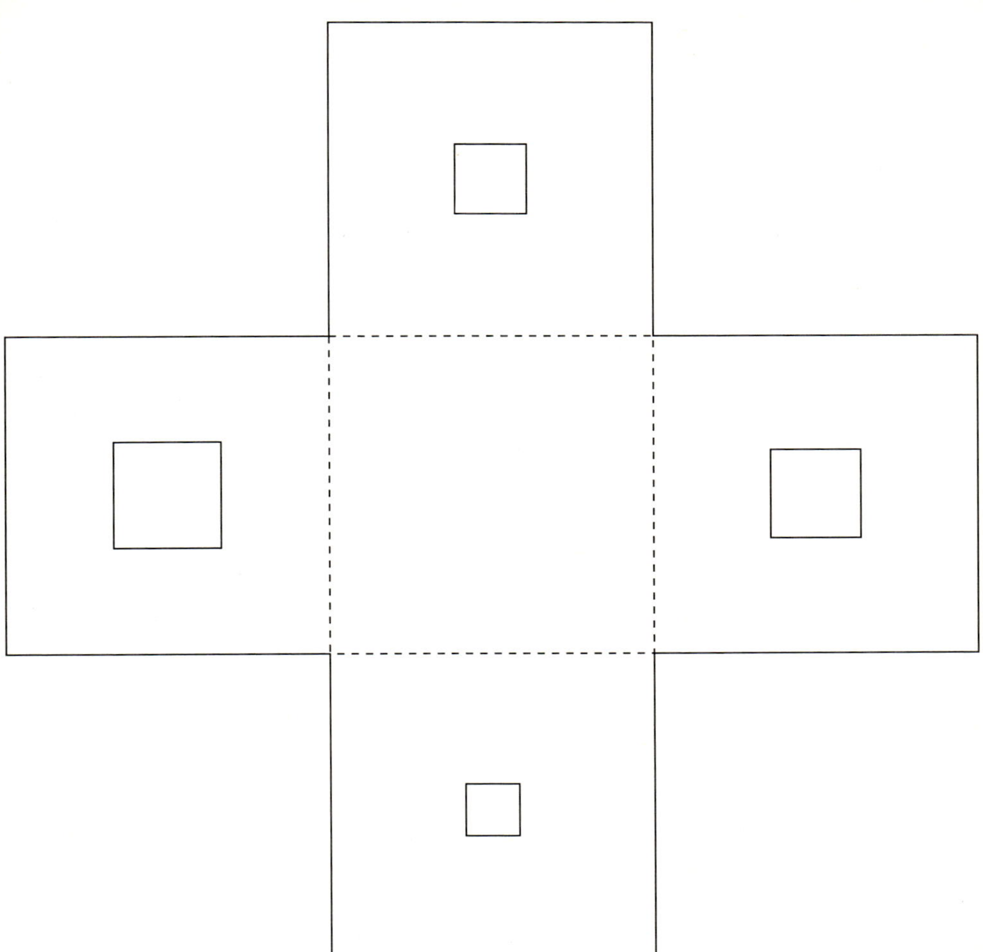

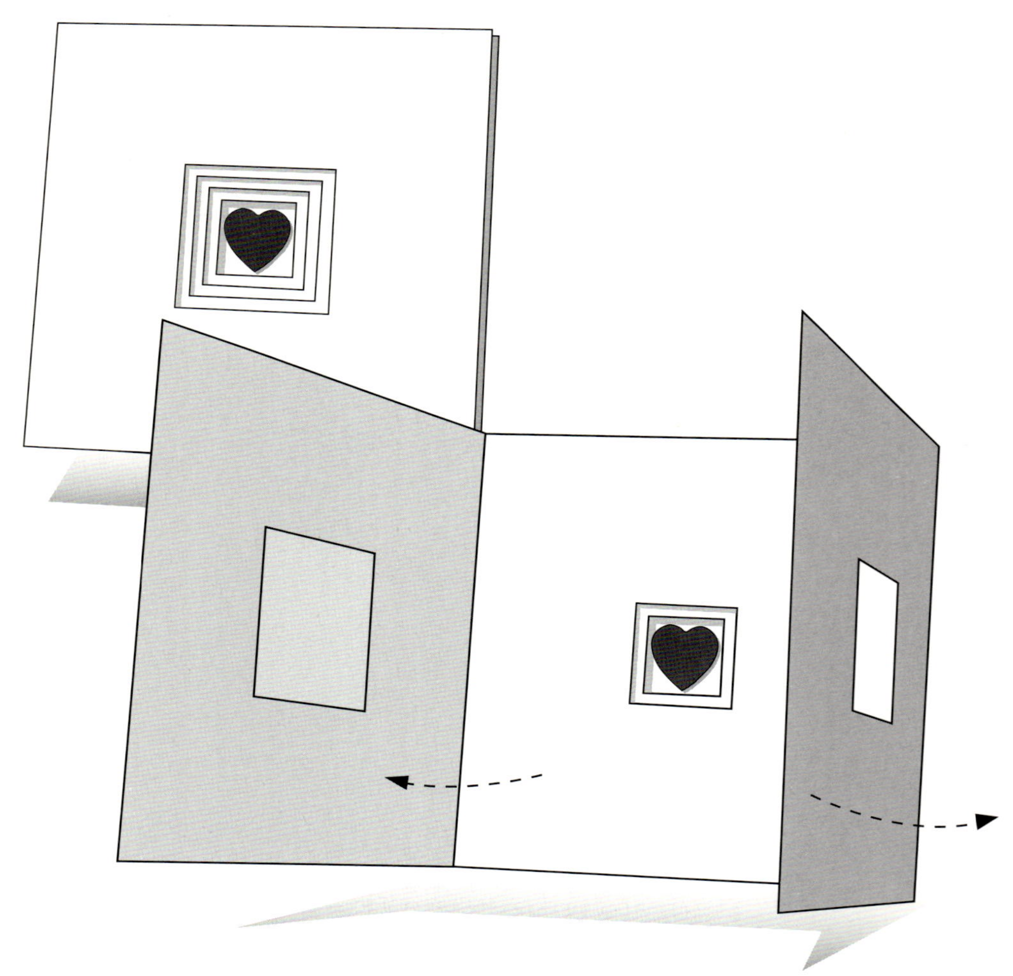

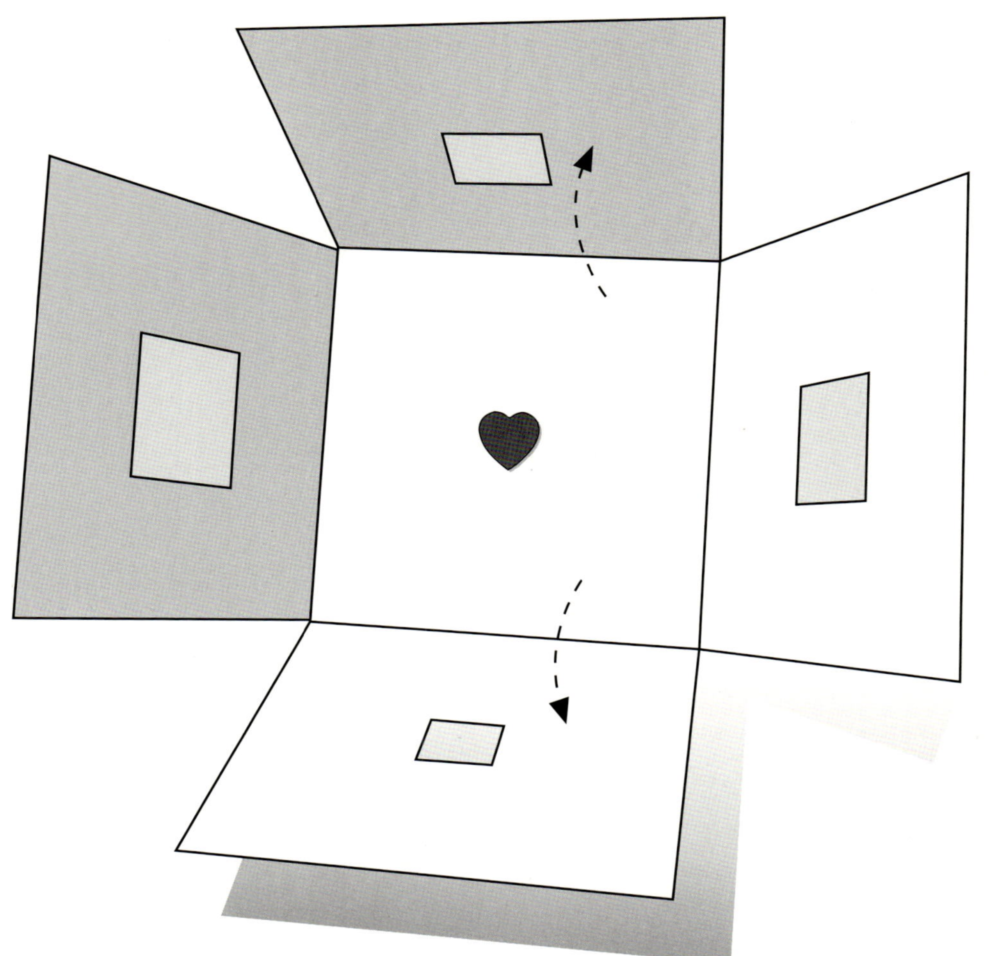

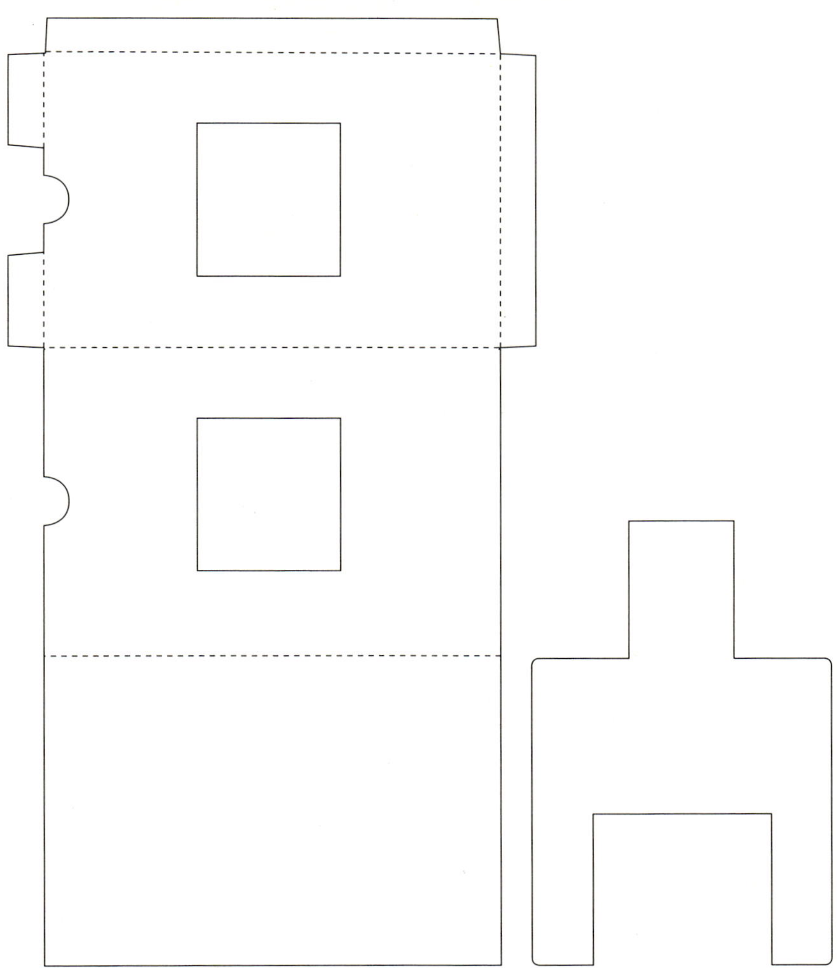

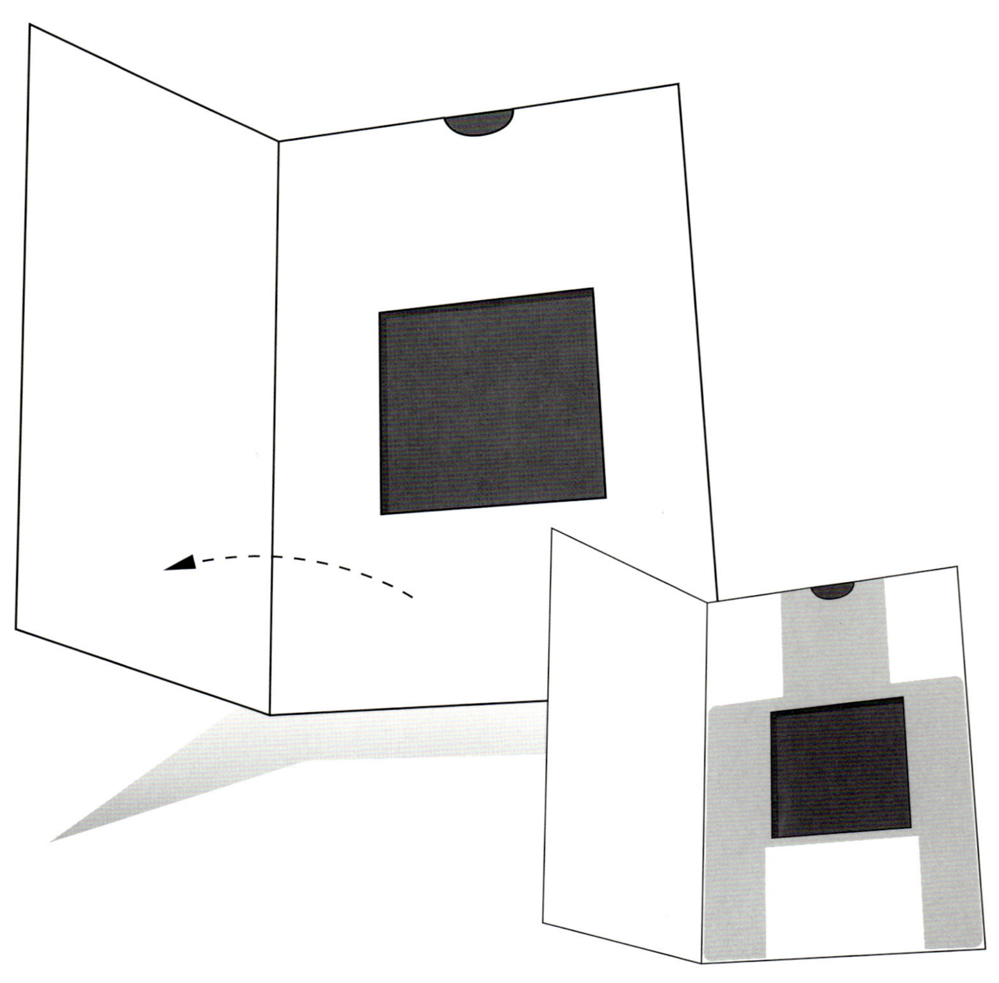

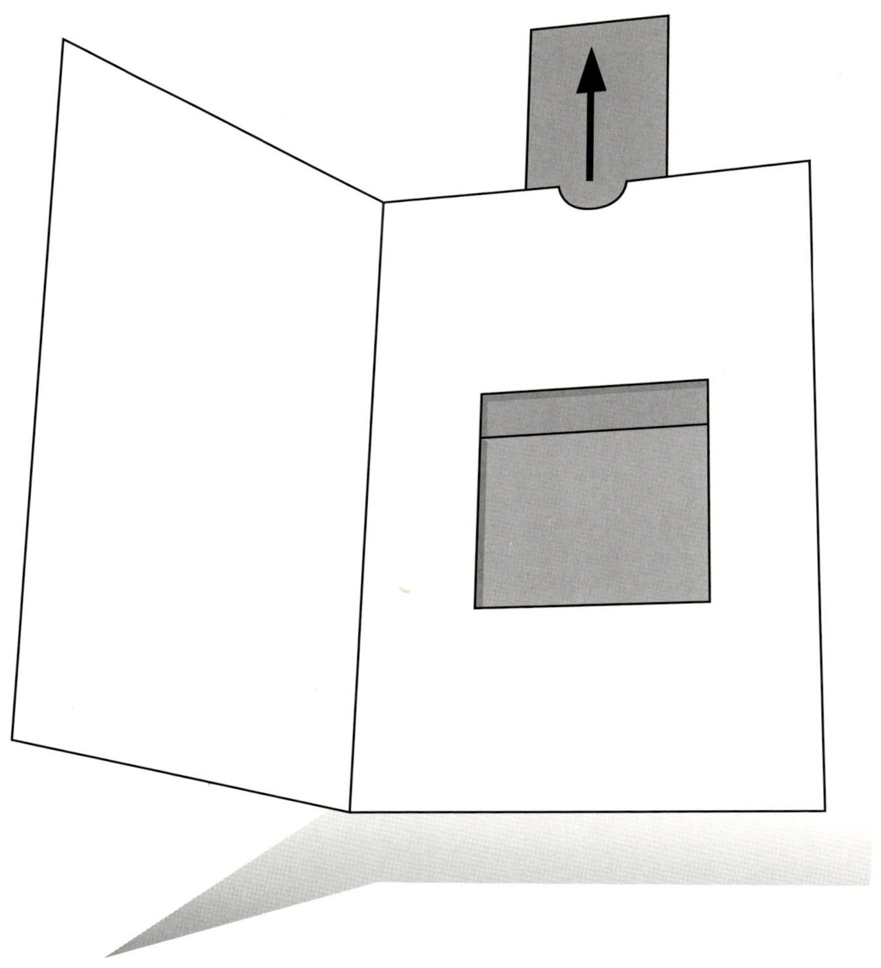

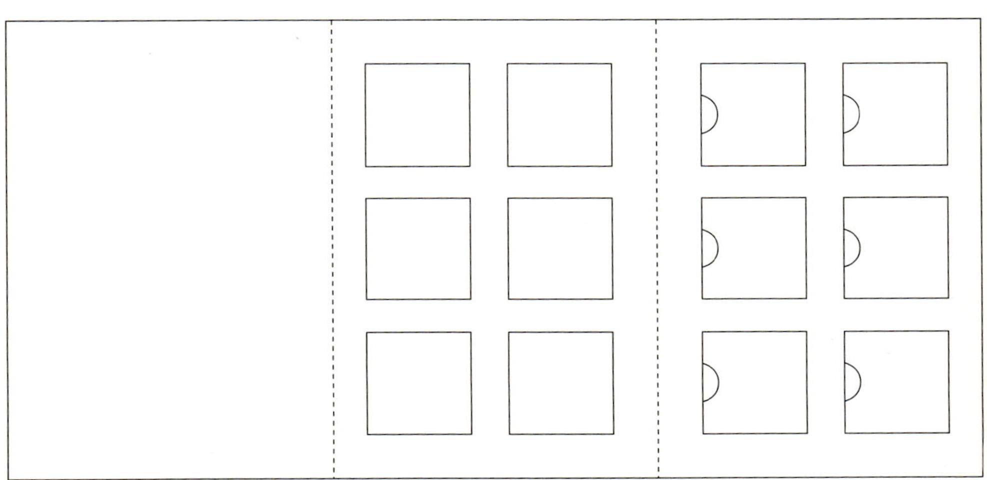

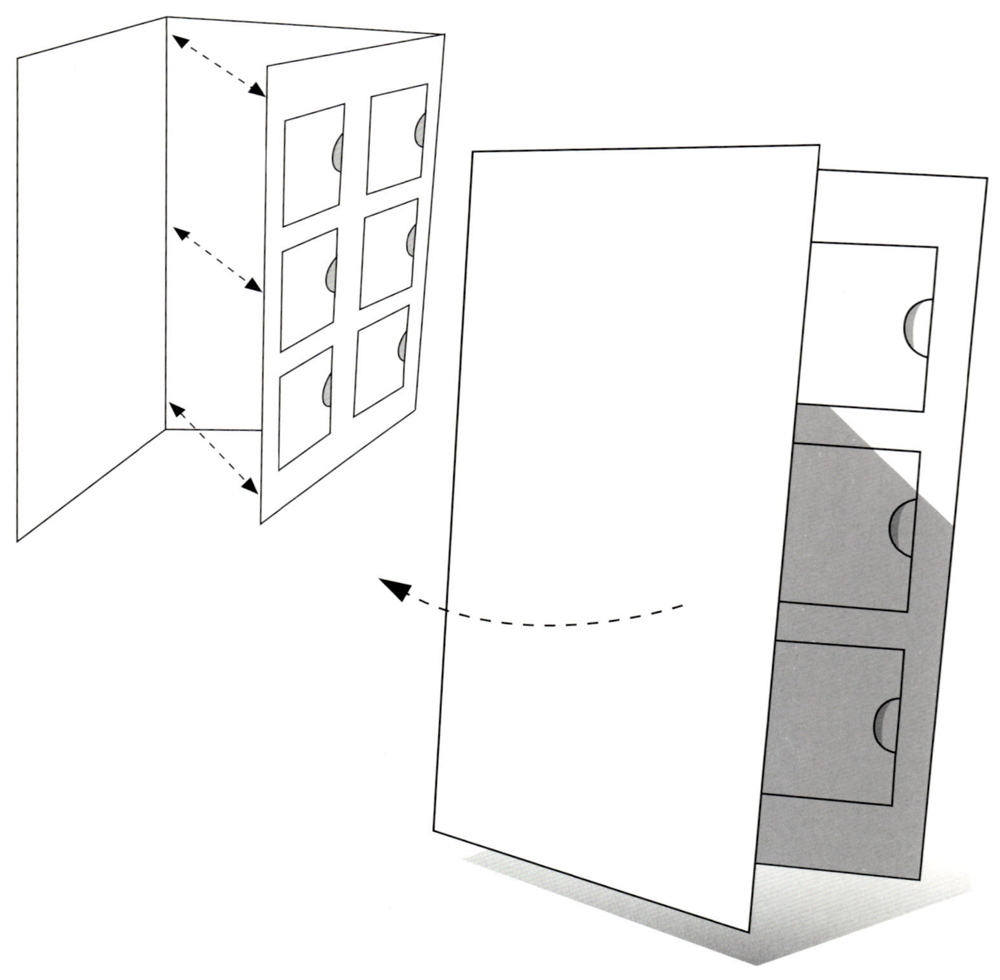

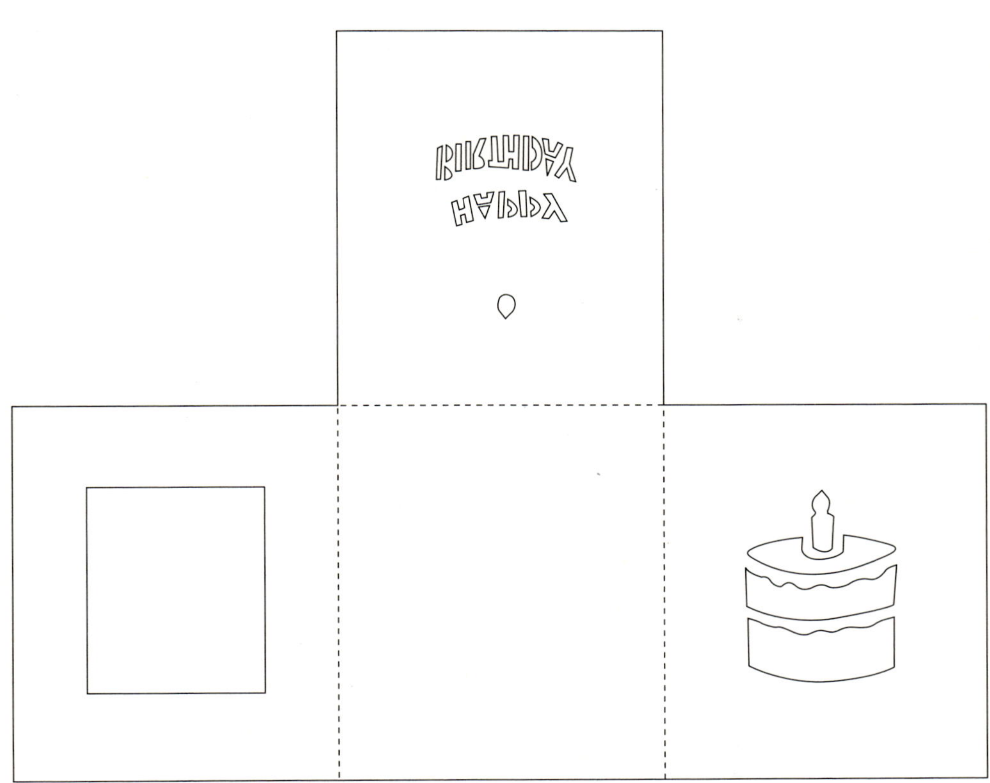
HAPPY BIRTHDAY

HAPPY
BIRTHDAY
HAPPY
BIRTHDAY

HAPPY
BIRTHDAY
HAPPY
BIRTHDAY

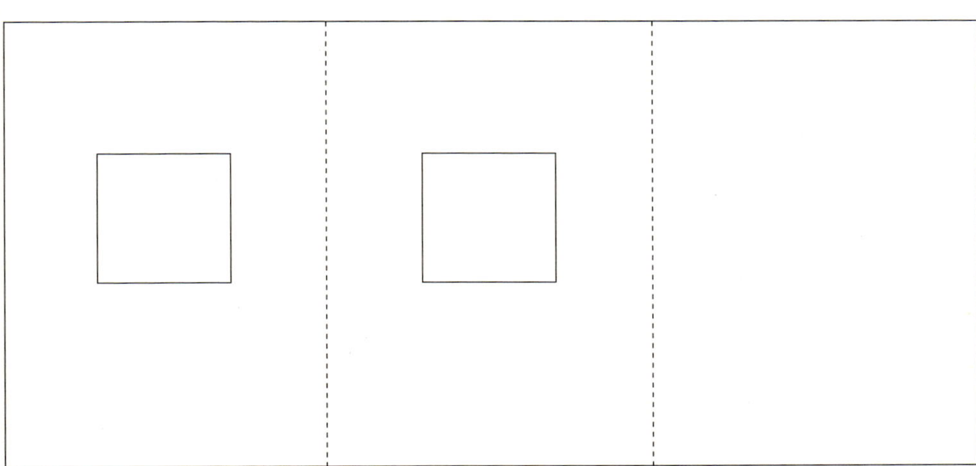

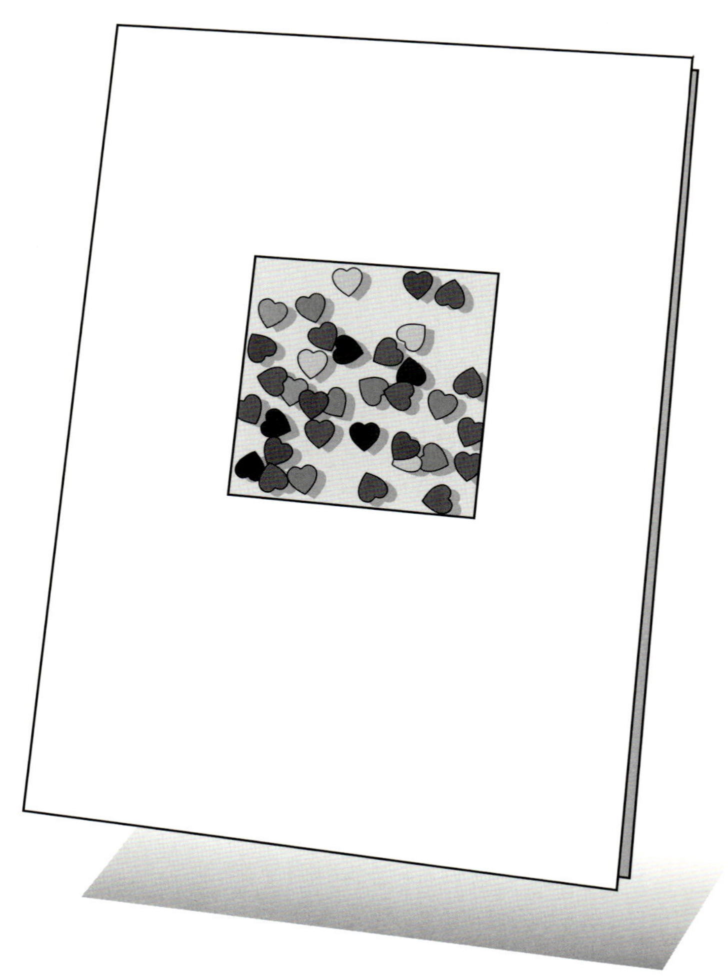

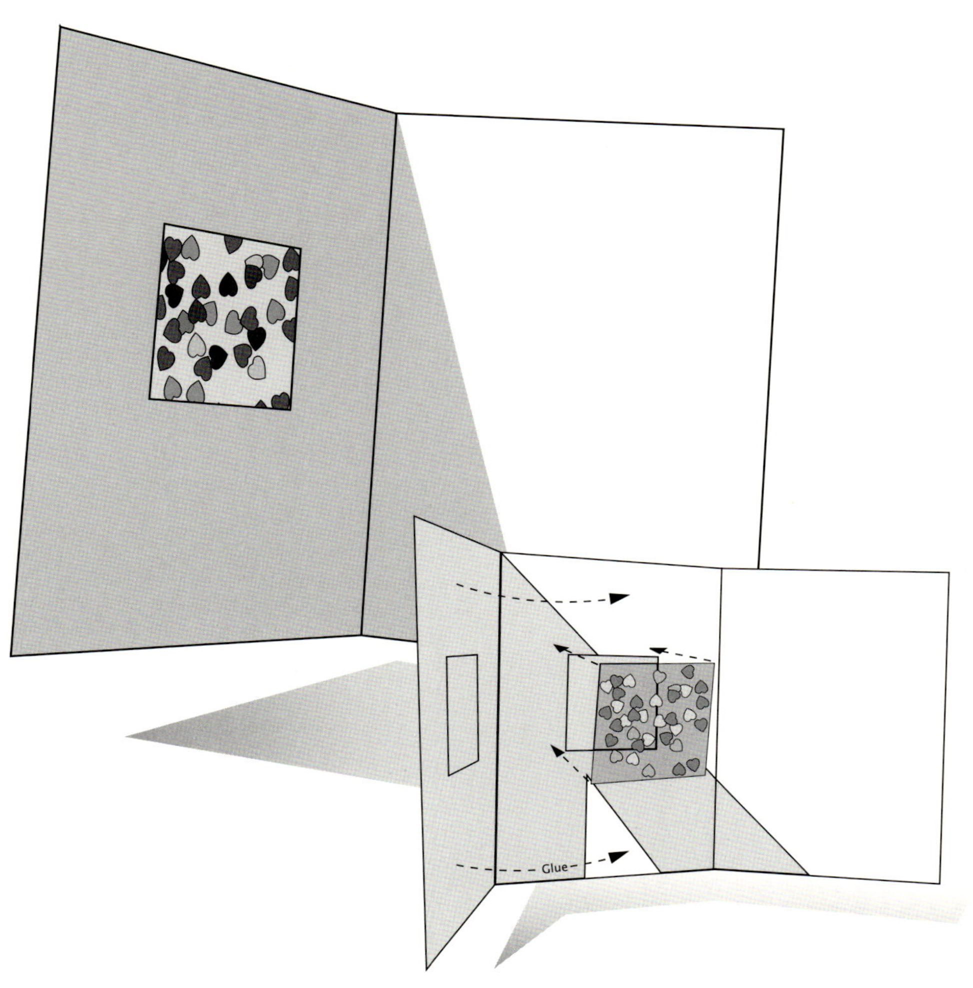

Glue

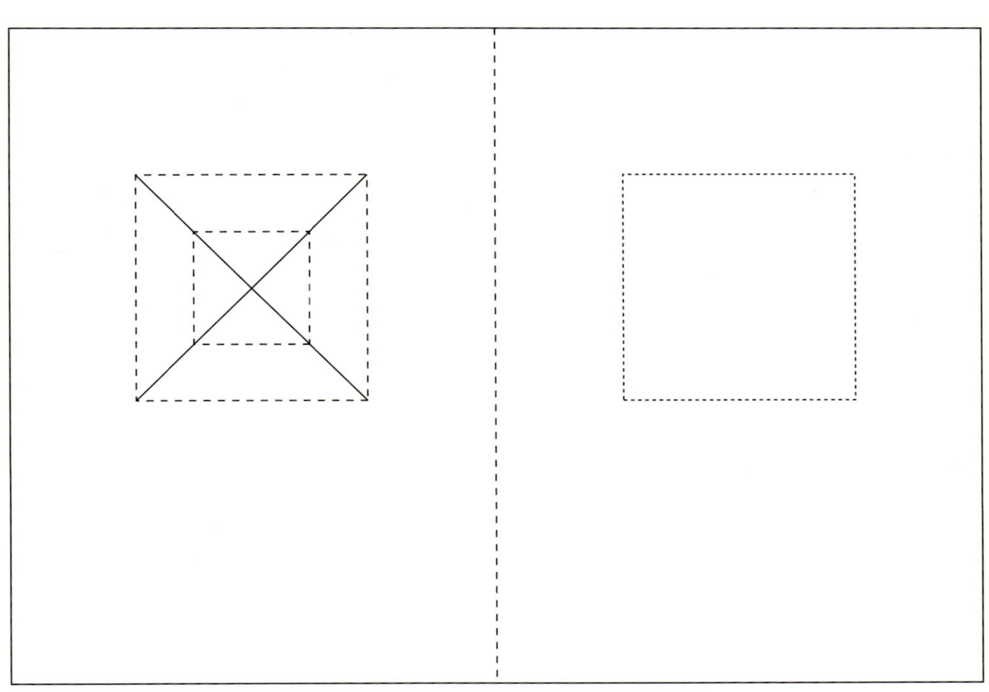

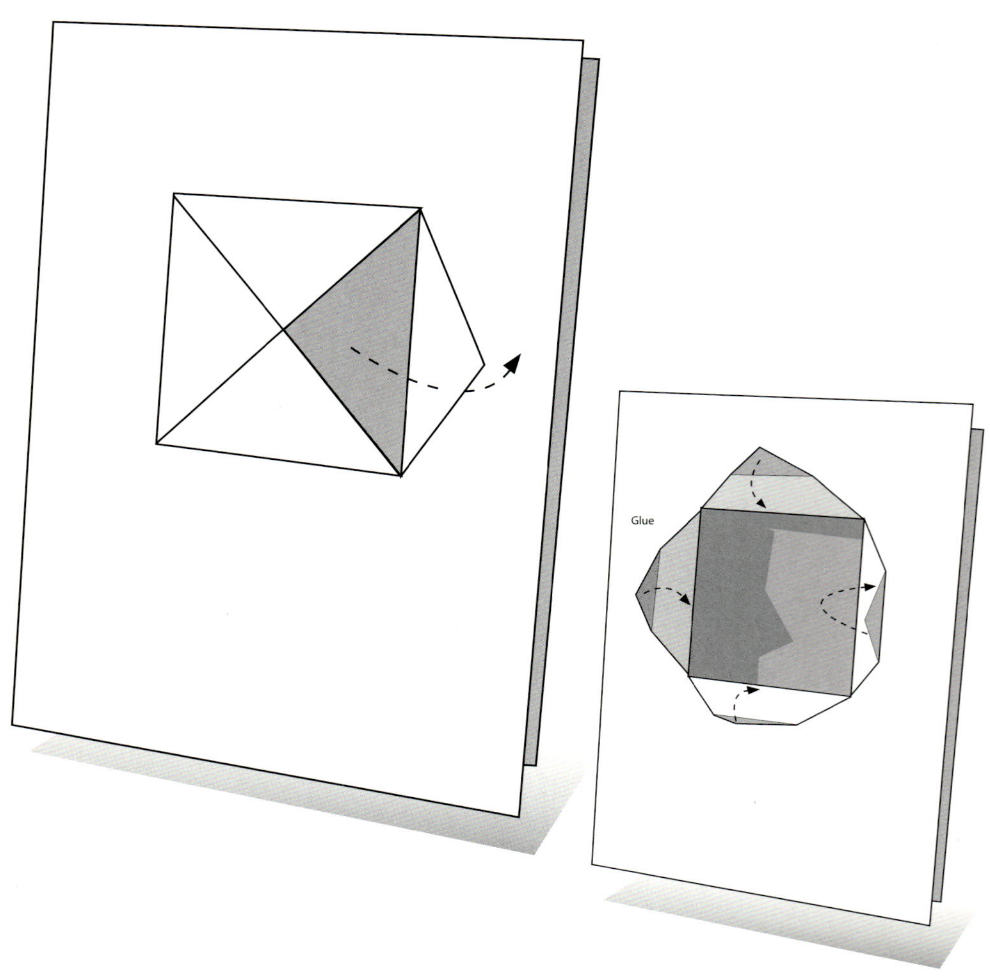

   Frames and Windows

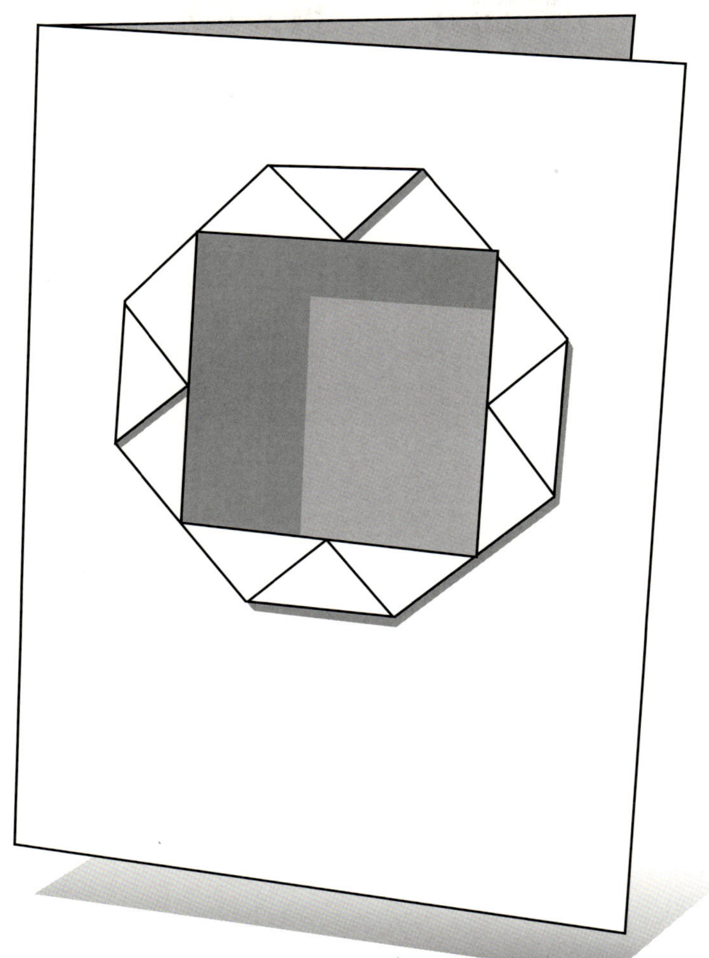

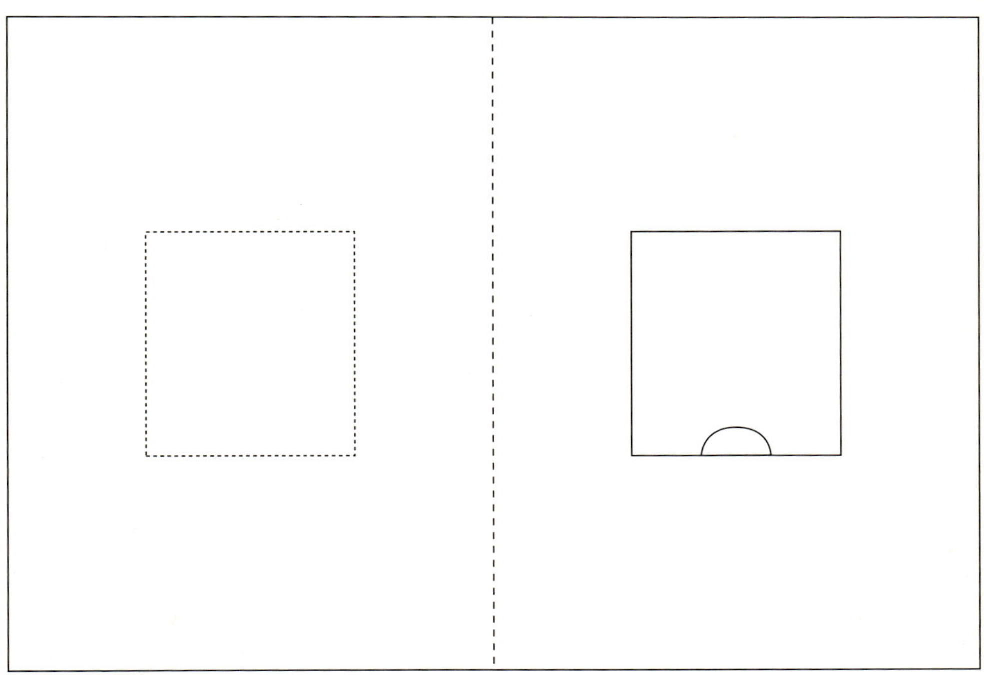

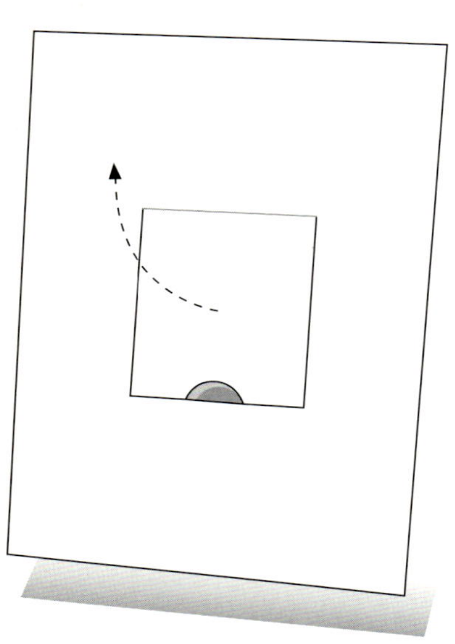

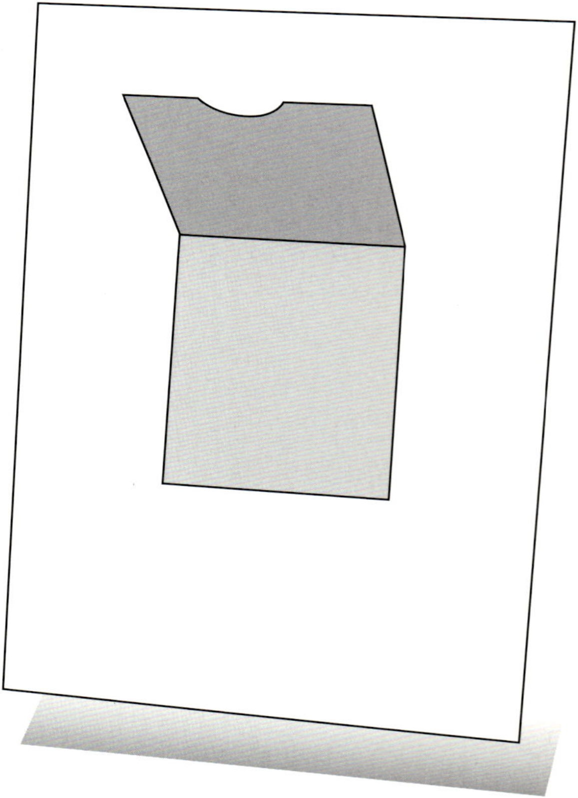

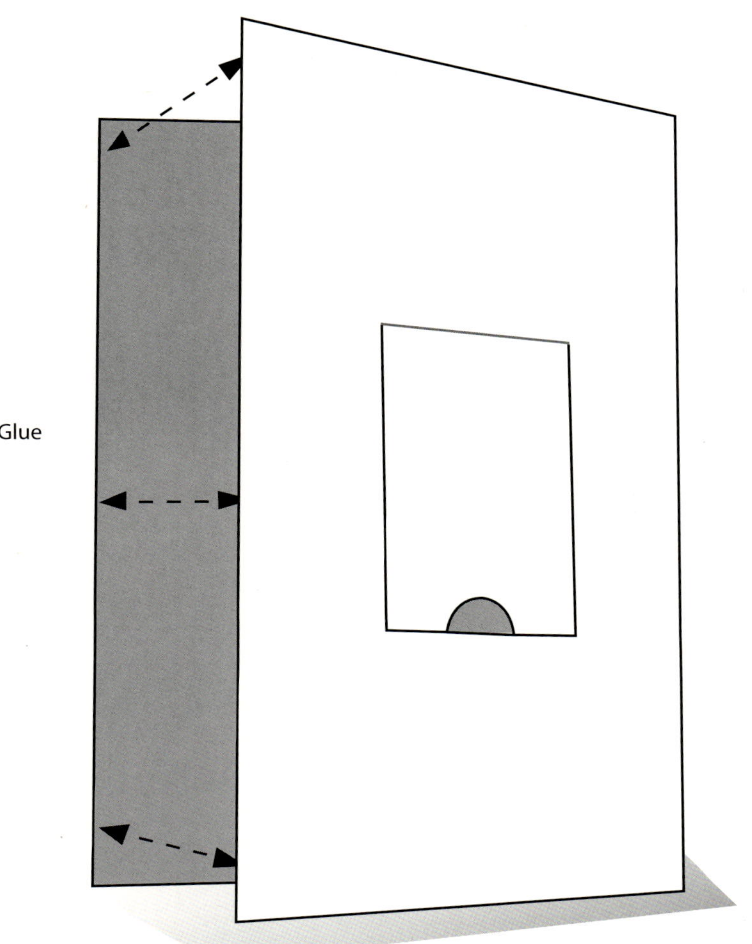

Glue

Locking Devices

固定部品
Systèmes de fermeture
Sistemas de cierre
Sistemi di chiusura
Verschlüsse

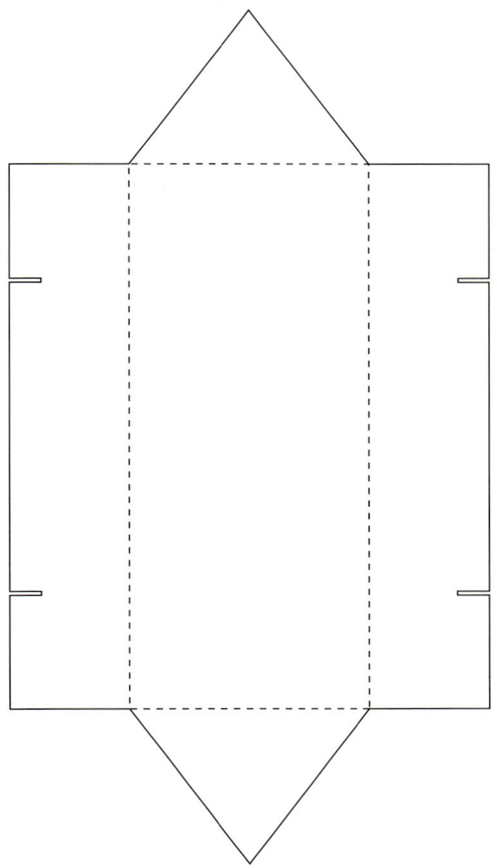

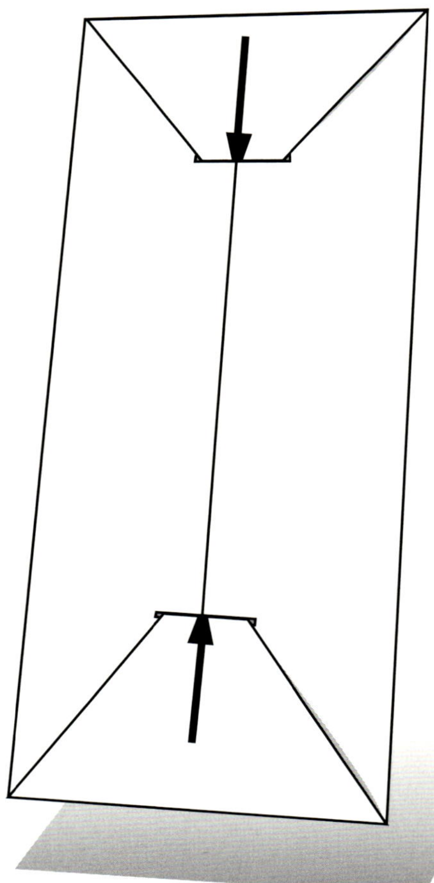

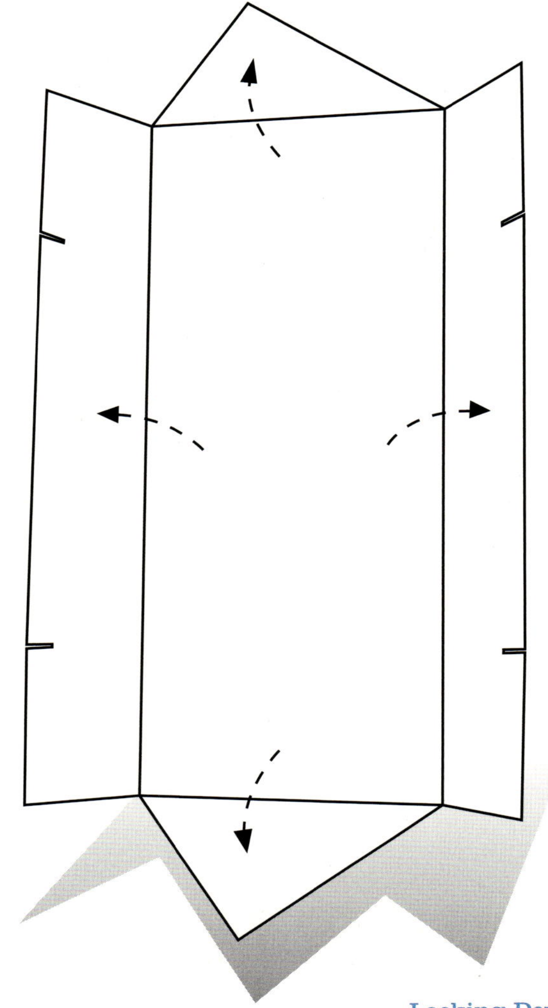

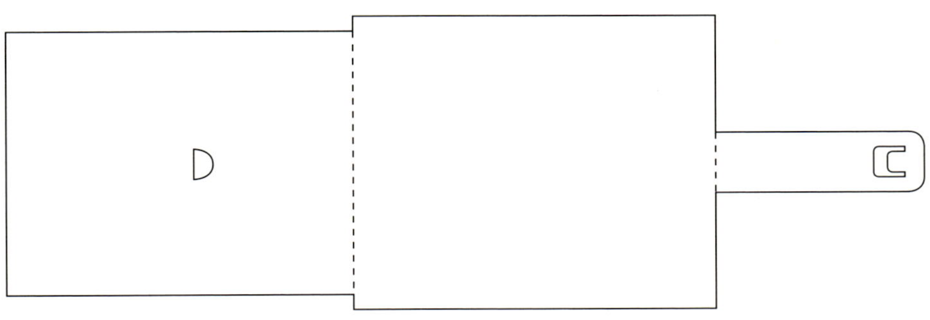

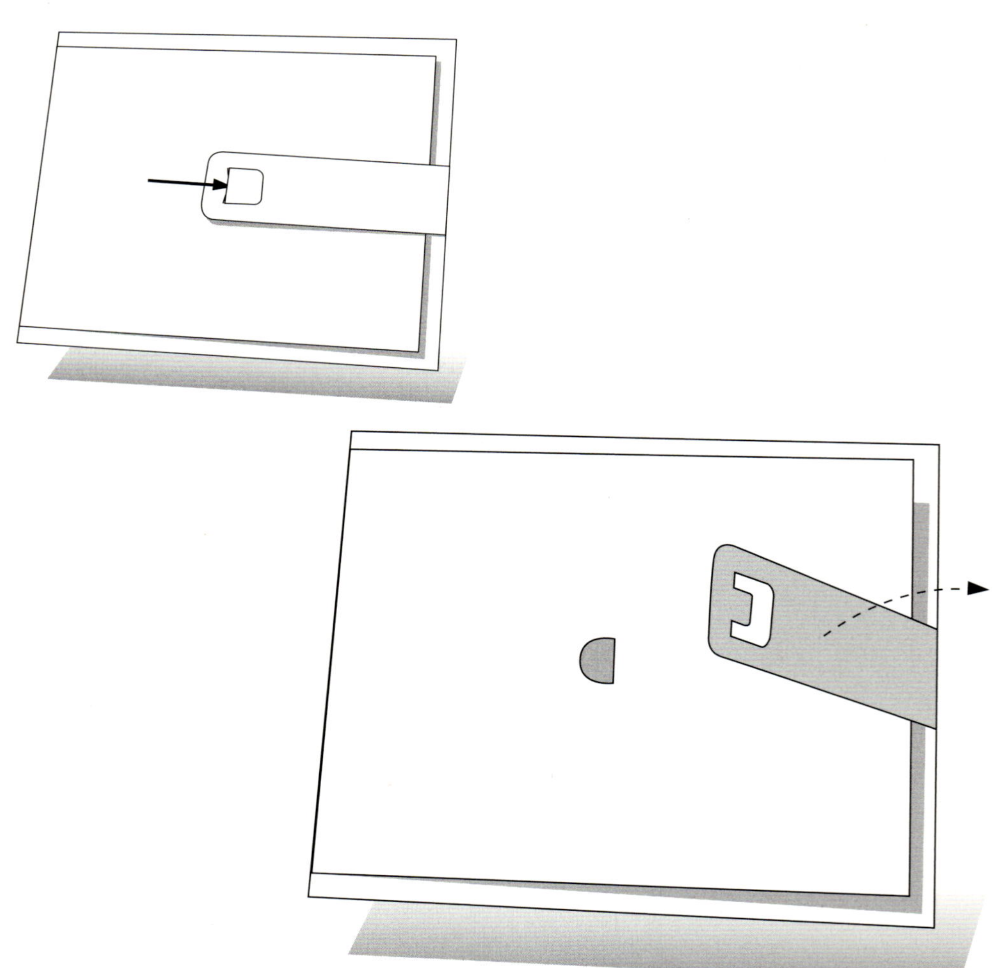

212   Locking Devices

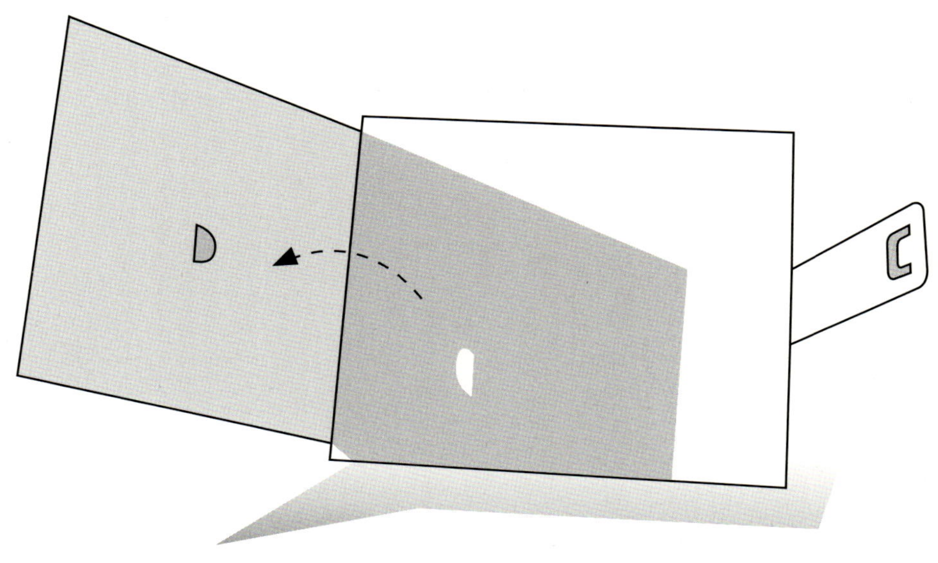

D
C

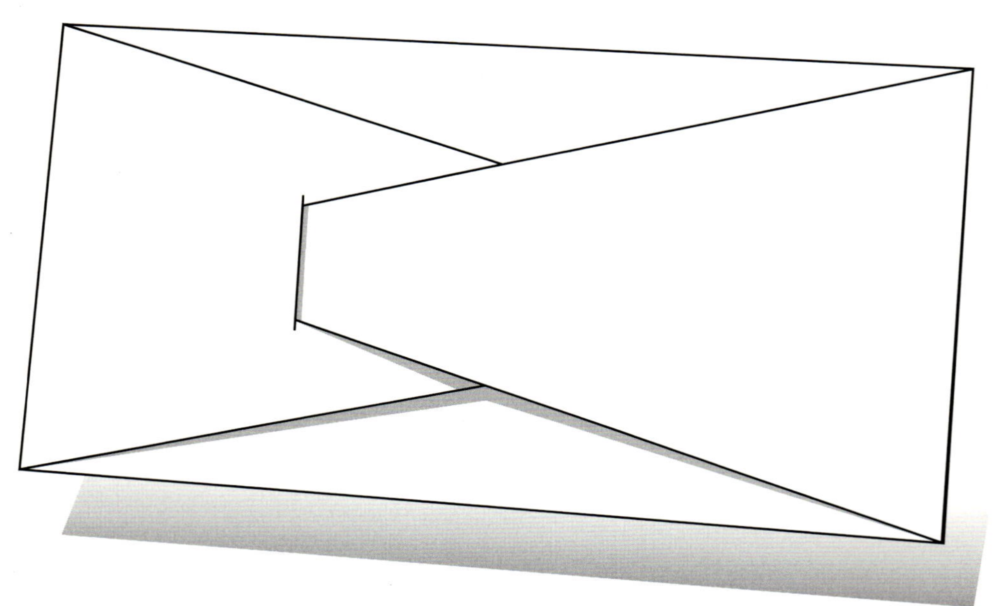

    Locking Devices

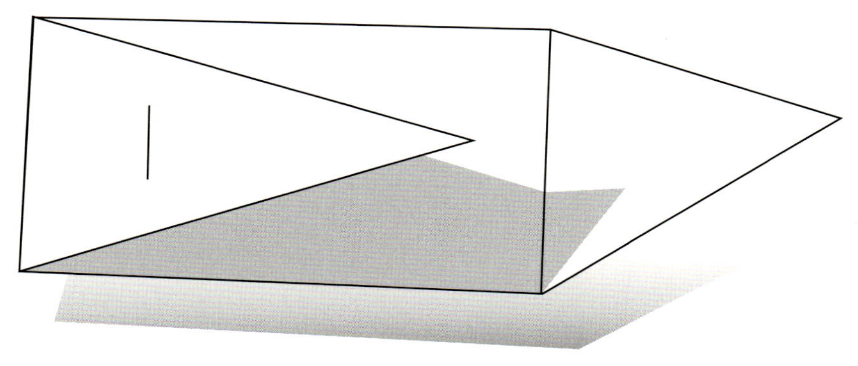

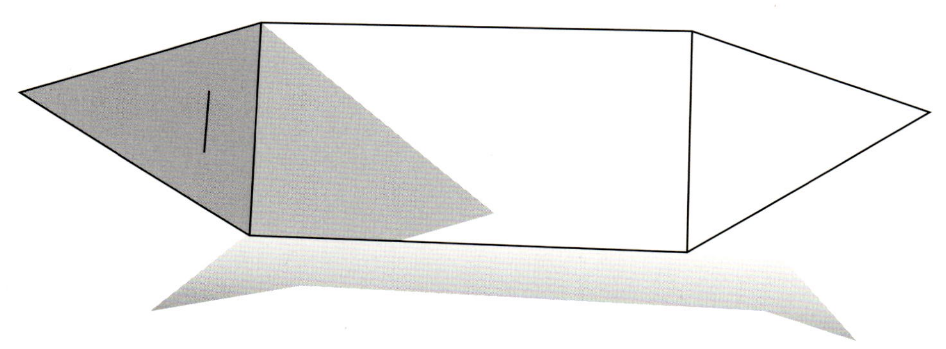

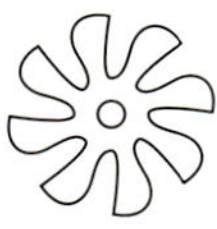

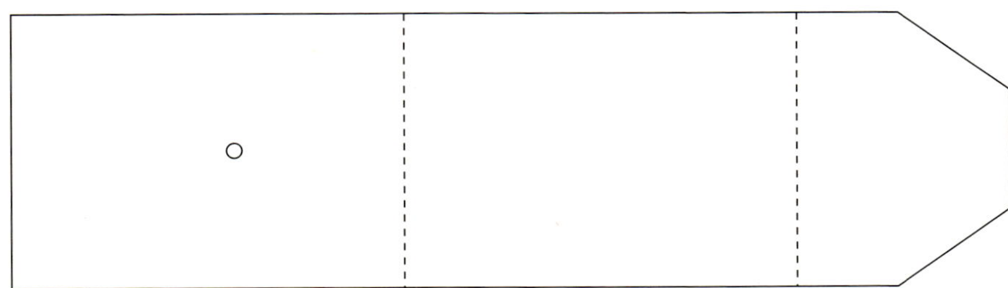

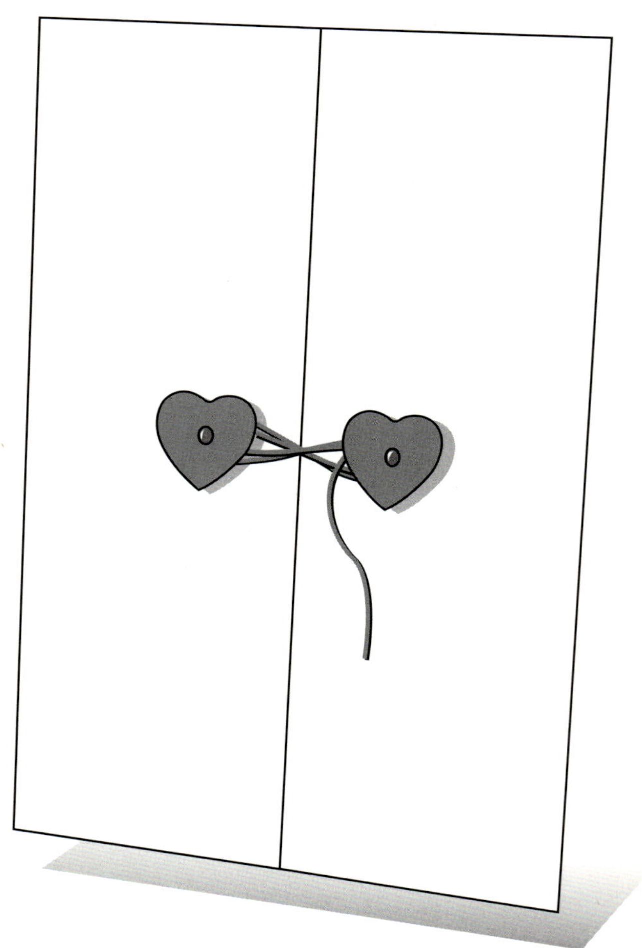

224   Locking Devices

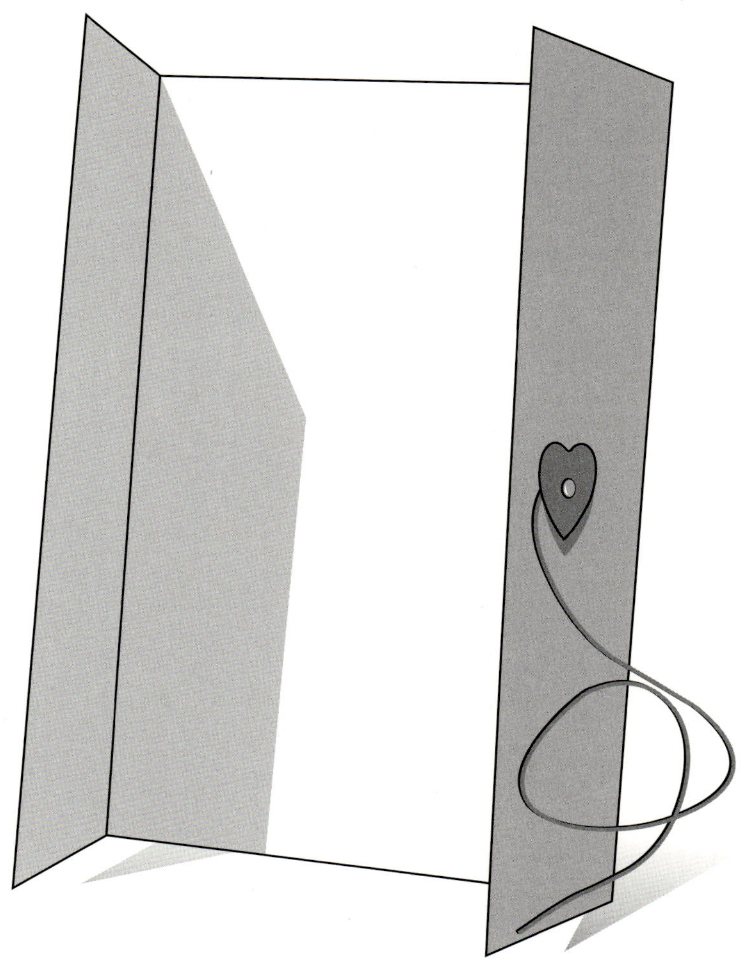

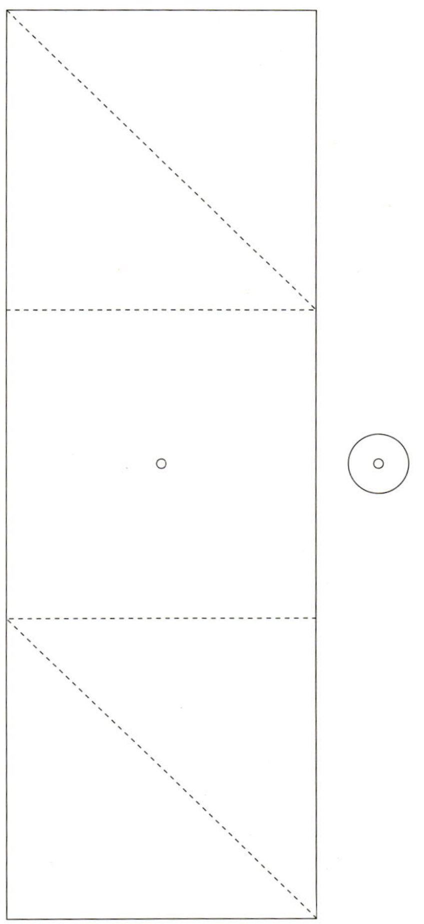

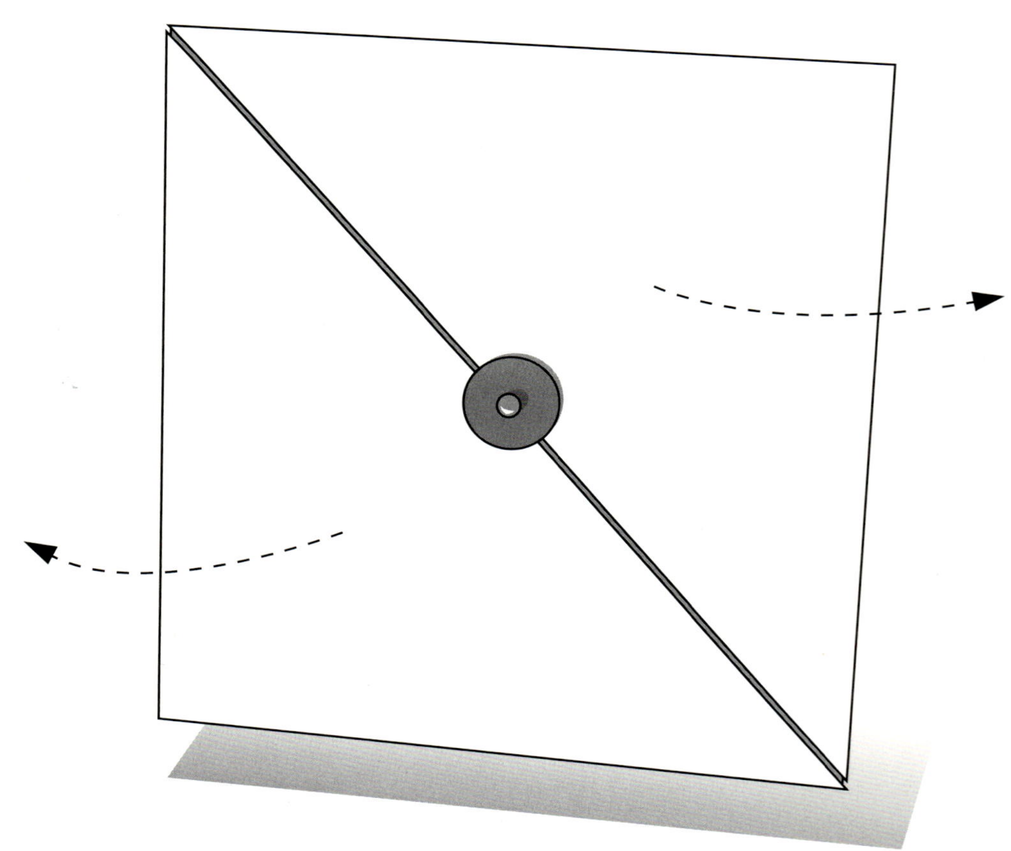

    Locking Devices

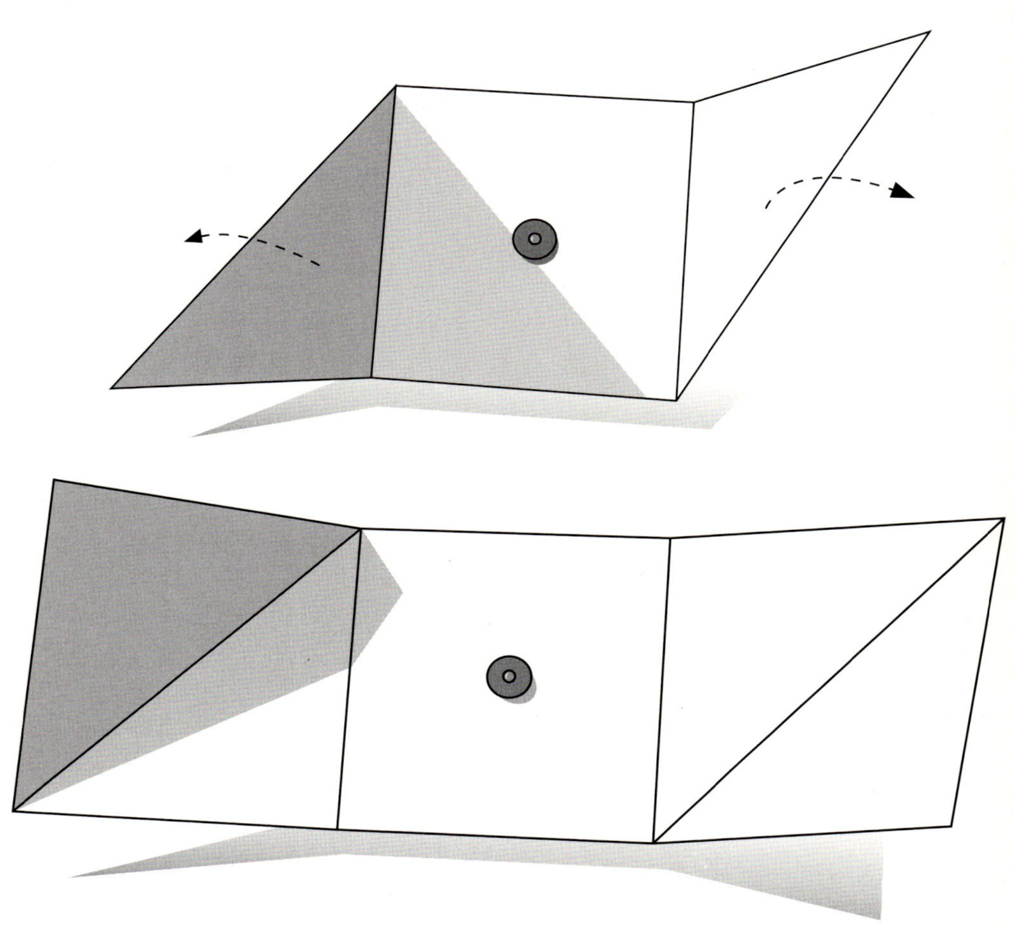

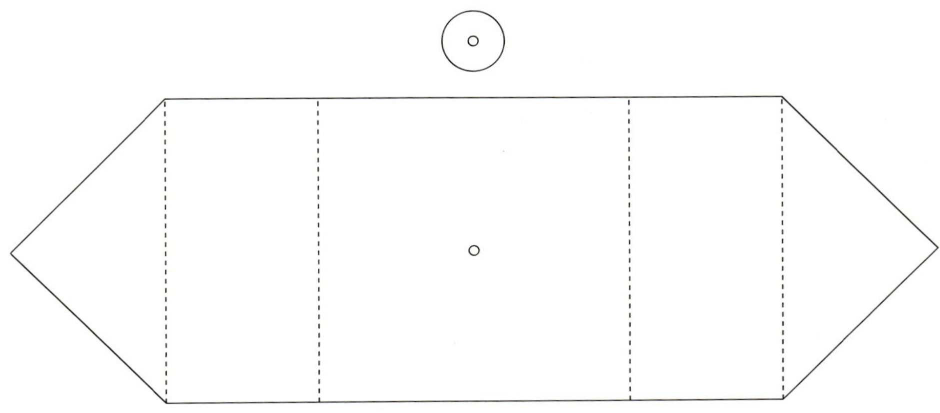

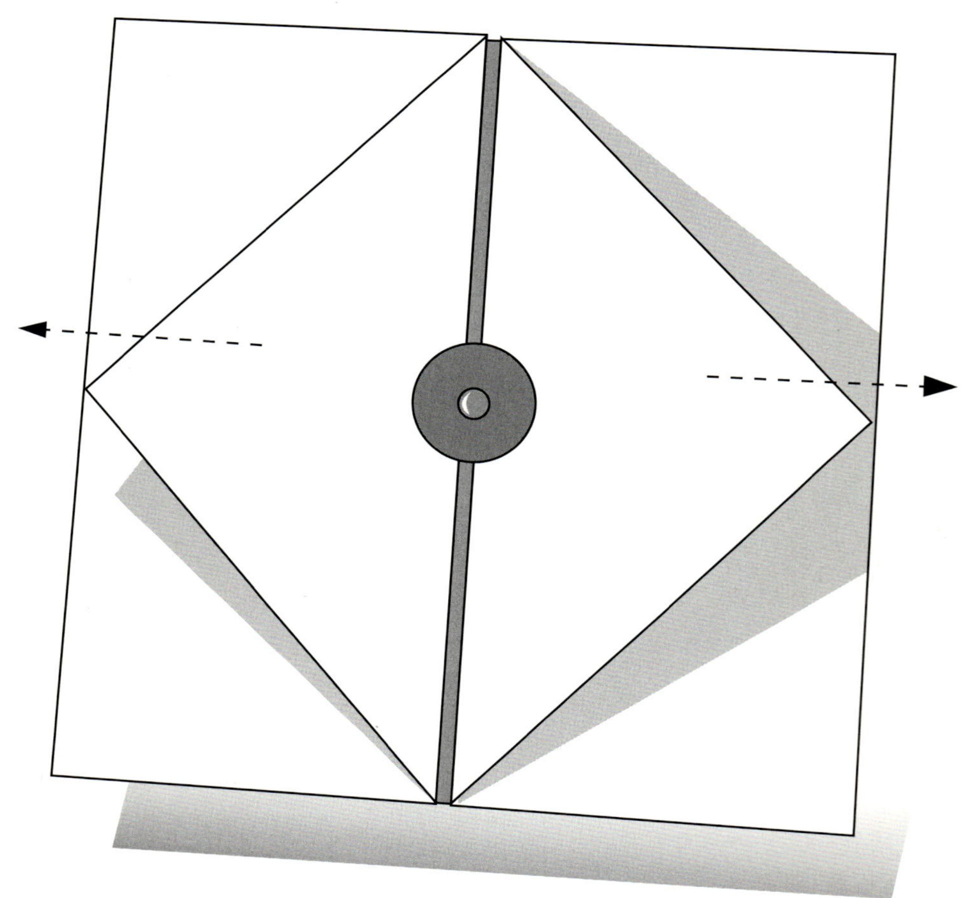

 Locking Devices

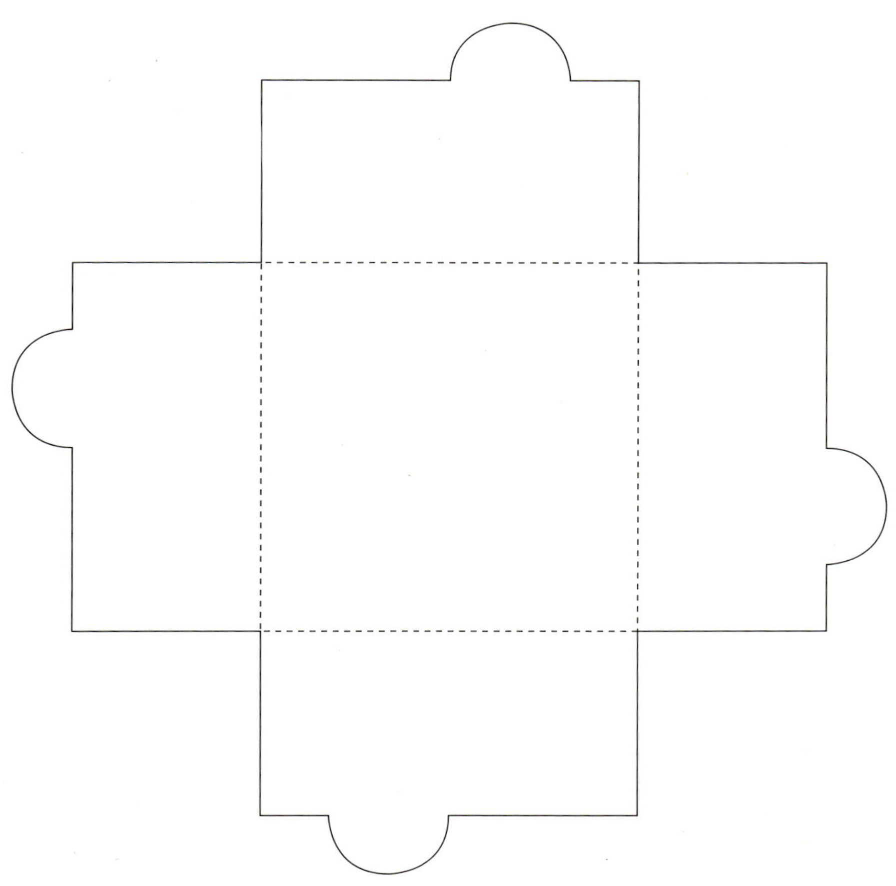

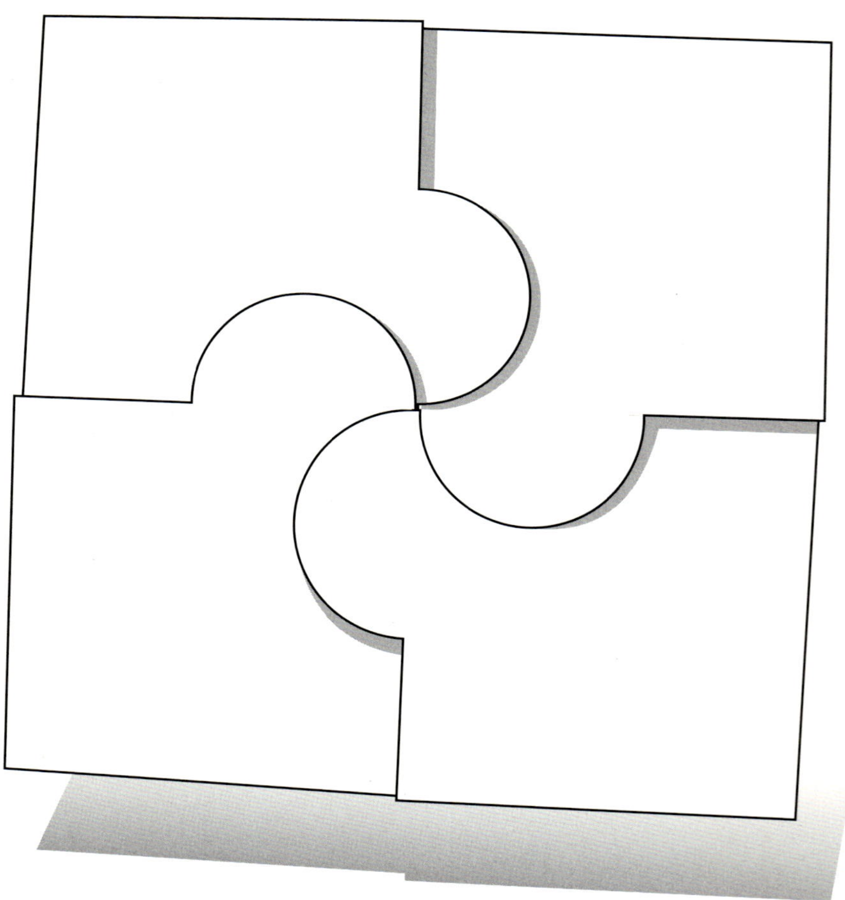

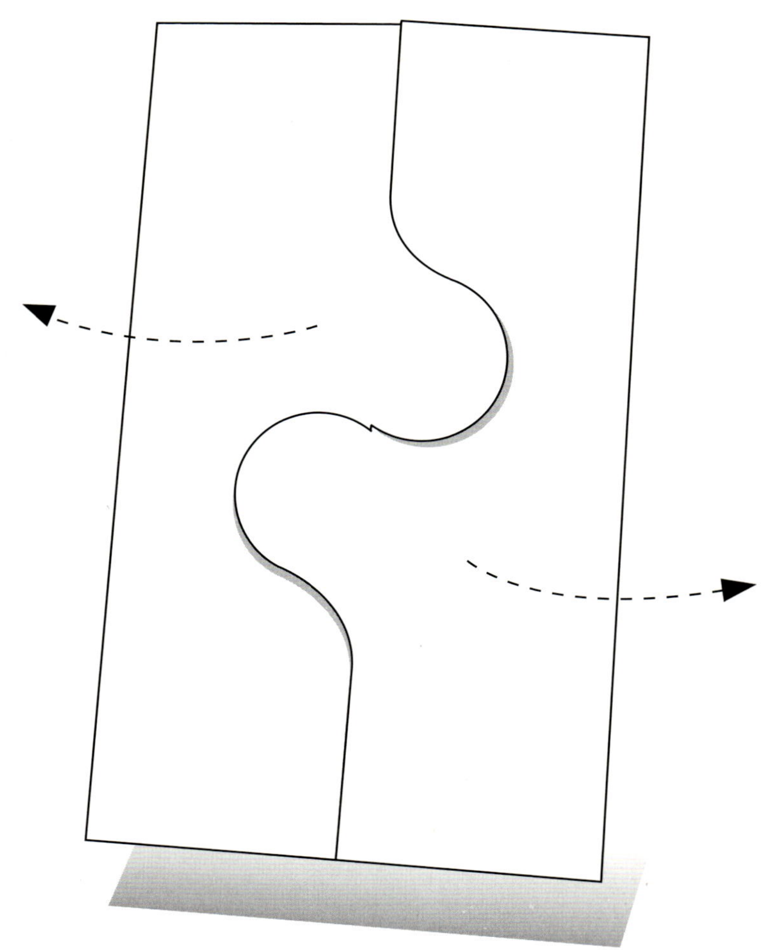

    Locking Devices

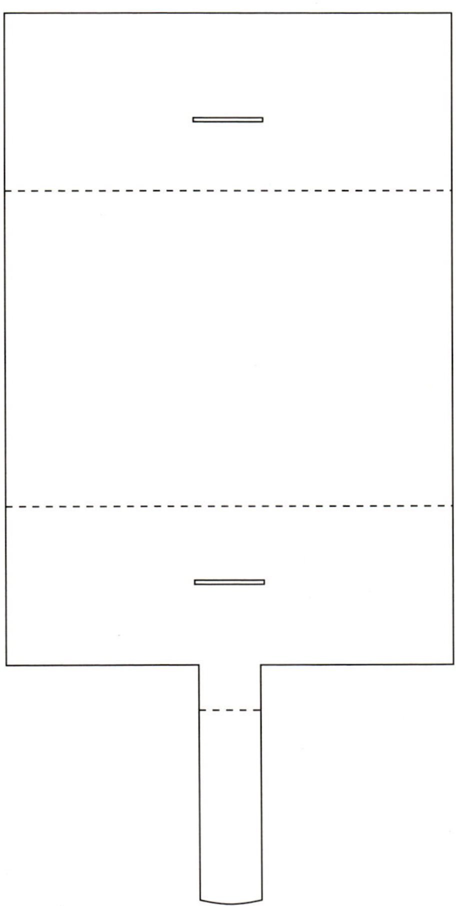

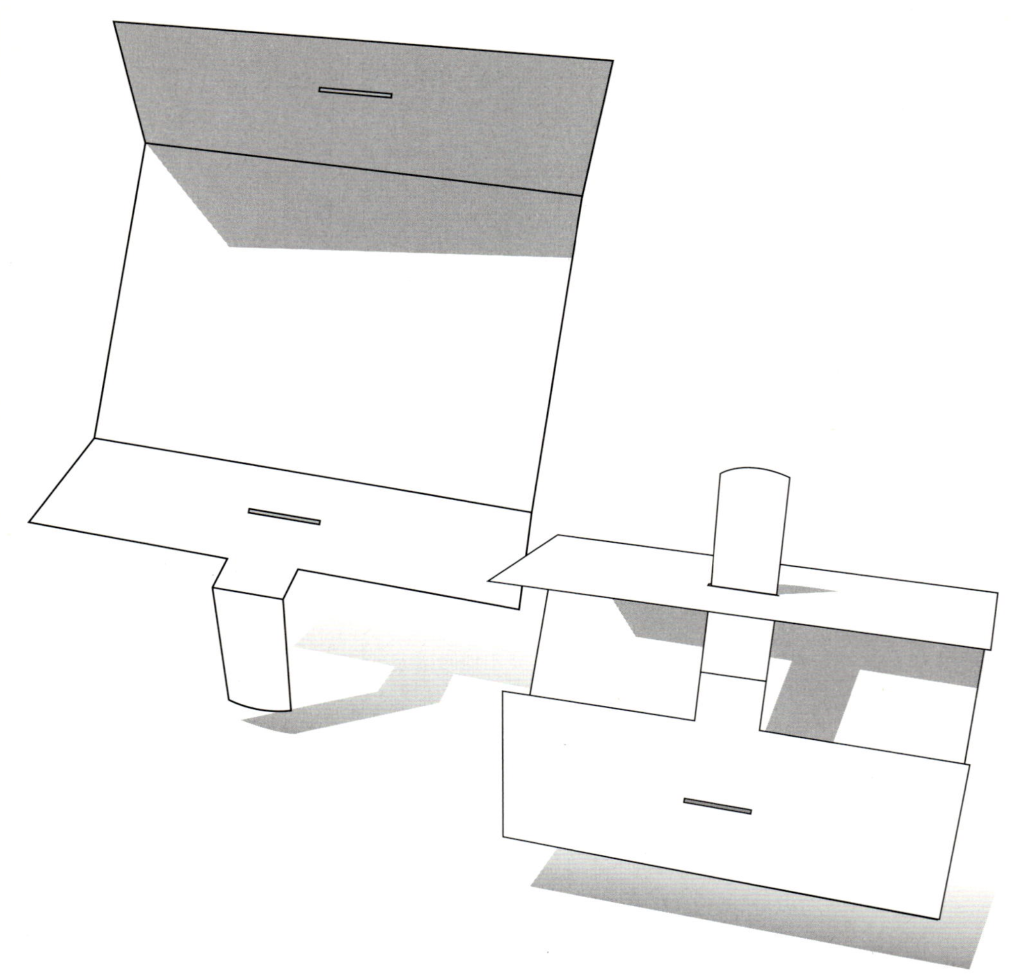

  Locking Devices

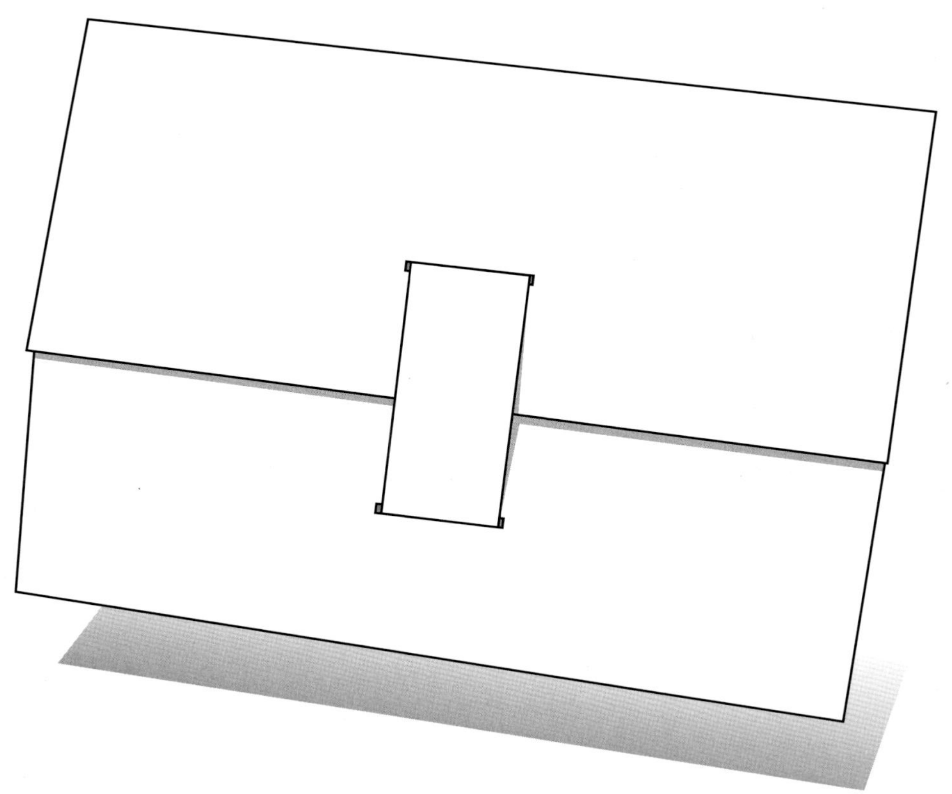

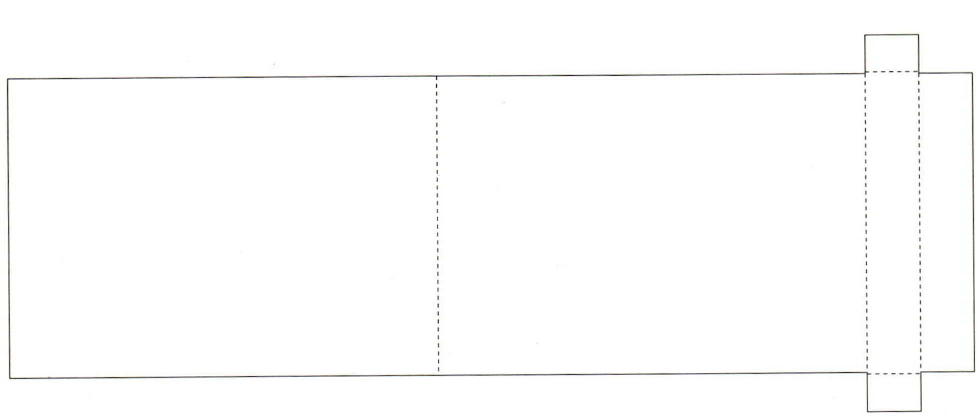

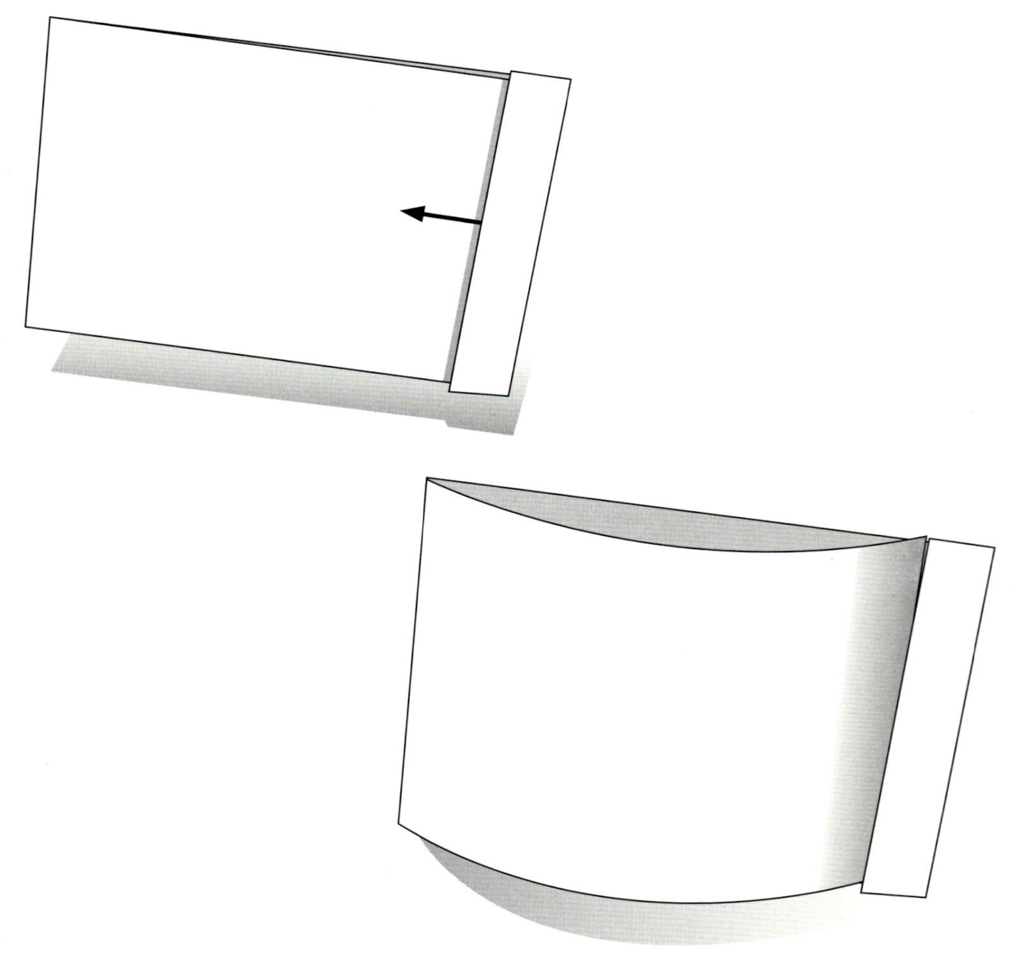

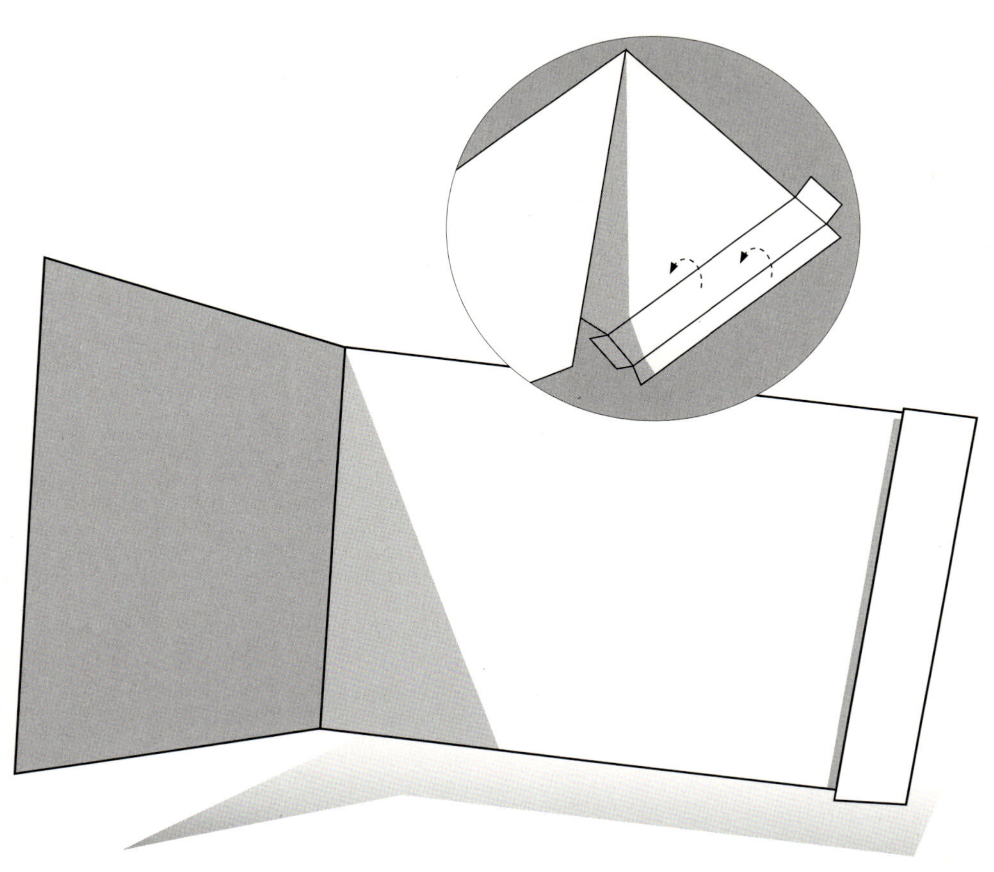

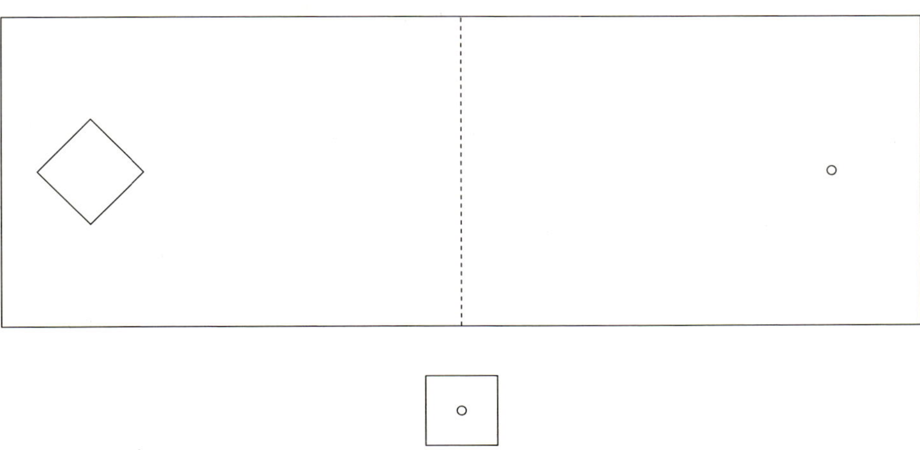

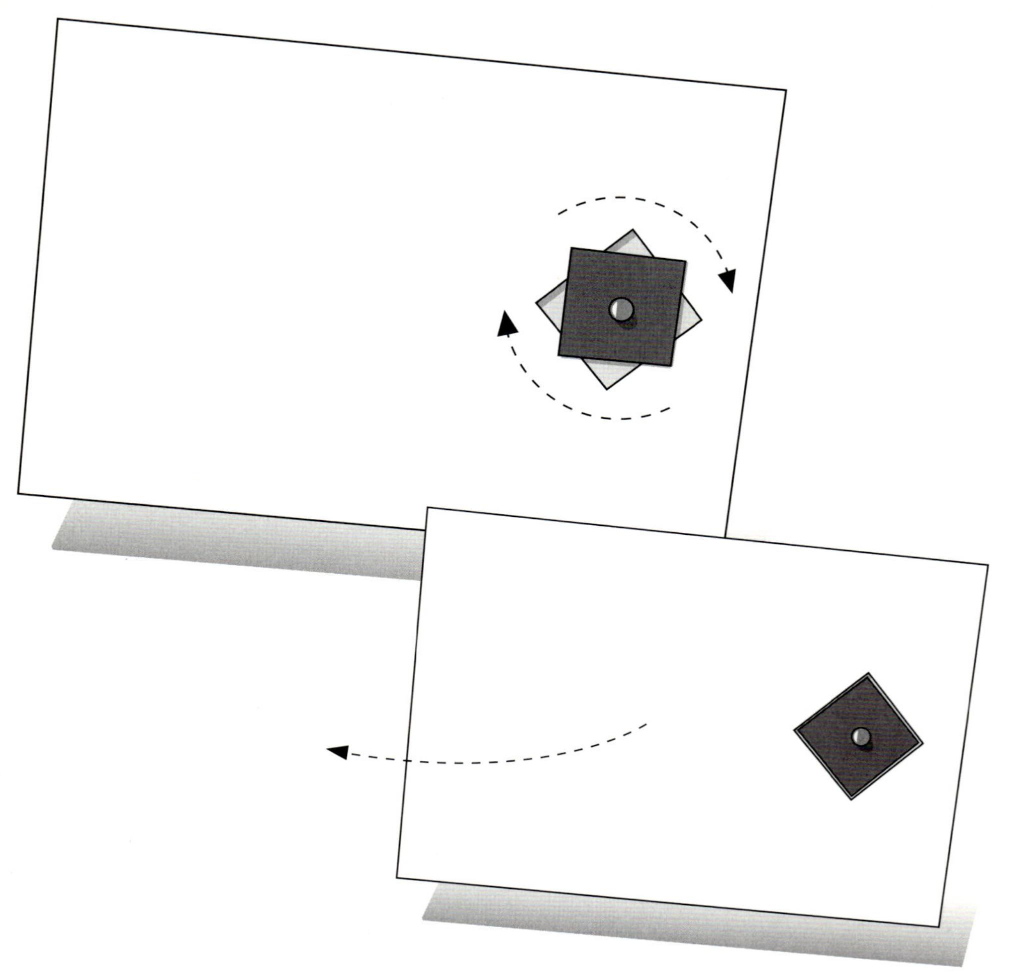

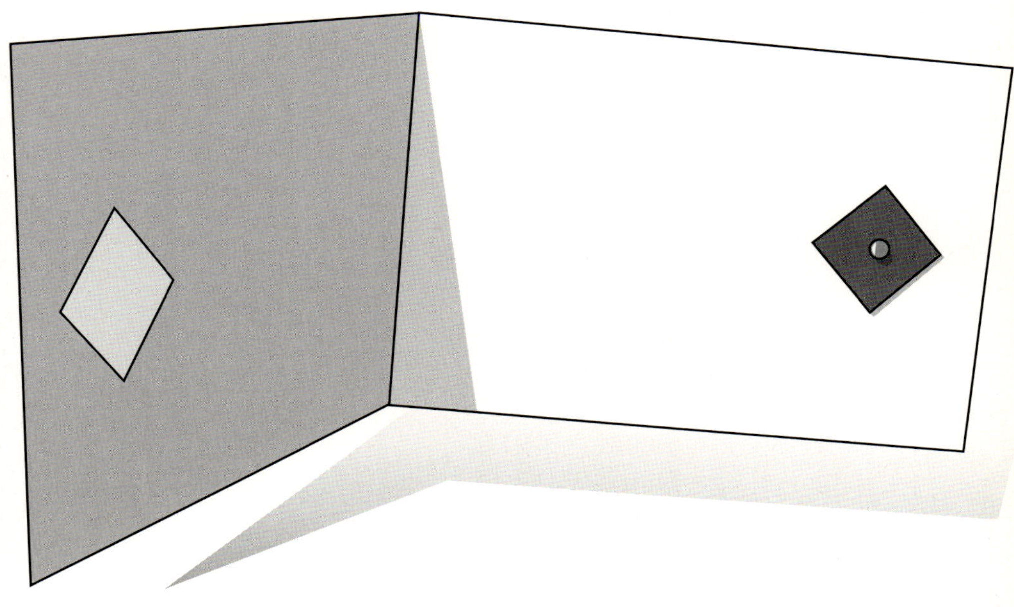

Pop-ups

ポップアップ
Dépliages
Desplegables
Biglietti pop-up
Pop-ups

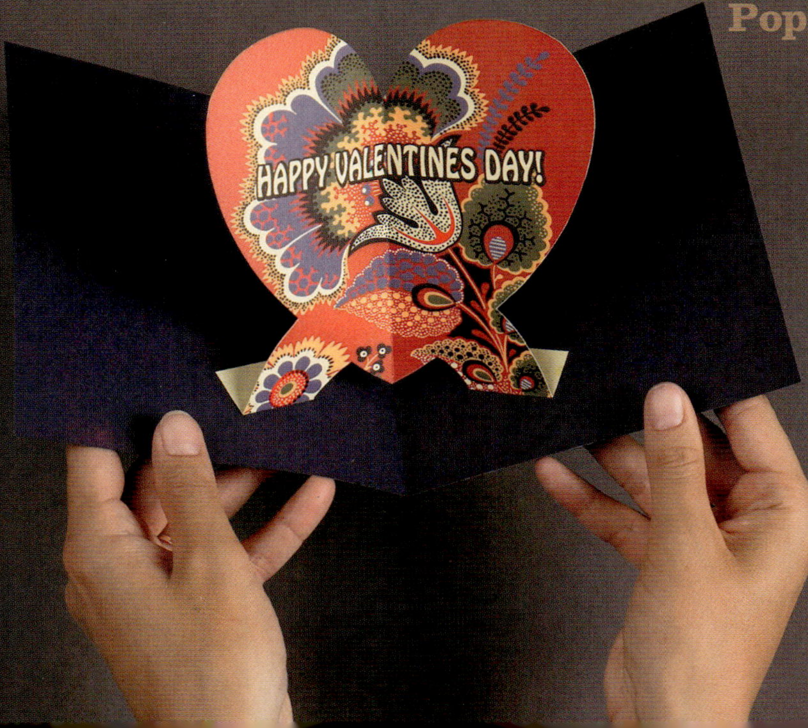
HAPPY VALENTINES DAY!

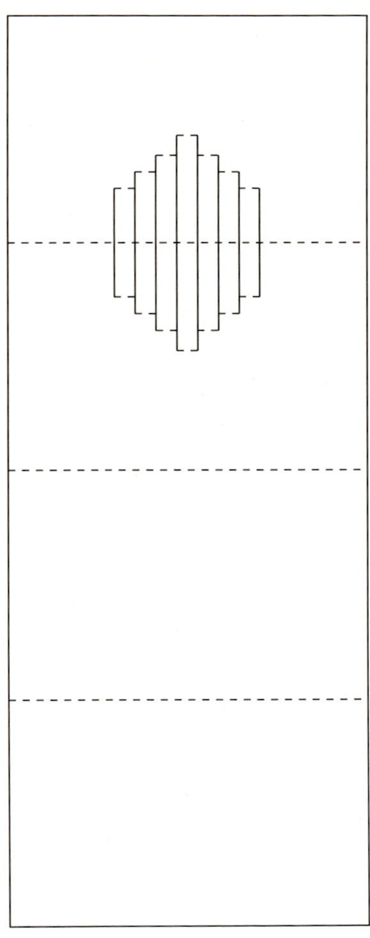

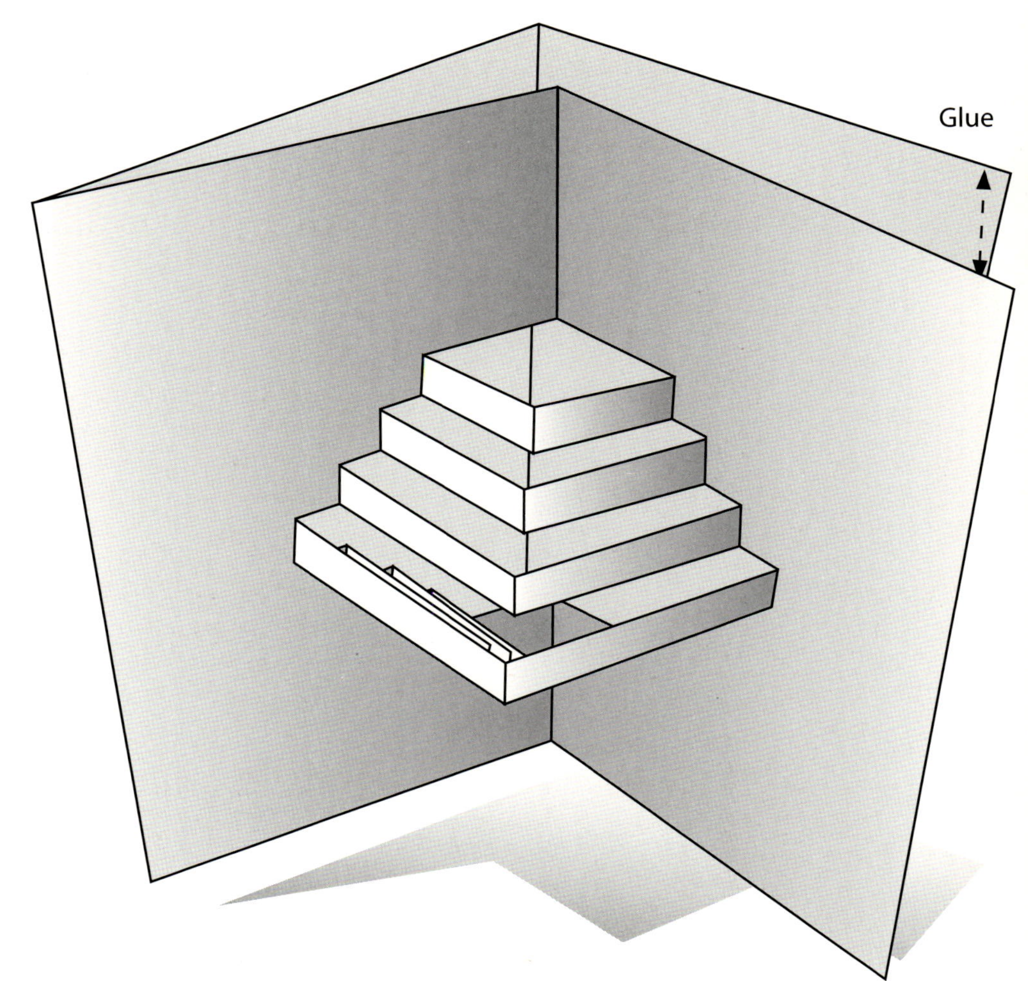

Glue

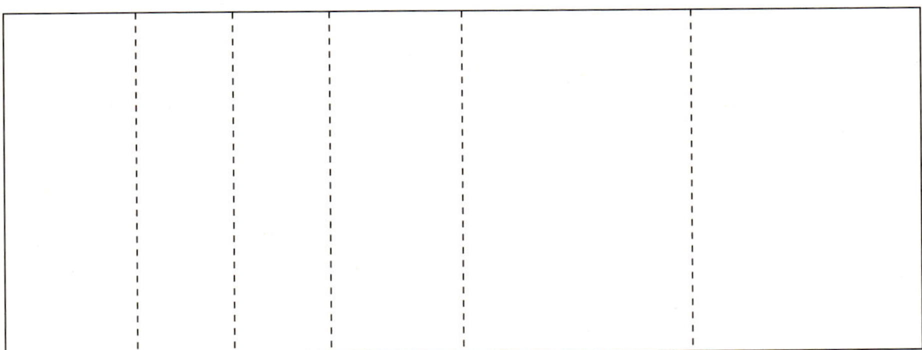

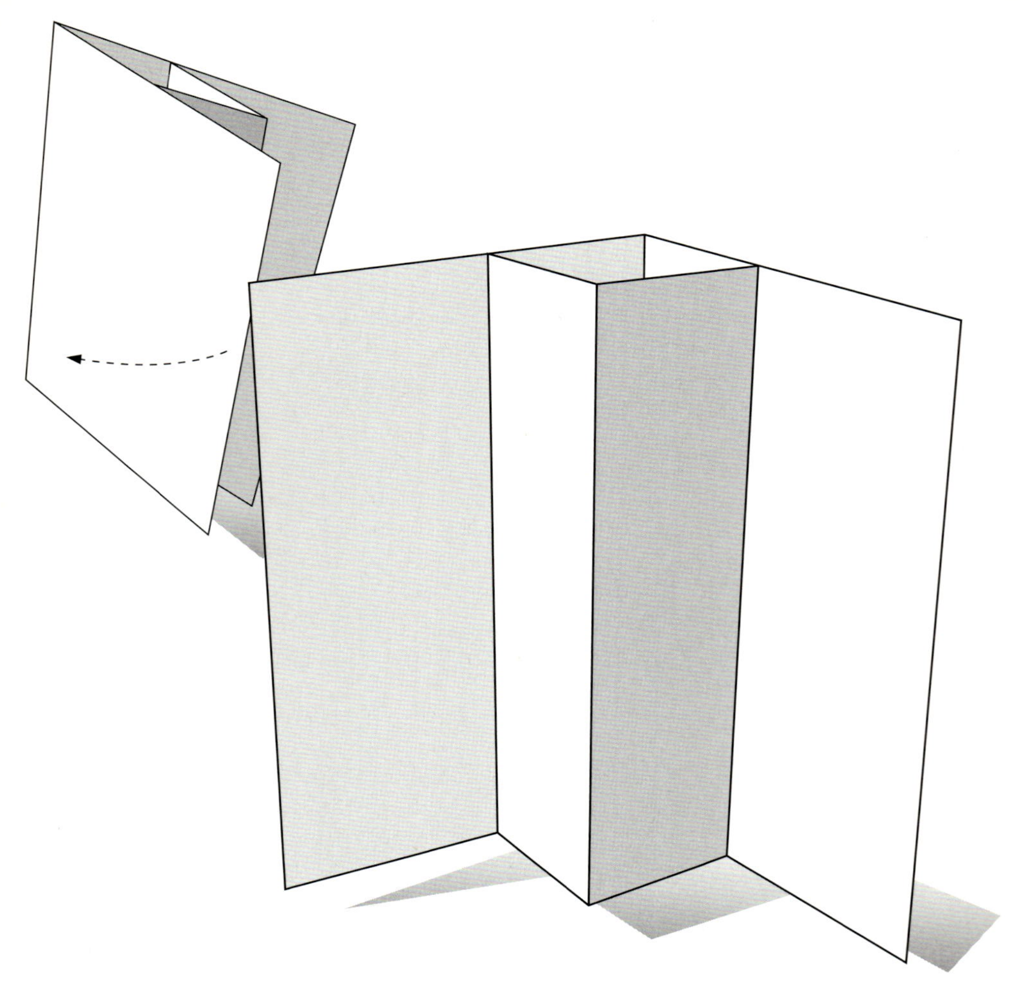

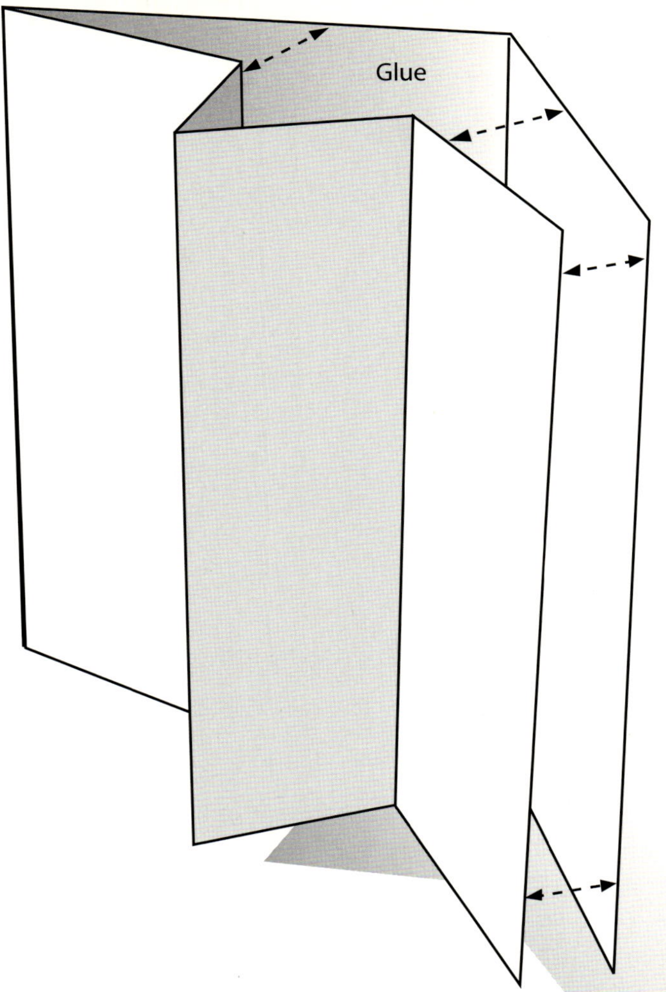

Glue

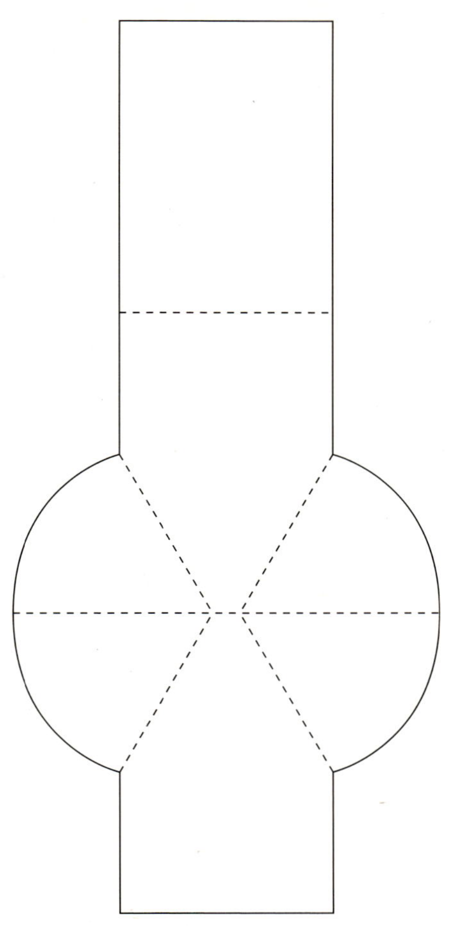

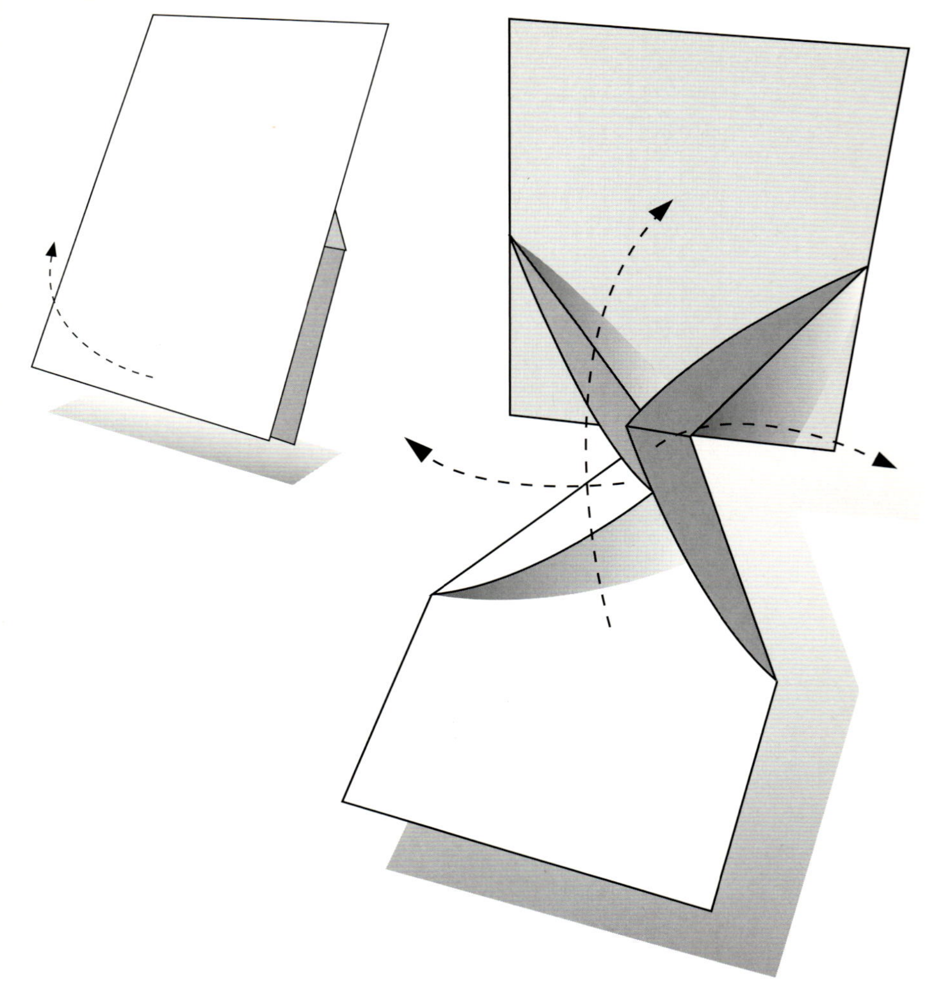

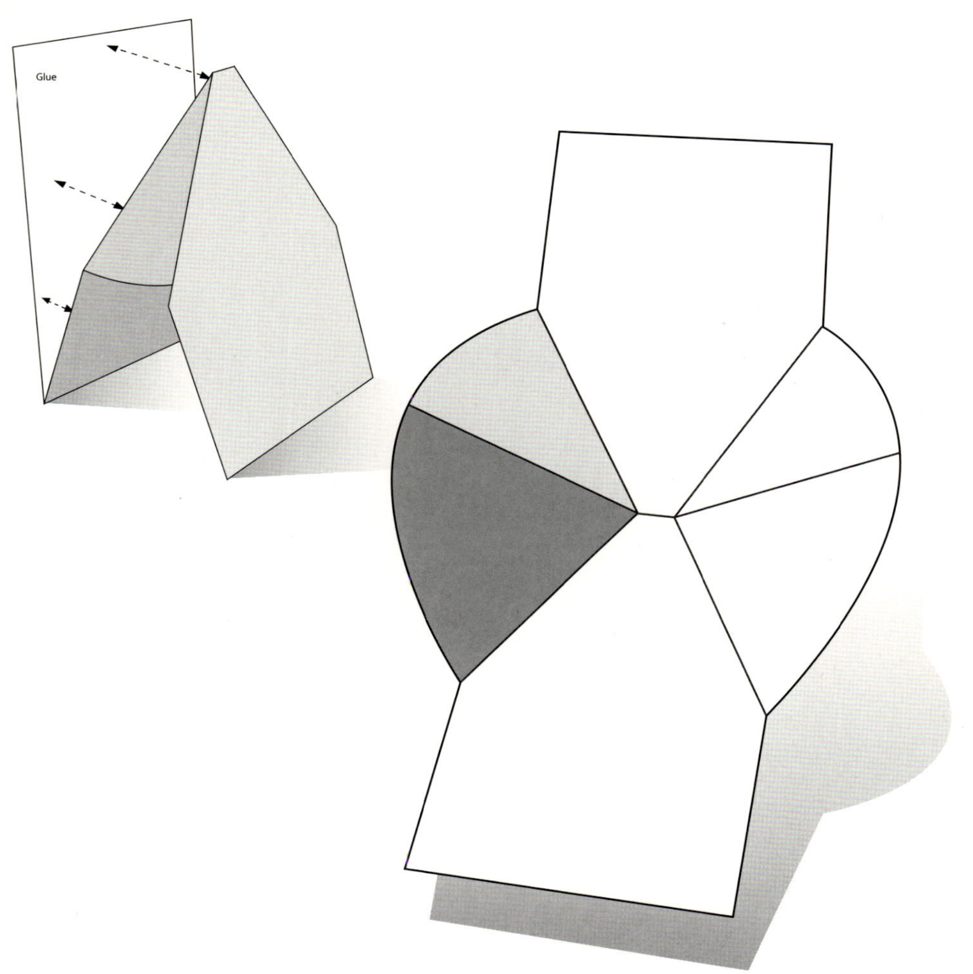
Glue

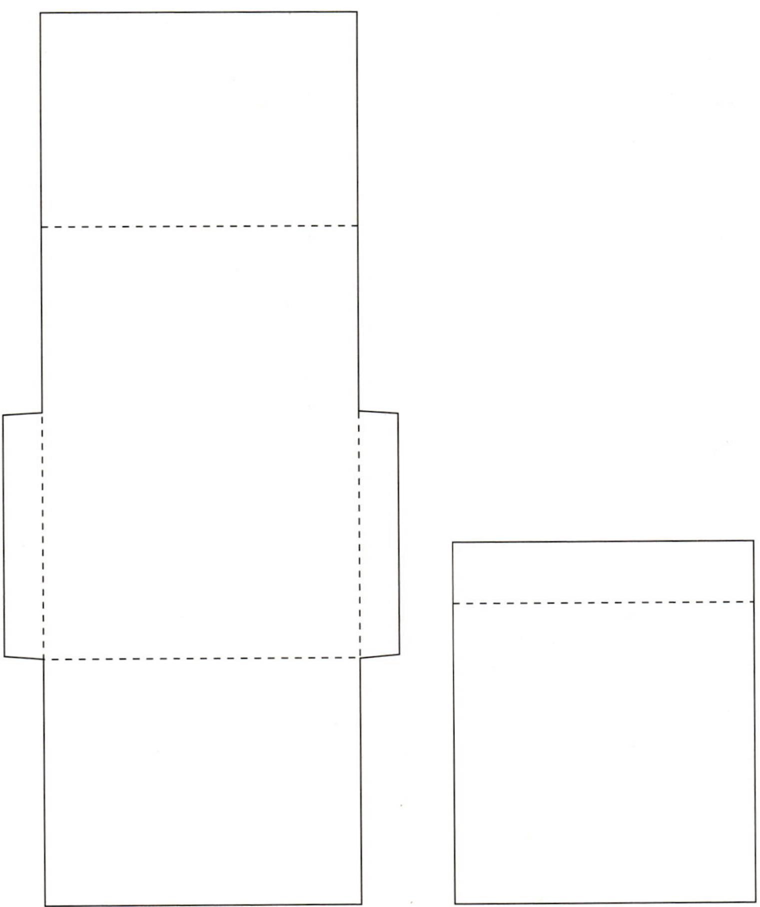

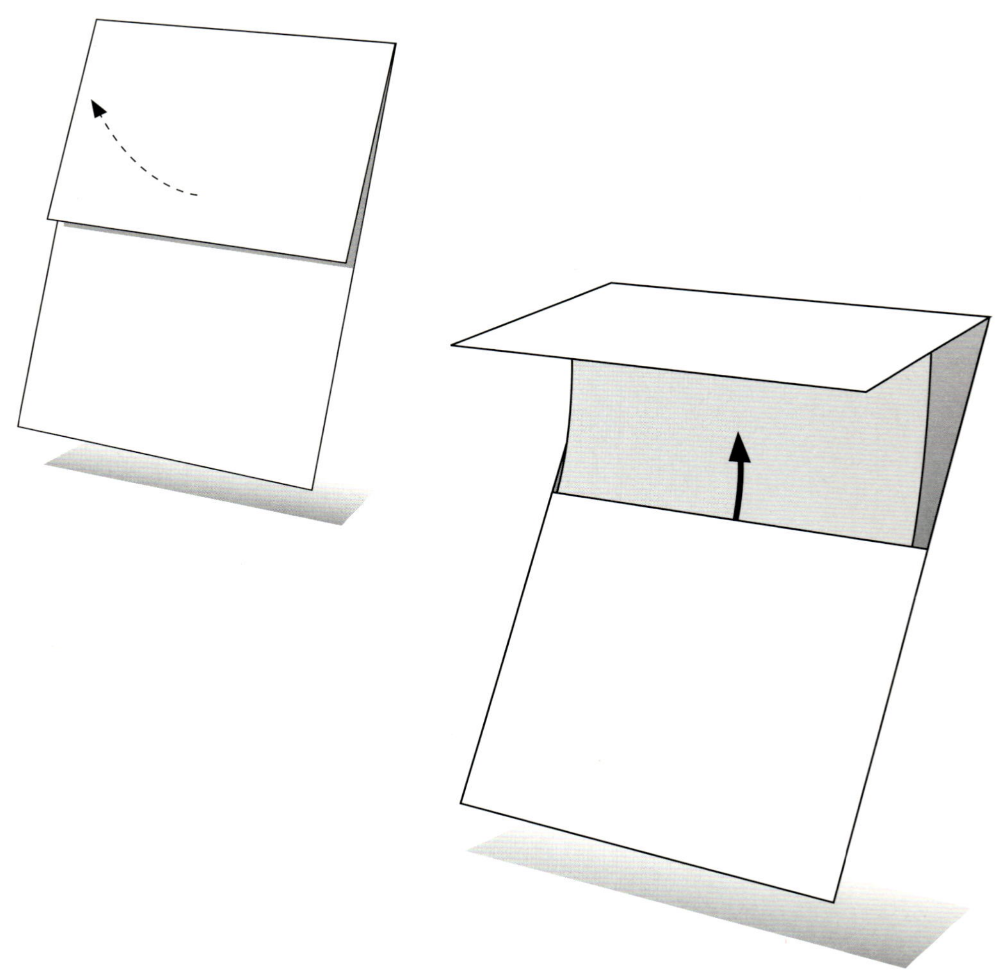

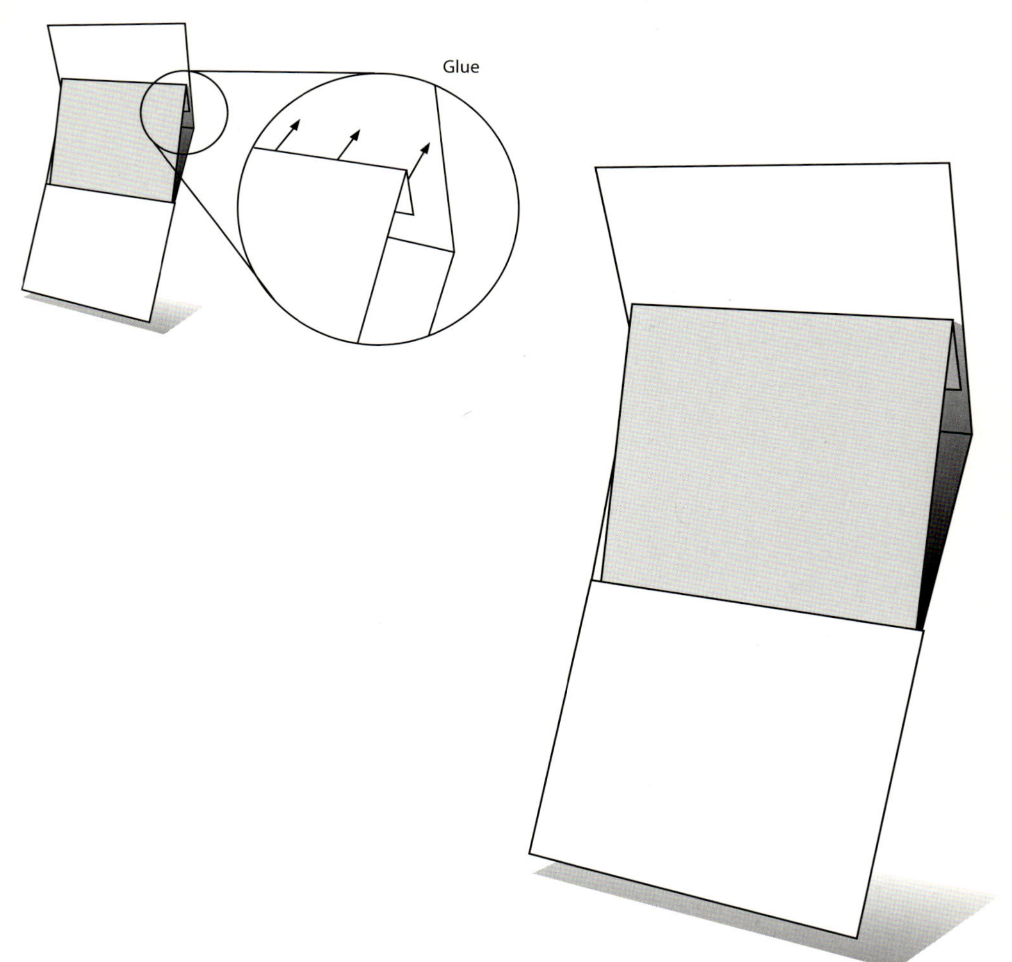

Glue

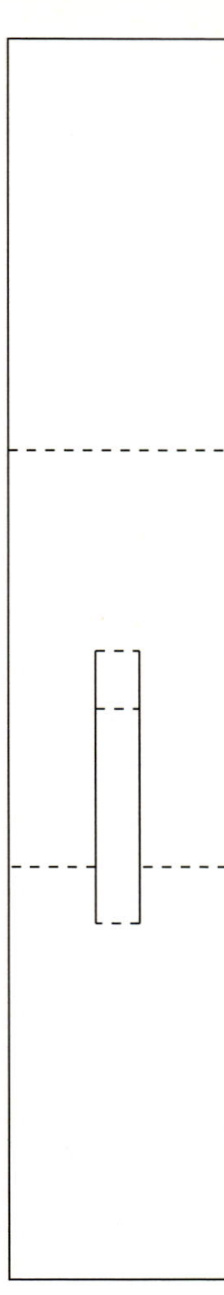

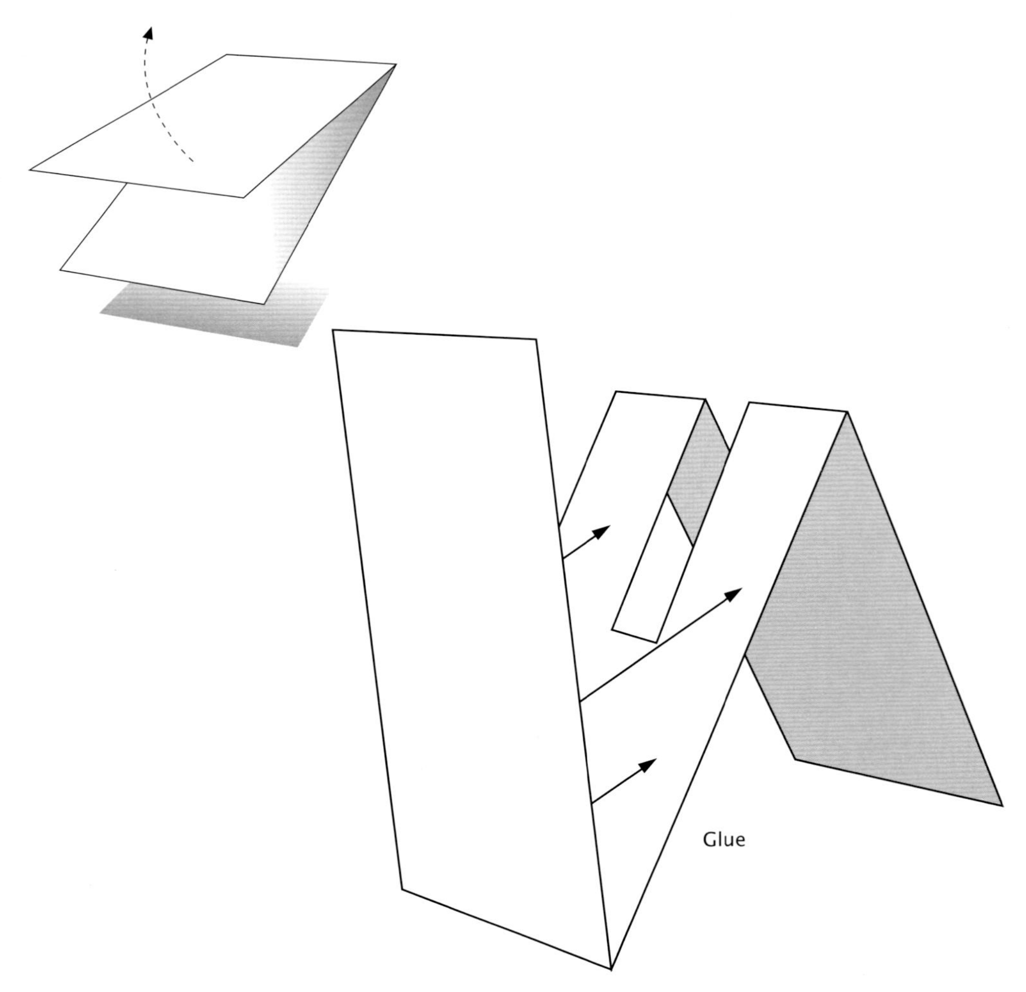

Glue

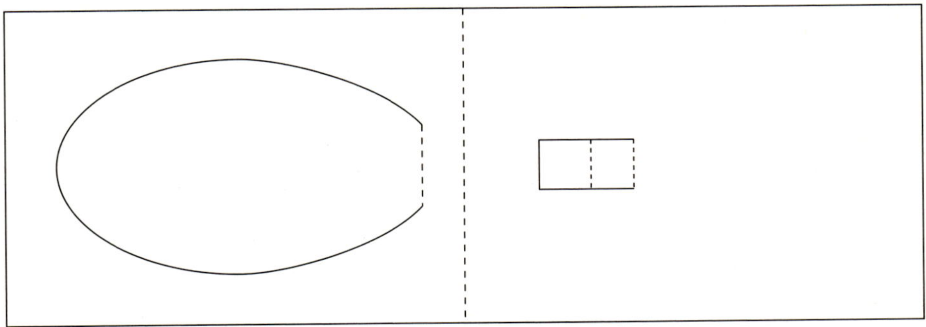

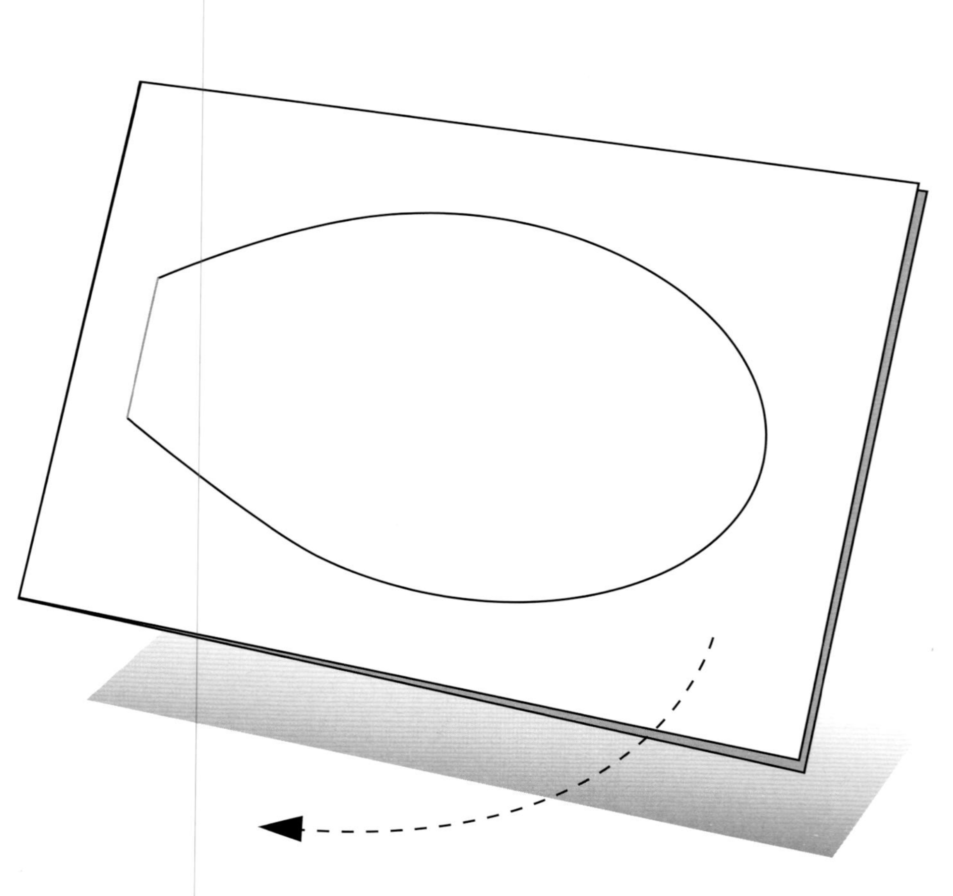

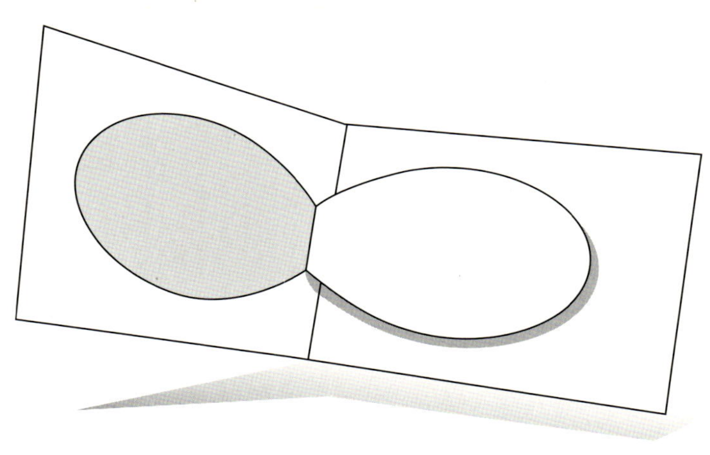

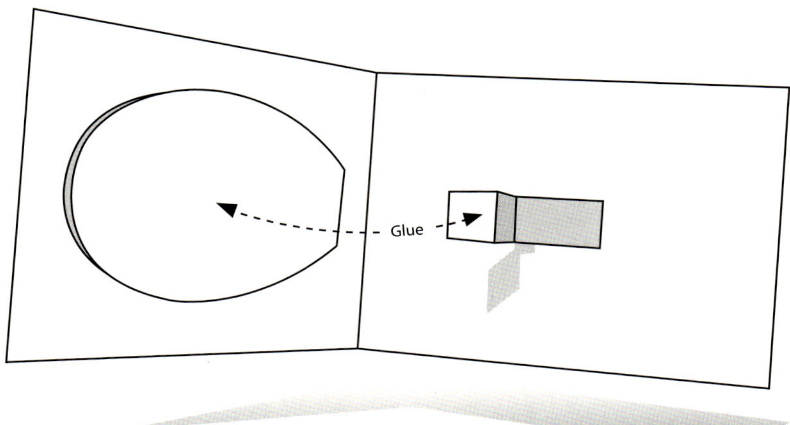
Glue

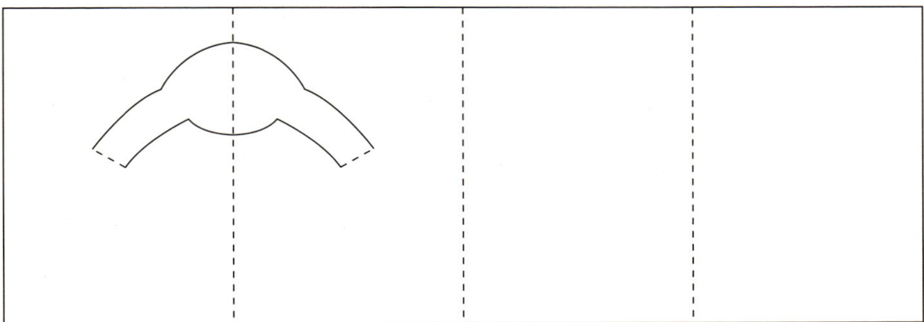

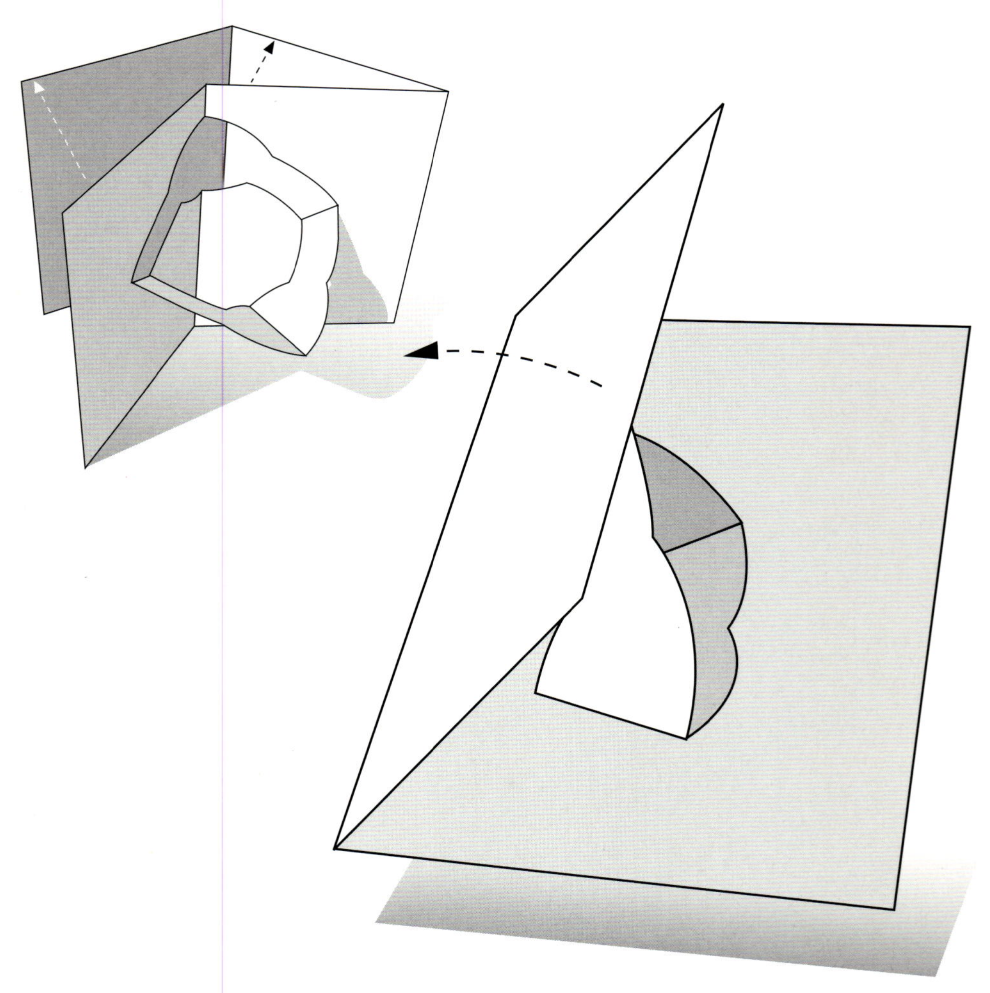

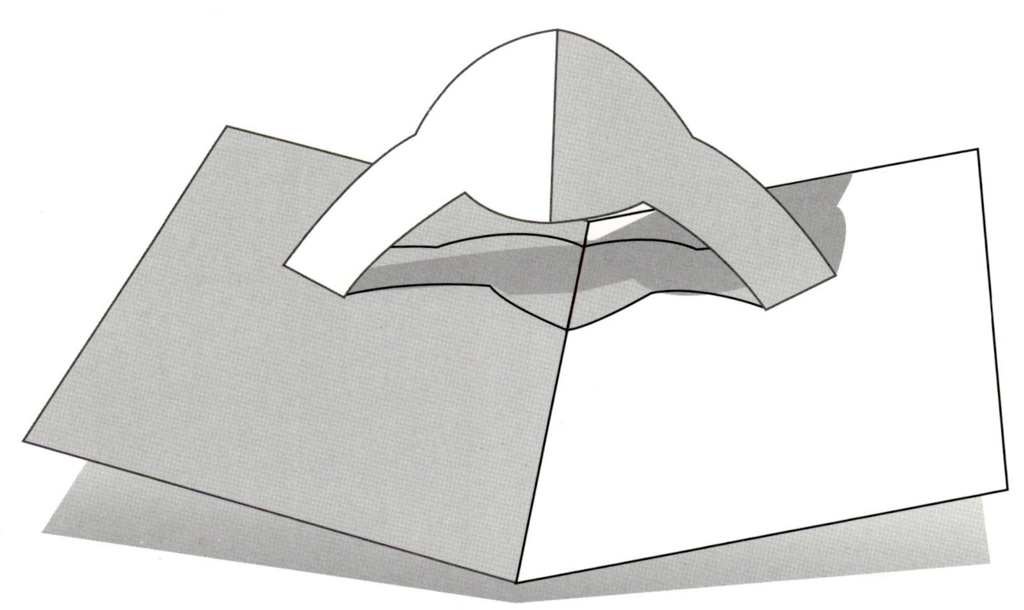

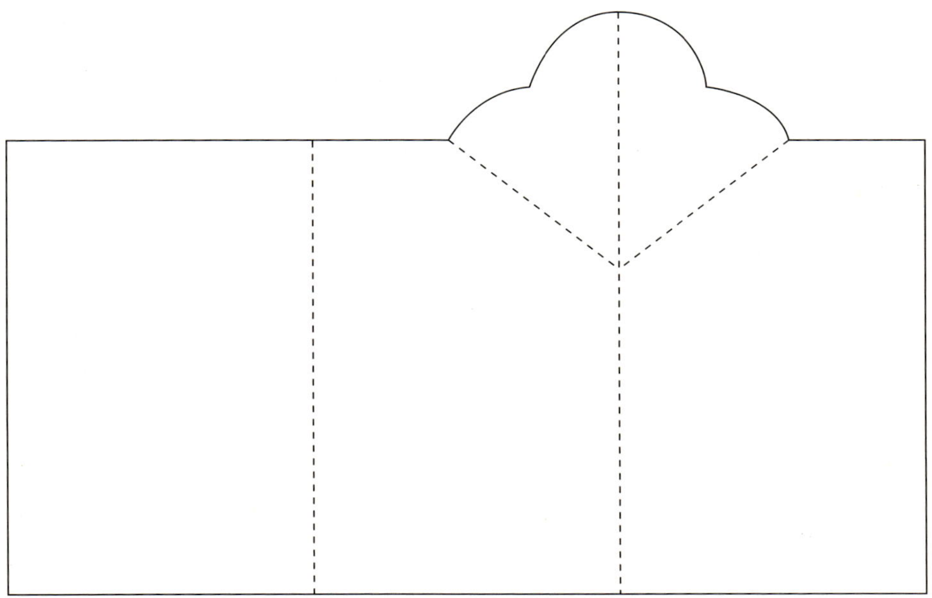

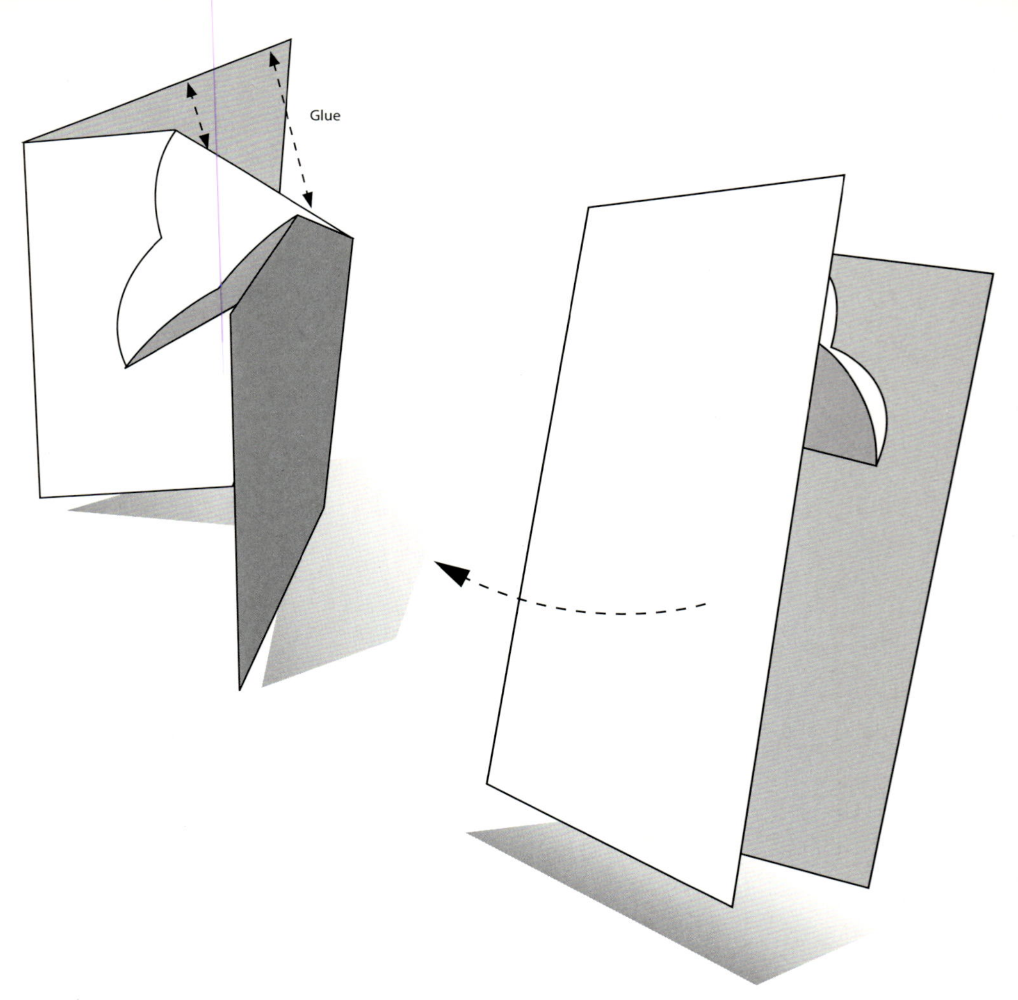
Glue

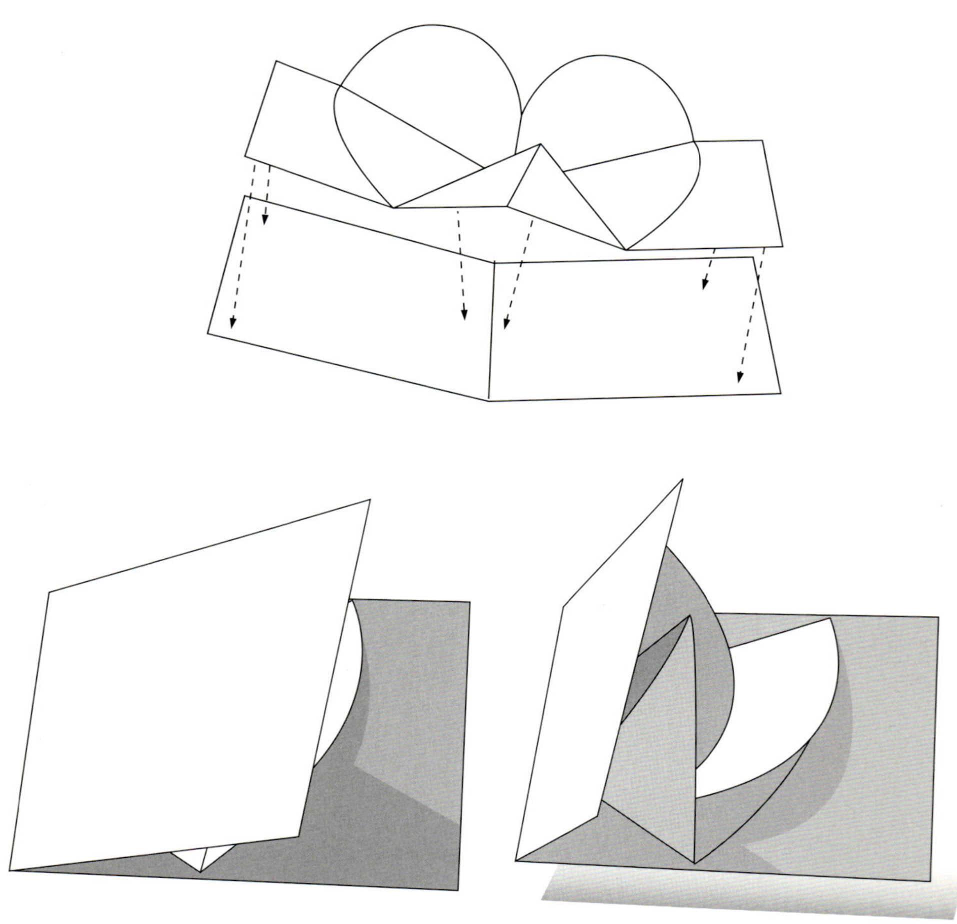

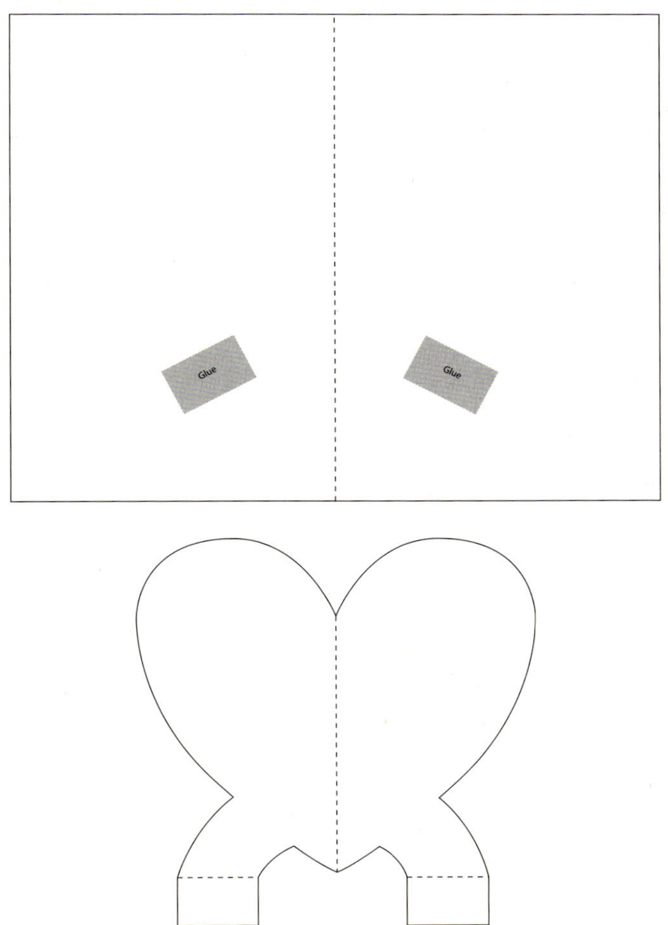

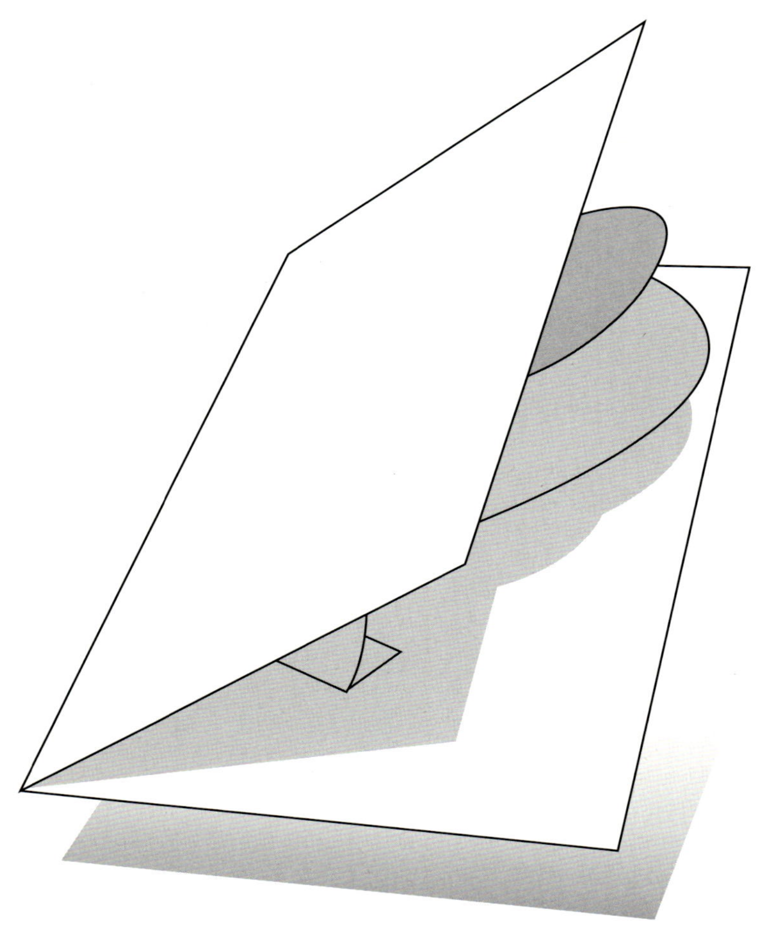

298　Pop-ups

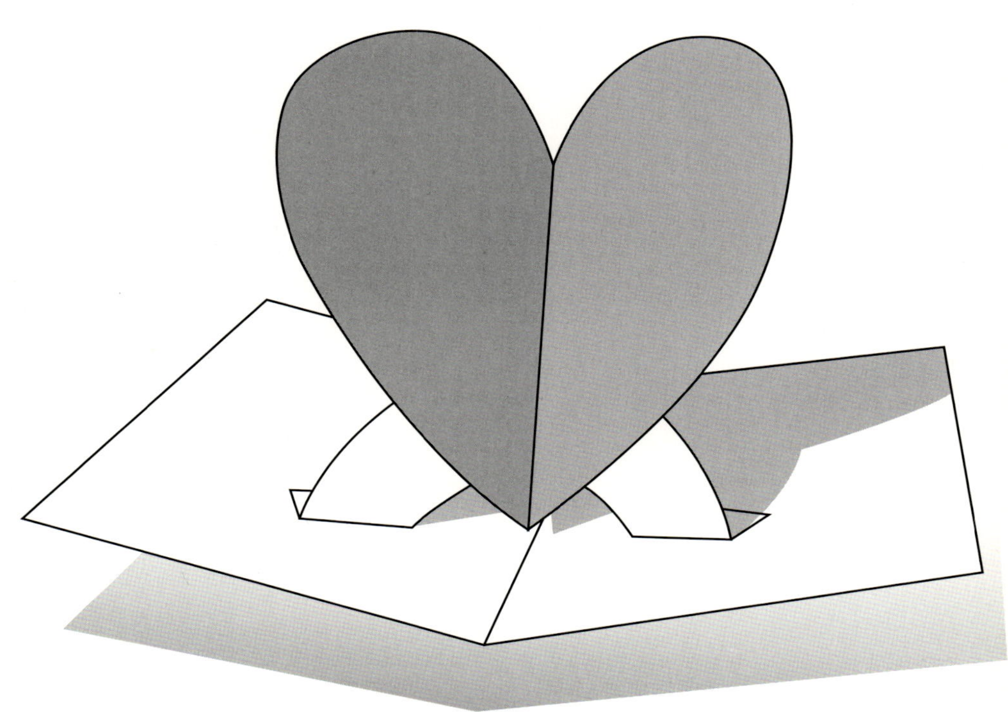

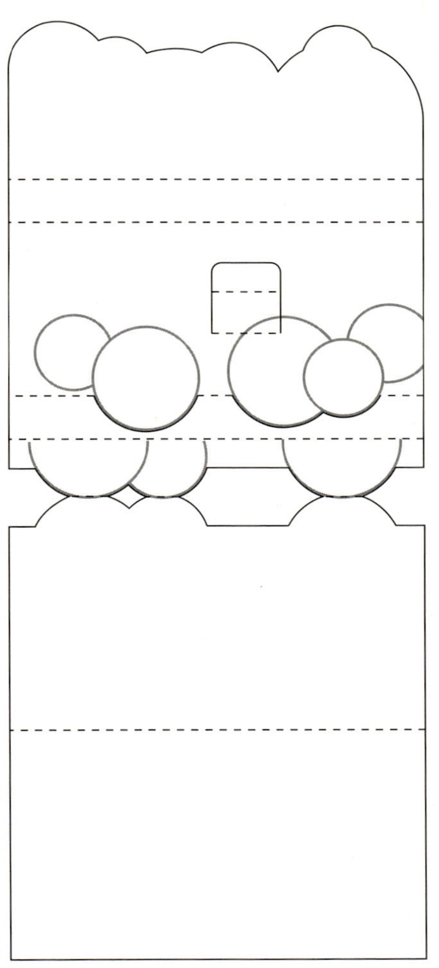

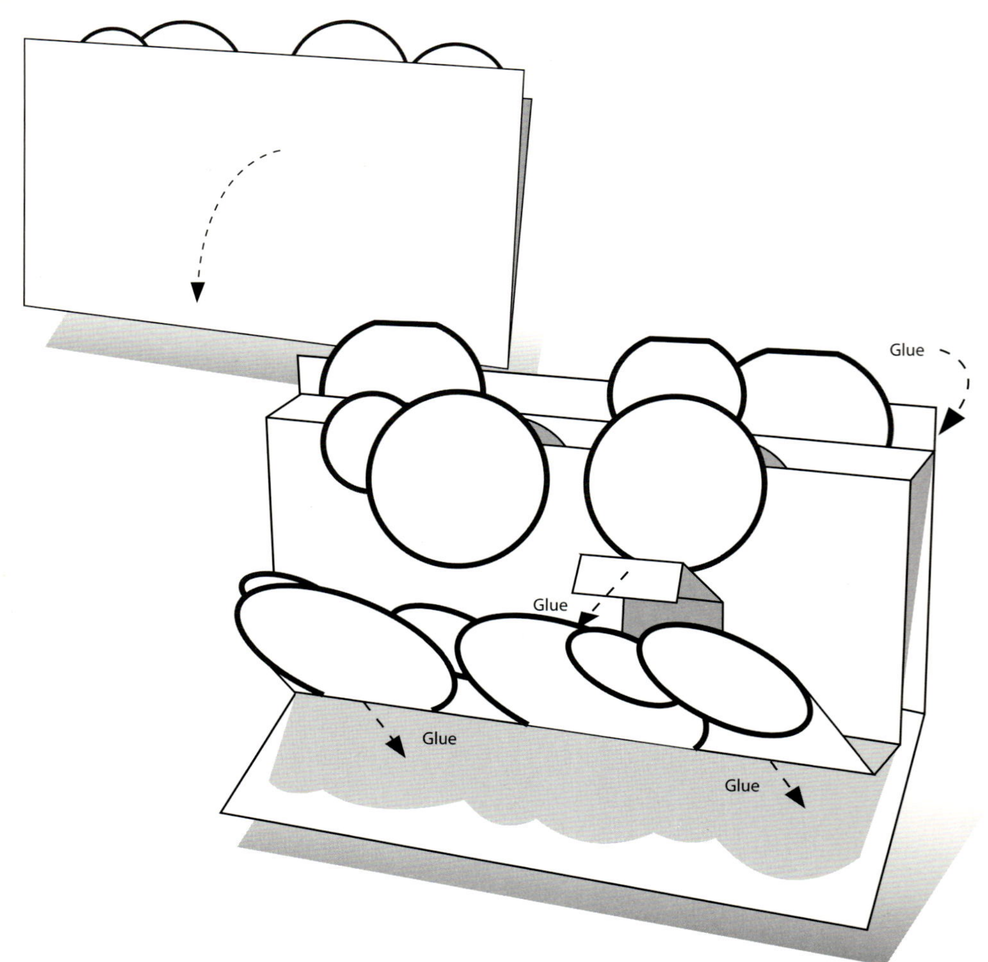

Glue
Glue
Glue
Glue

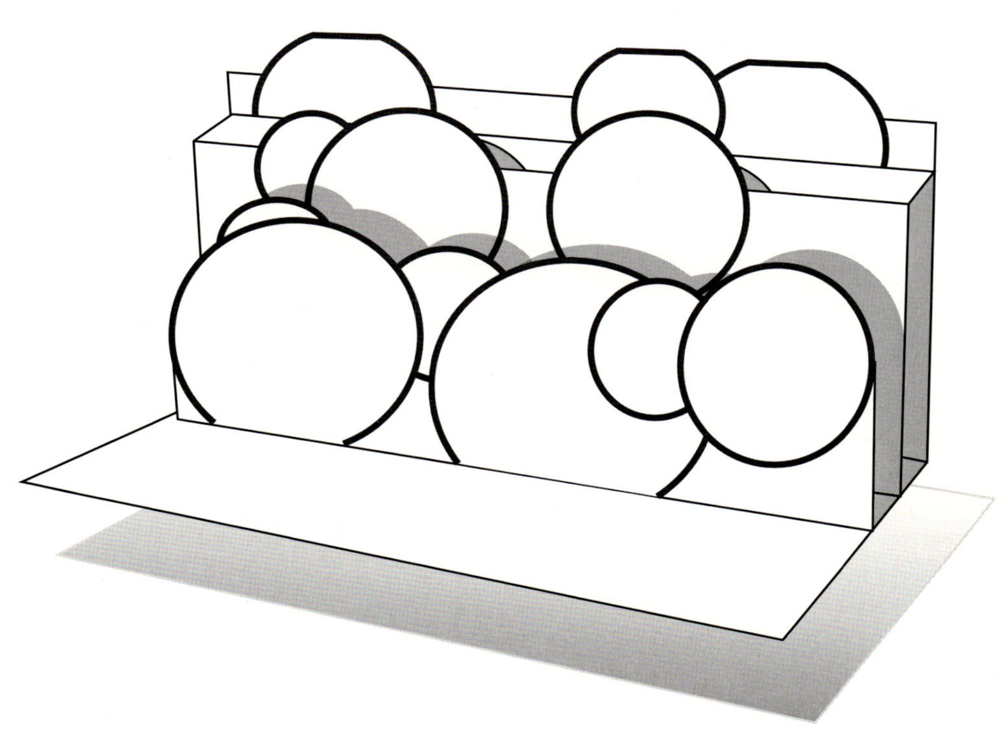

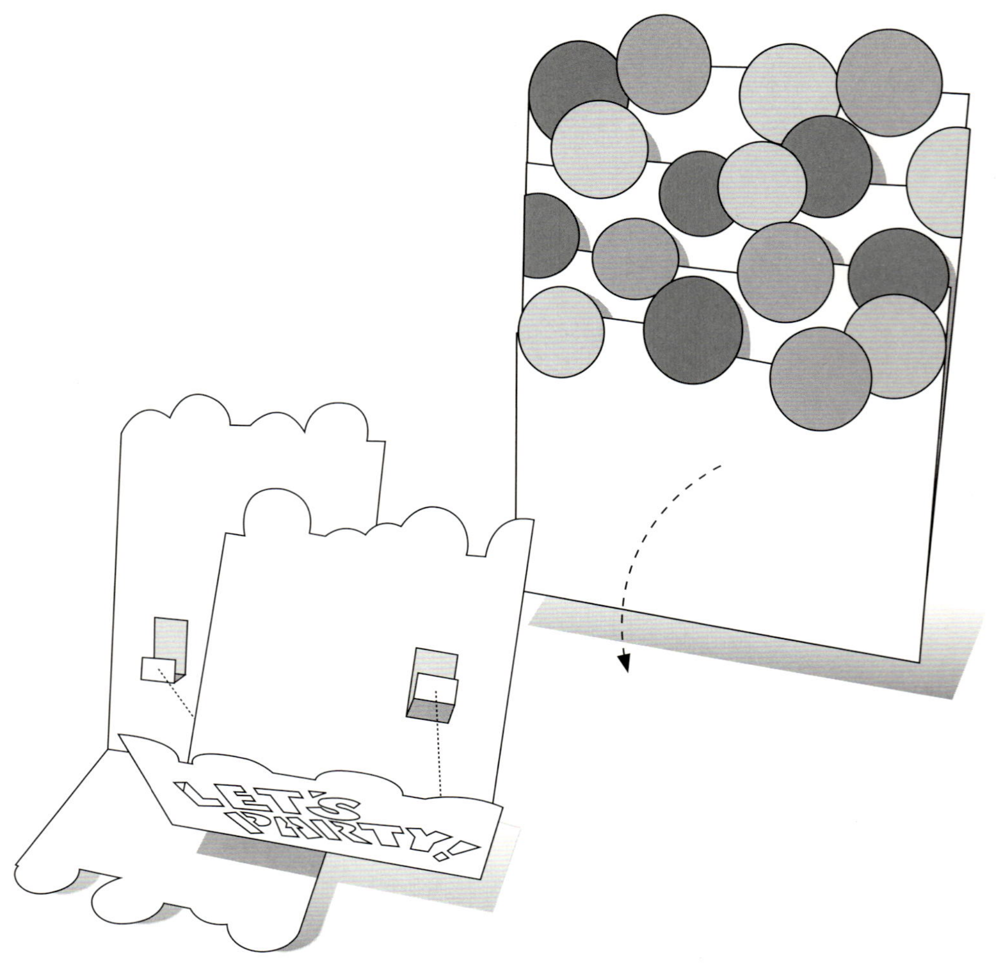
LET'S PARTY!

LET'S PARTY!

310   Pop-ups

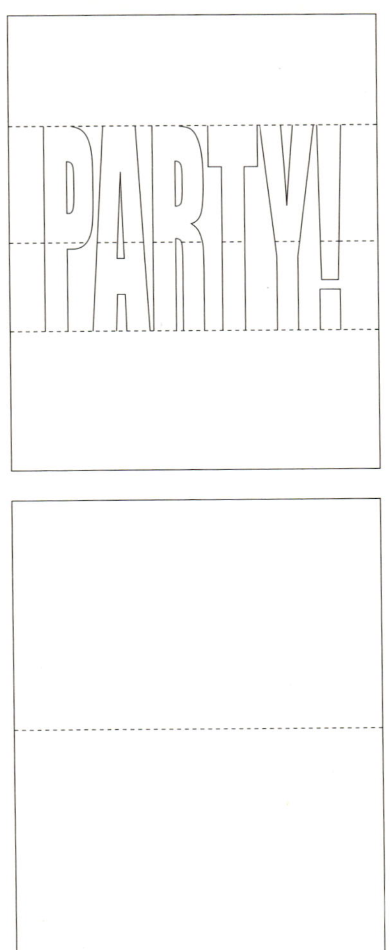

Glue

PARTY!

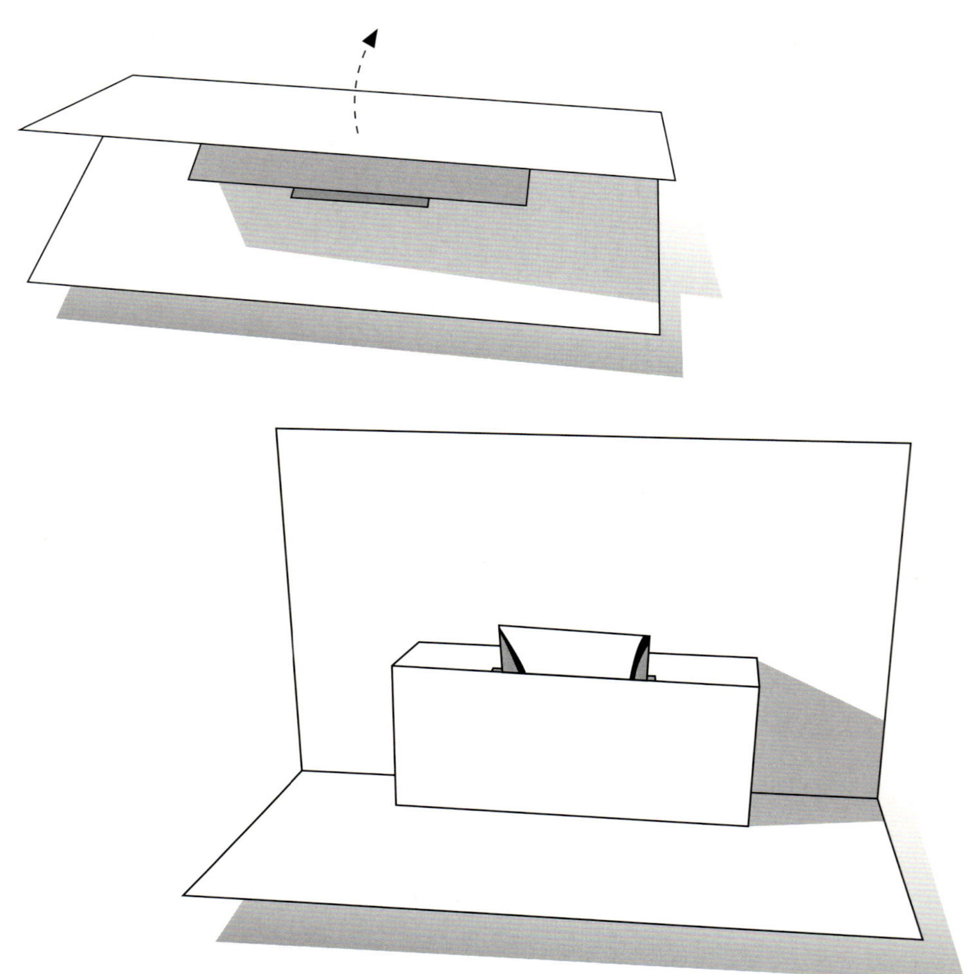

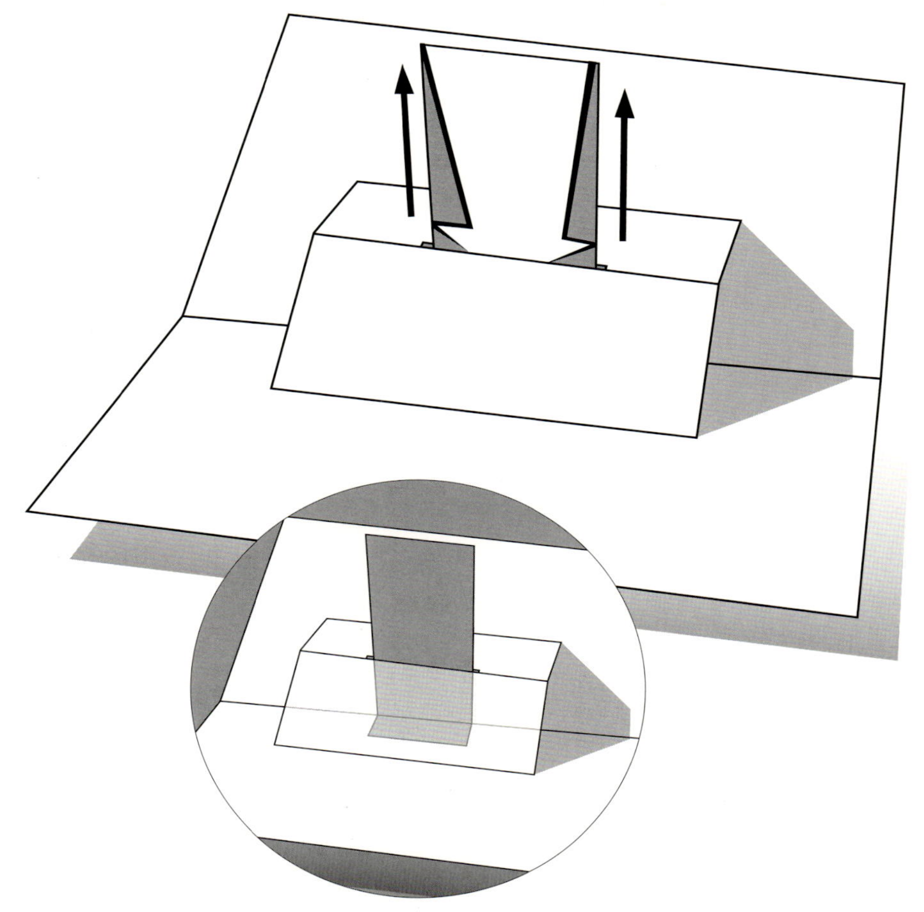

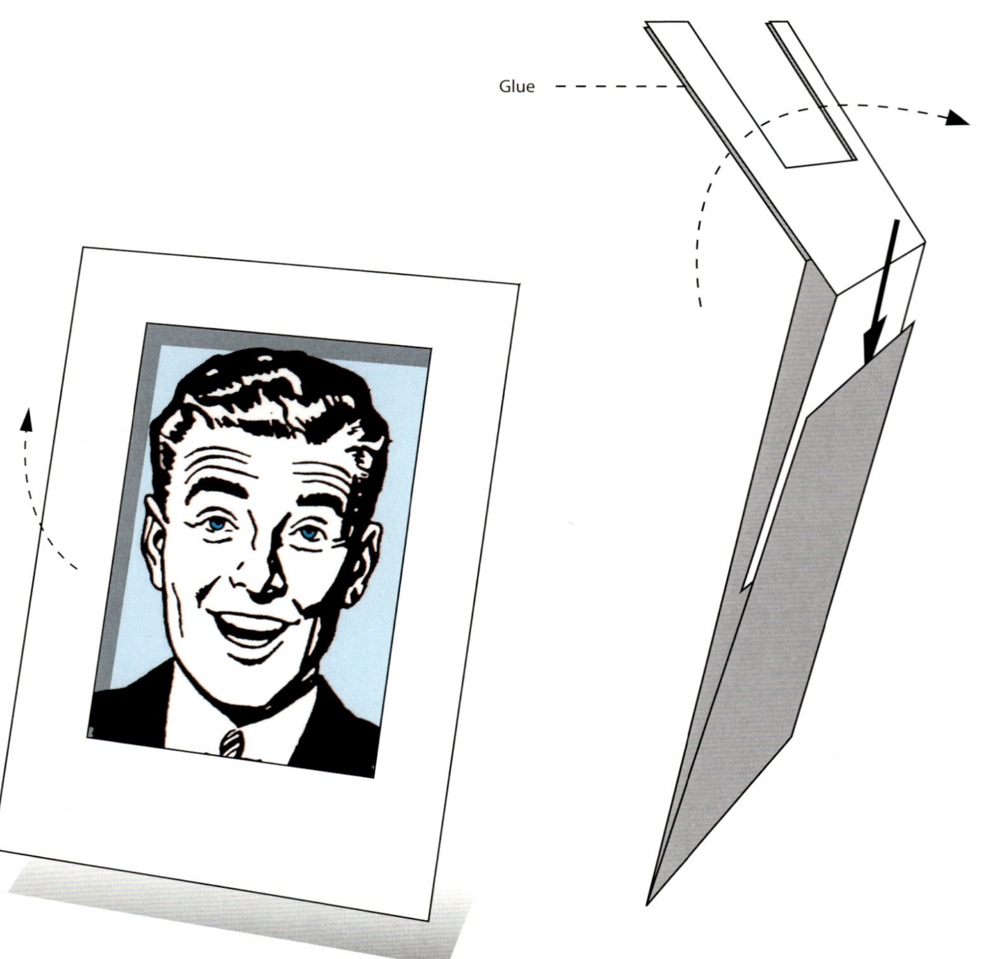
Glue

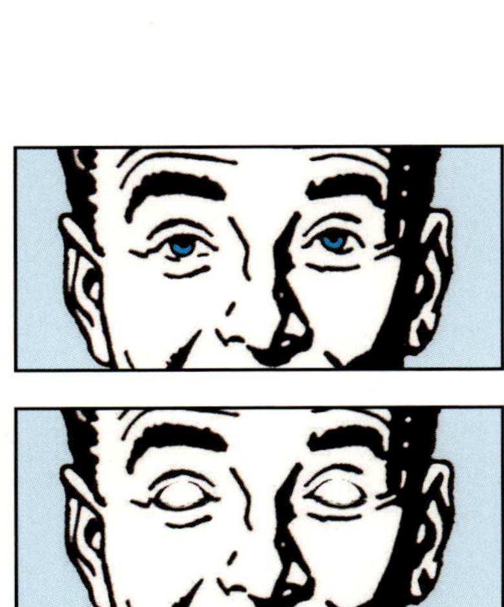

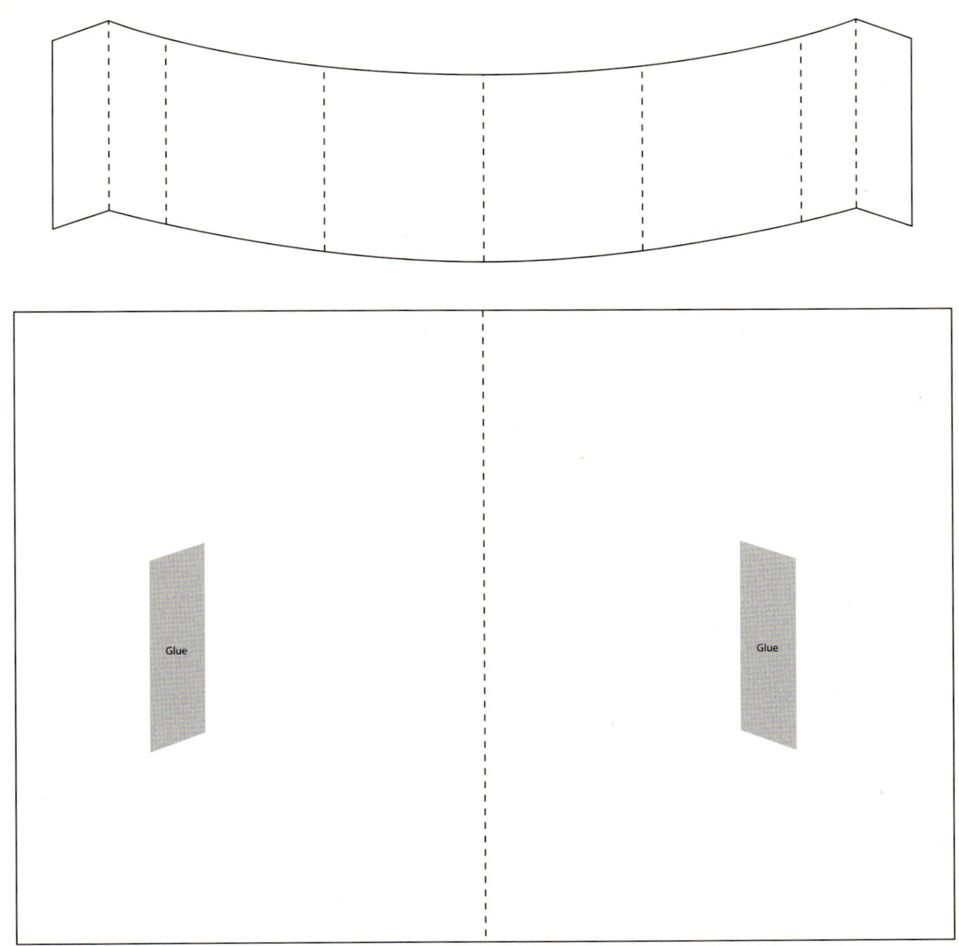

Glue
Glue

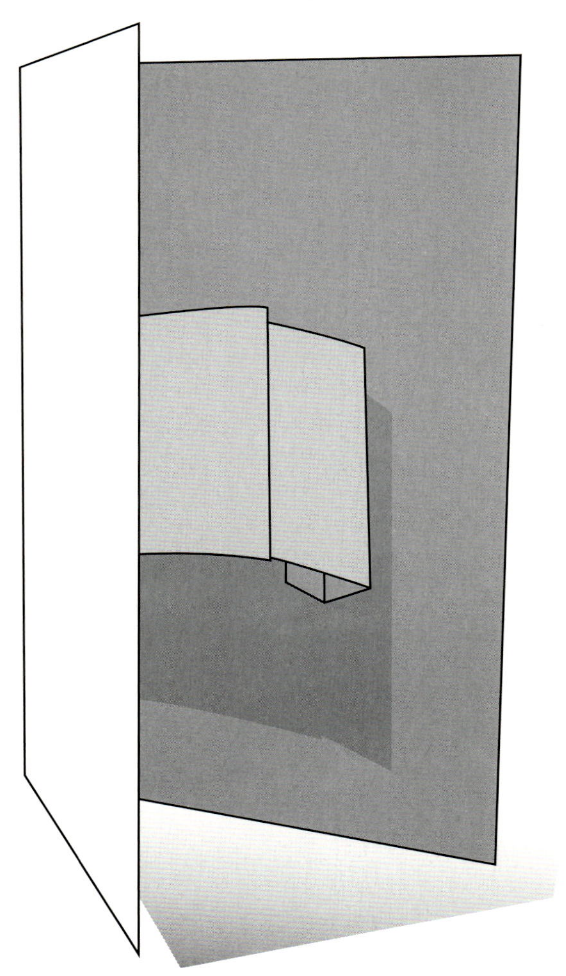

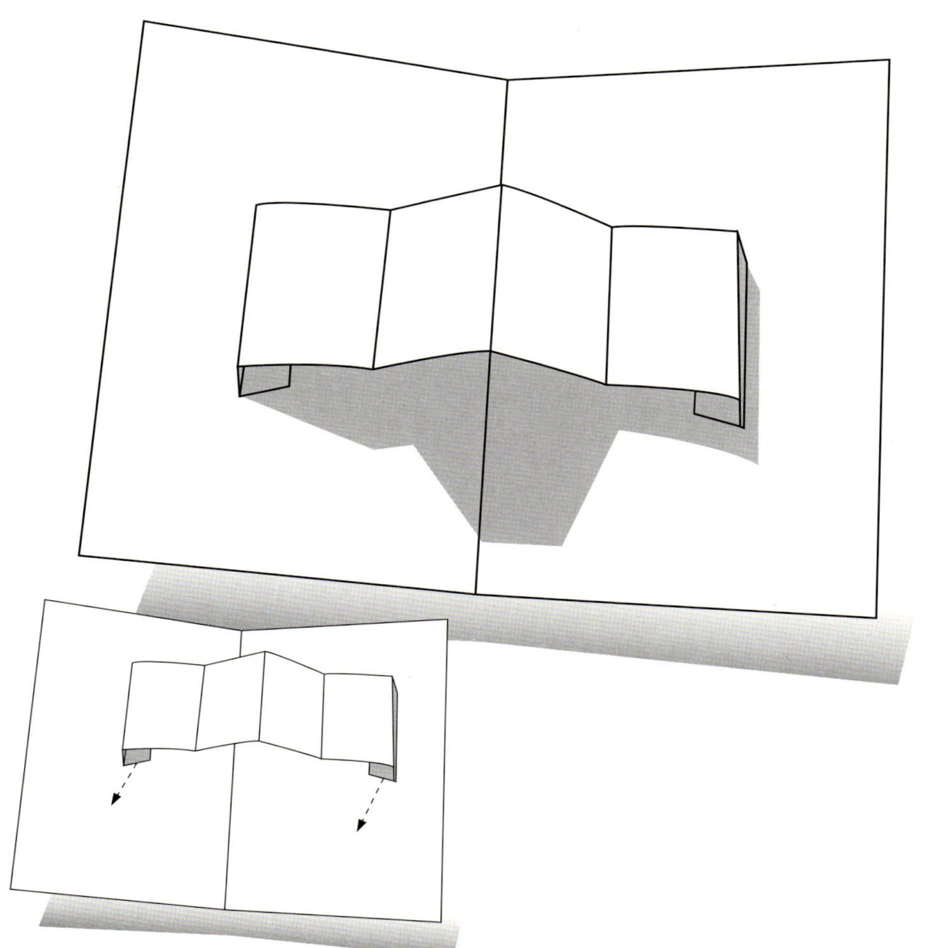

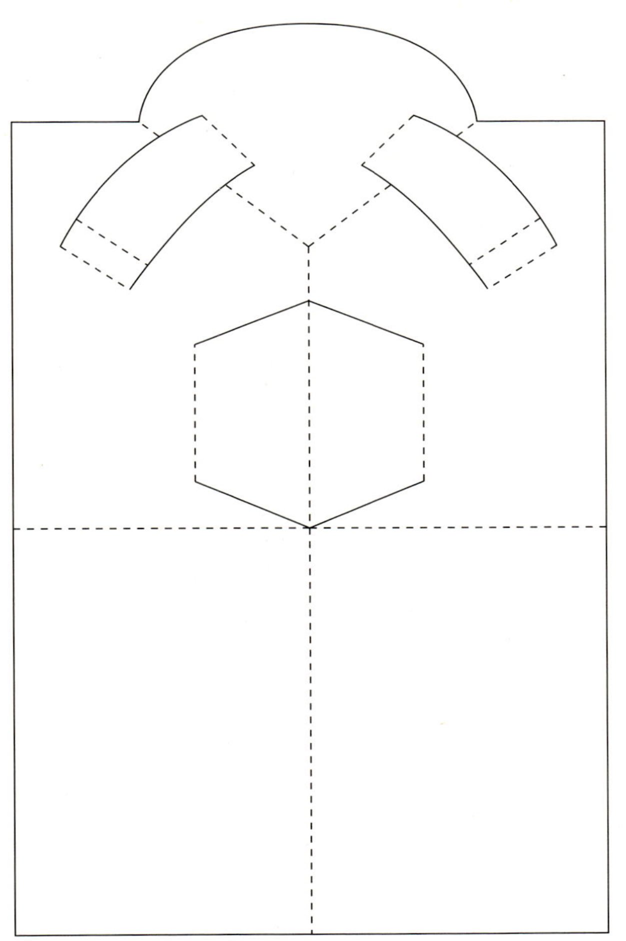

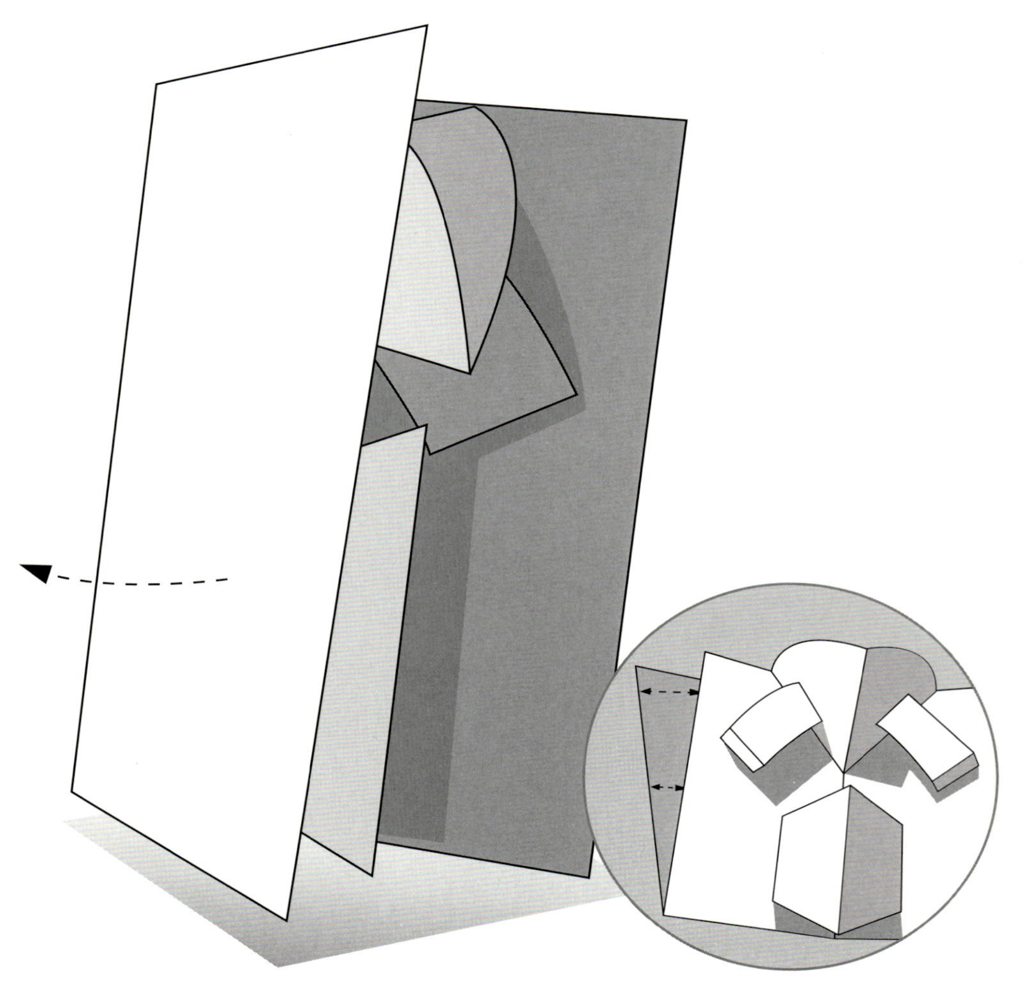

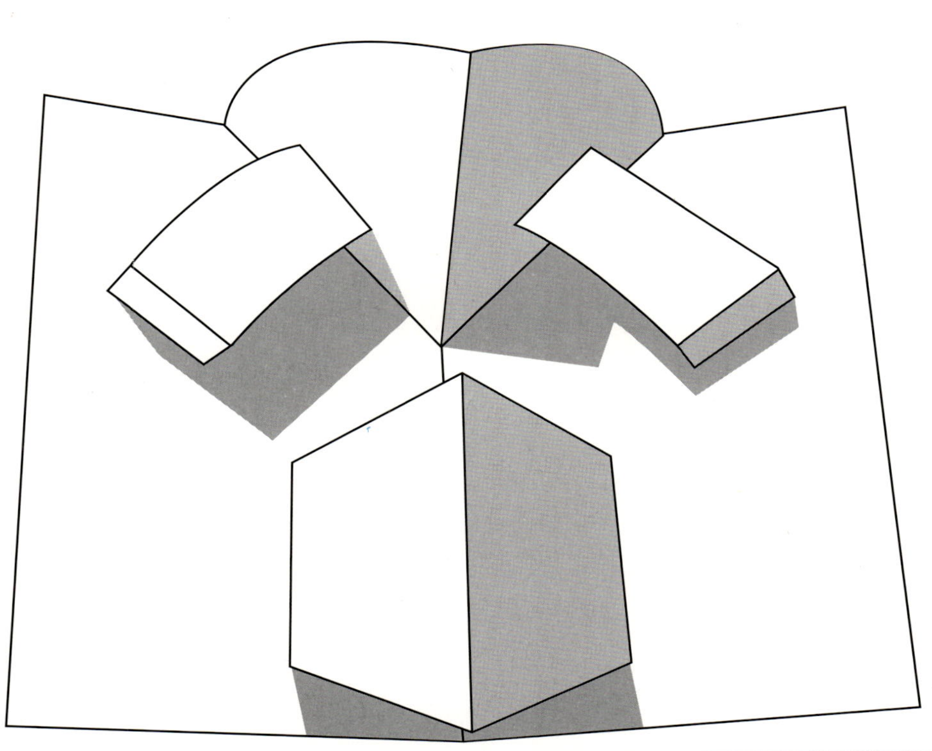

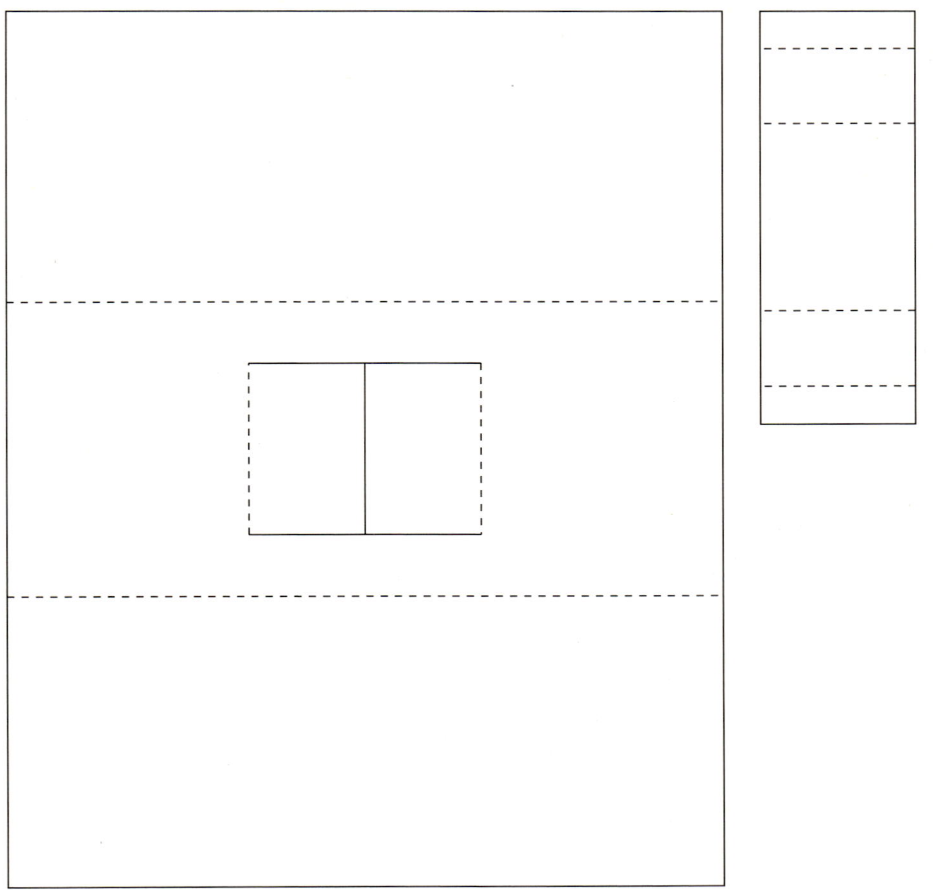

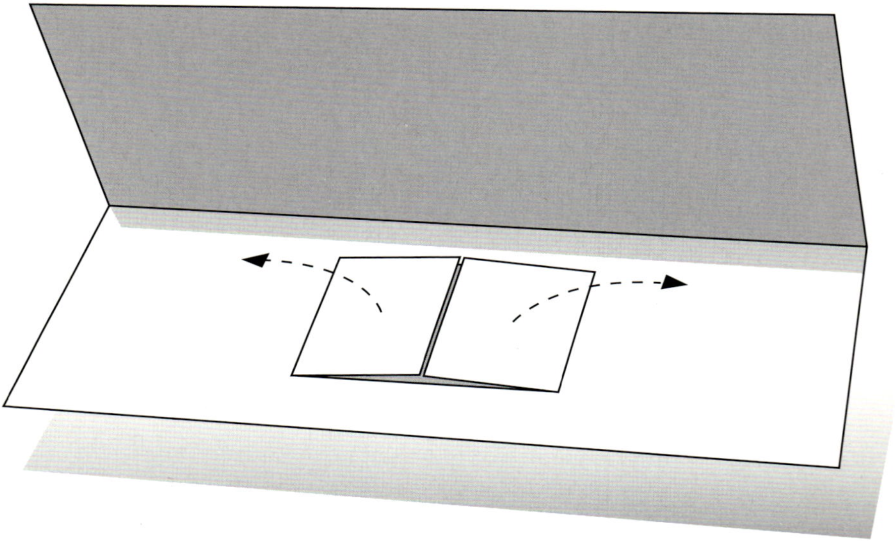

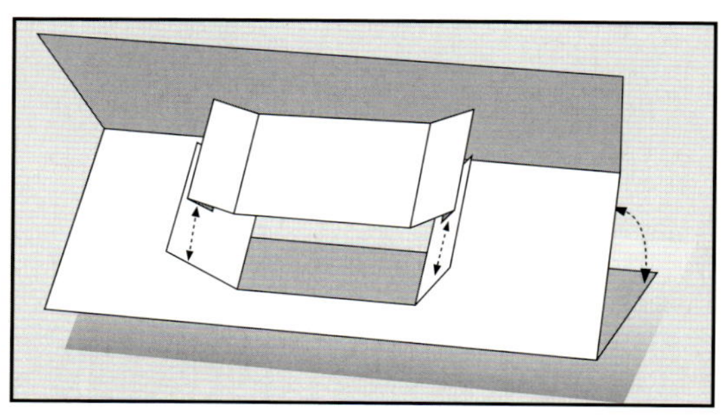

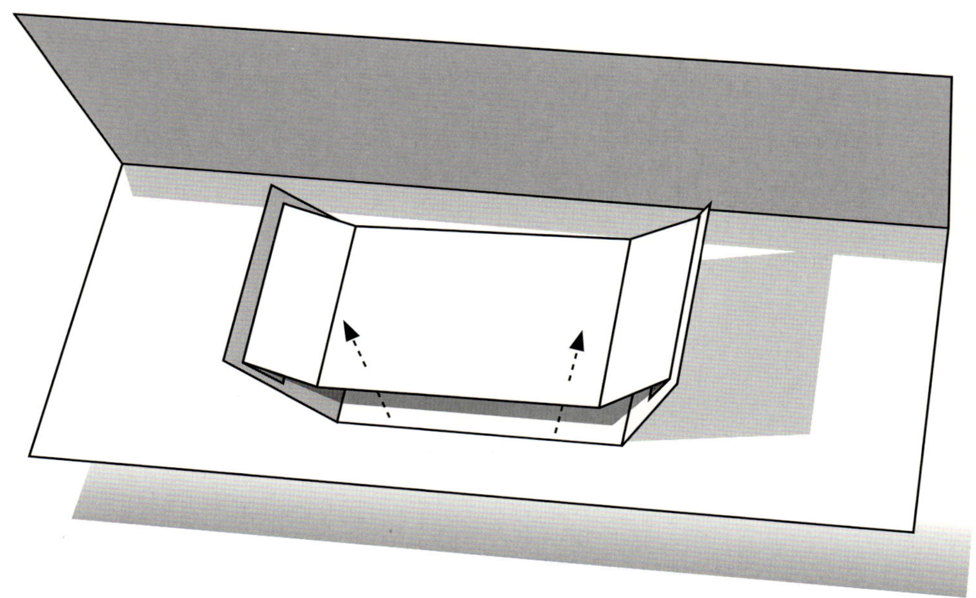

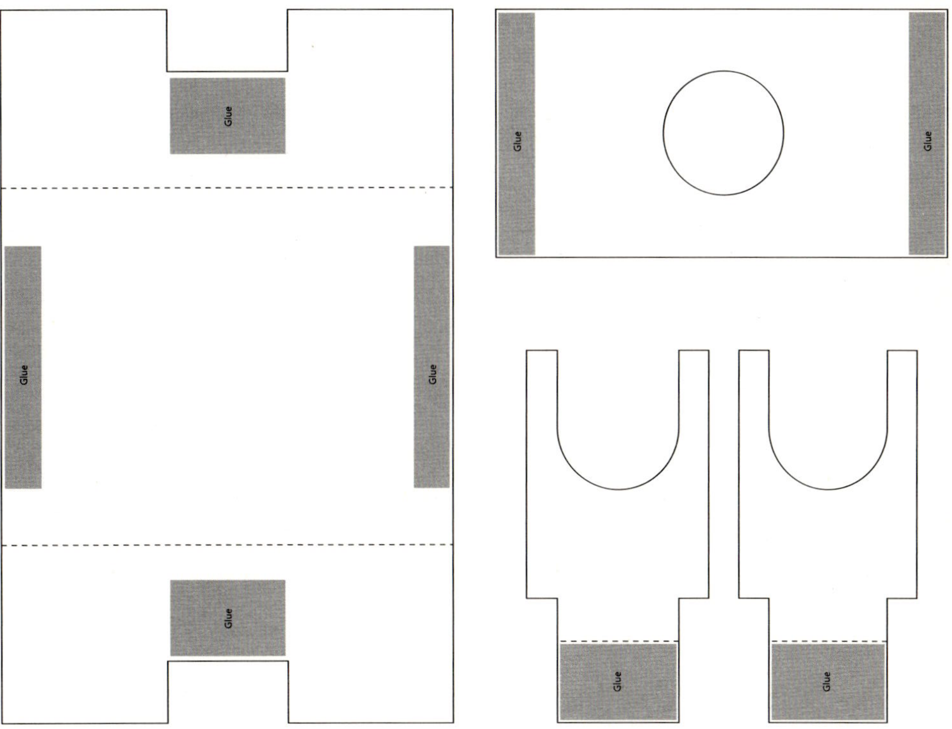

Glue
Glue
Glue
Glue
Glue
Glue
Glue
Glue
Glue

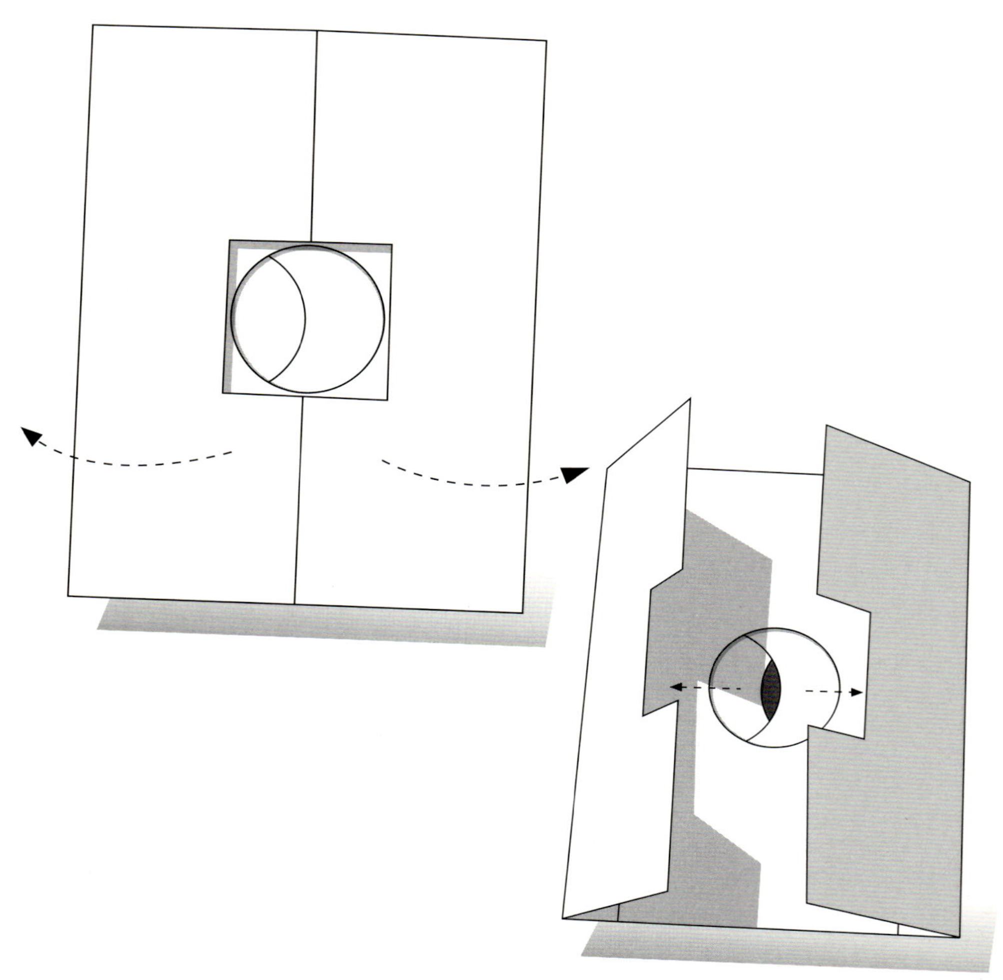

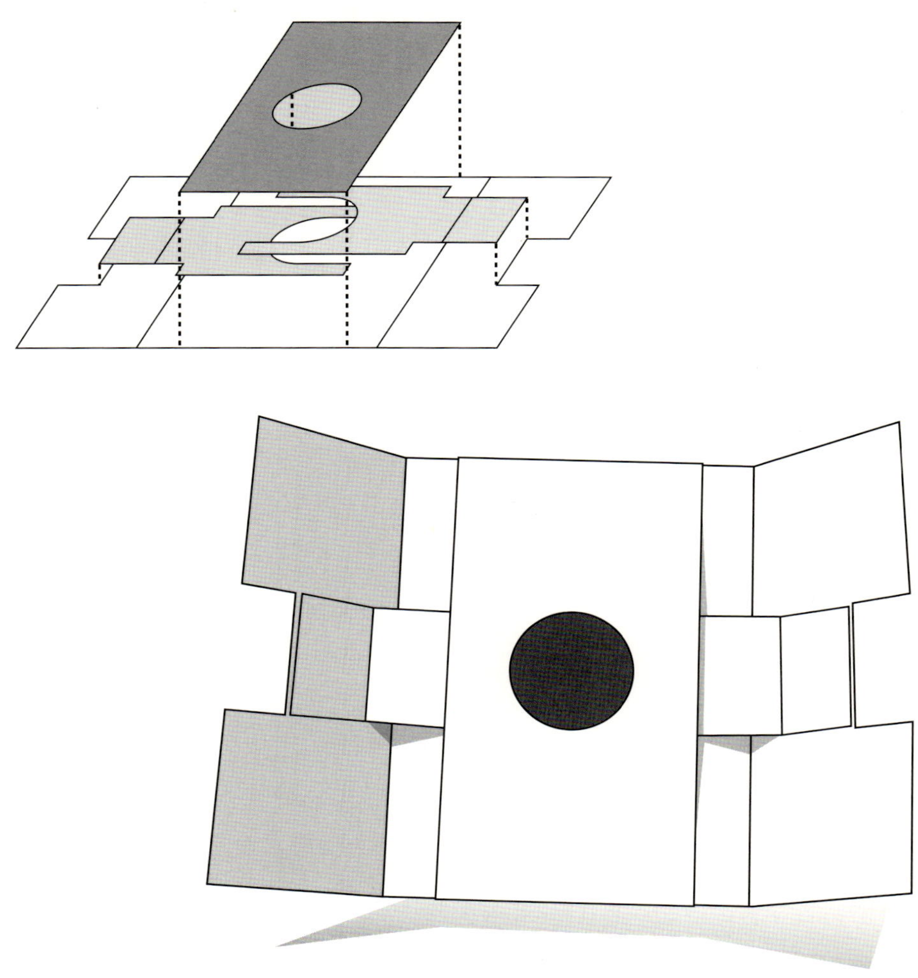

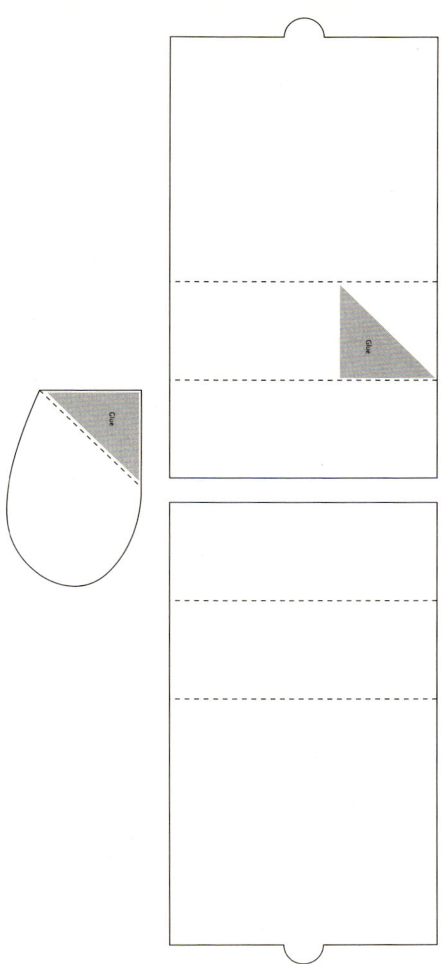
Glue
Glue

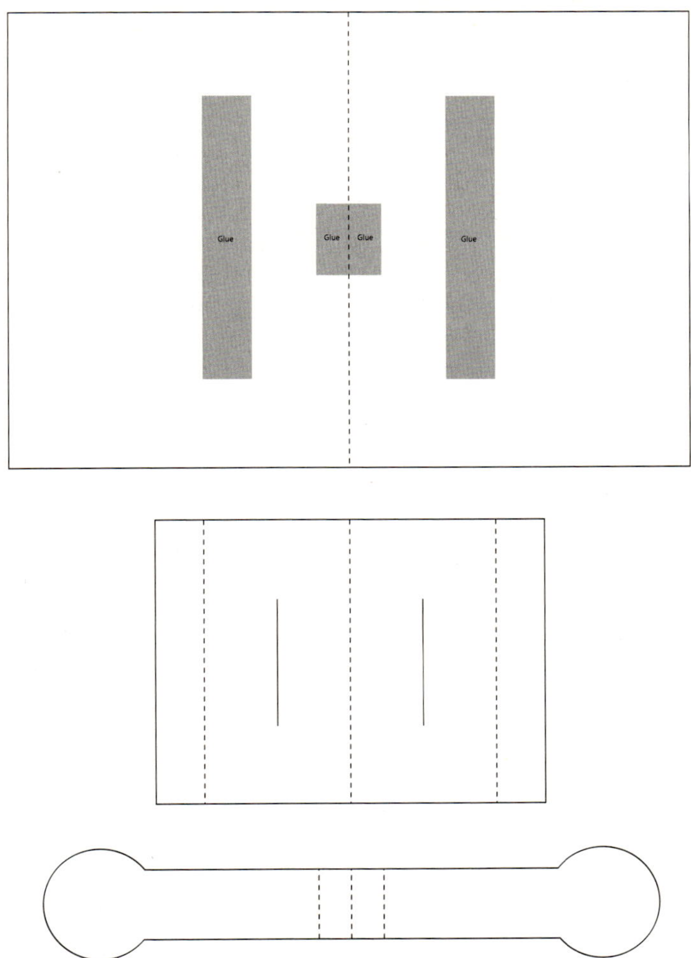

Glue
Glue
Glue
Glue

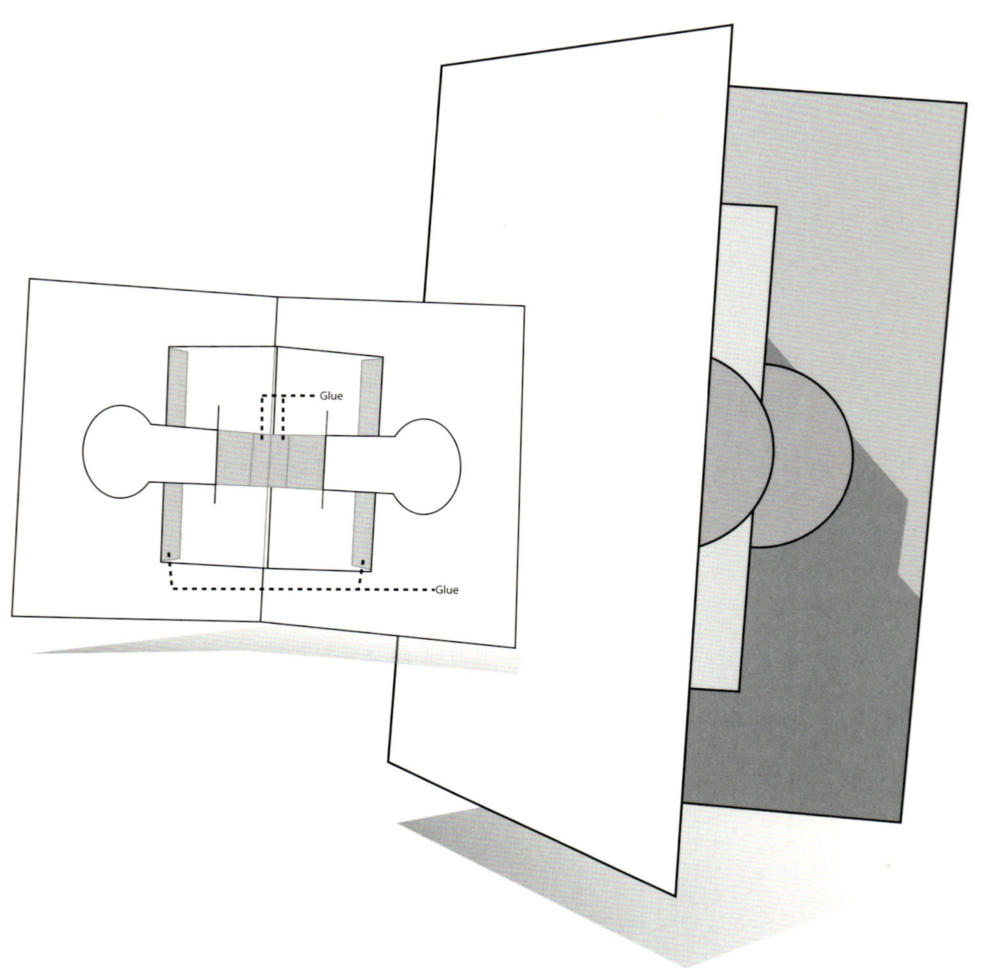
Glue
Glue

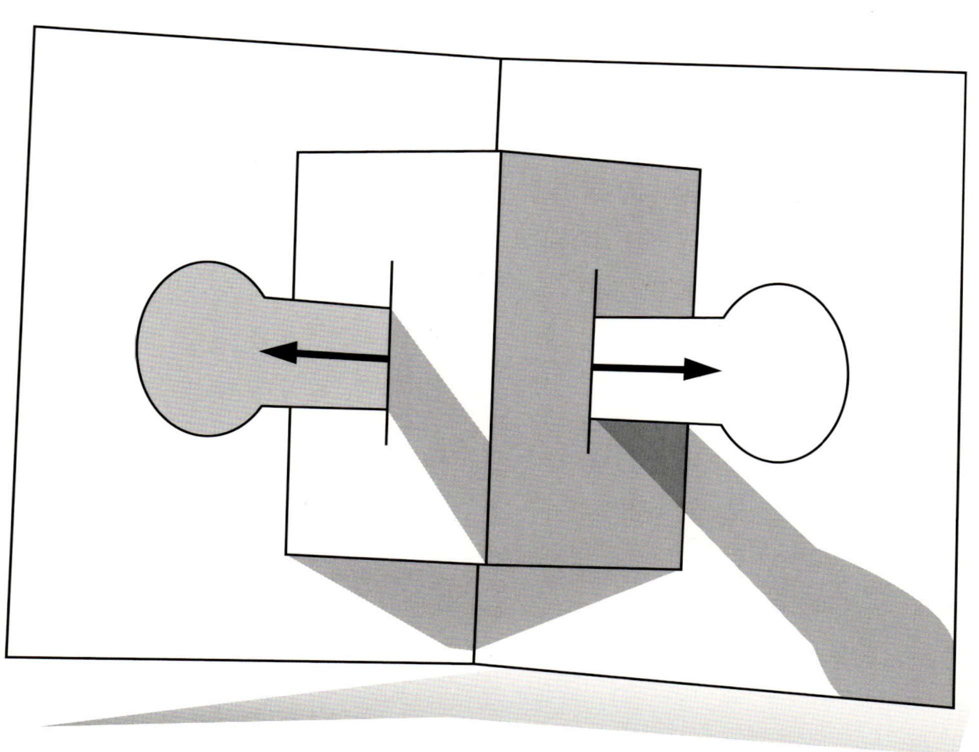

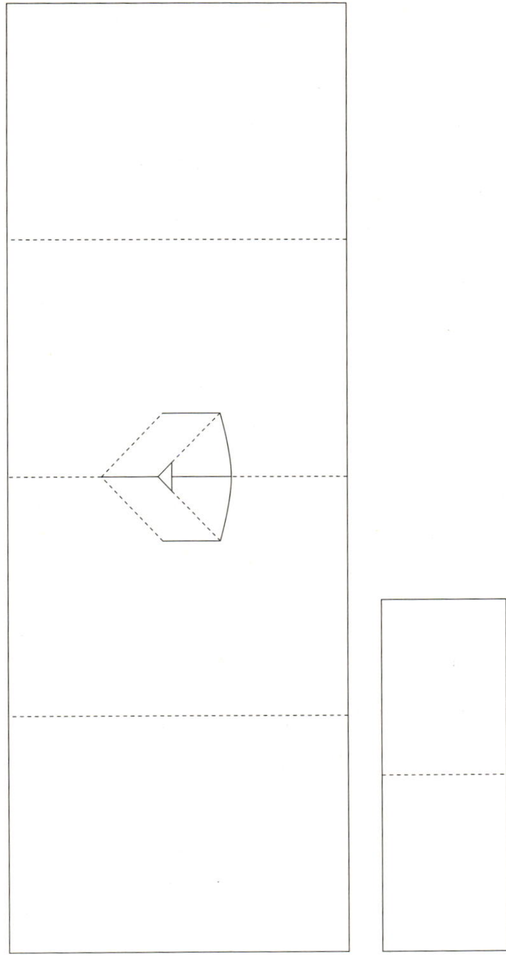

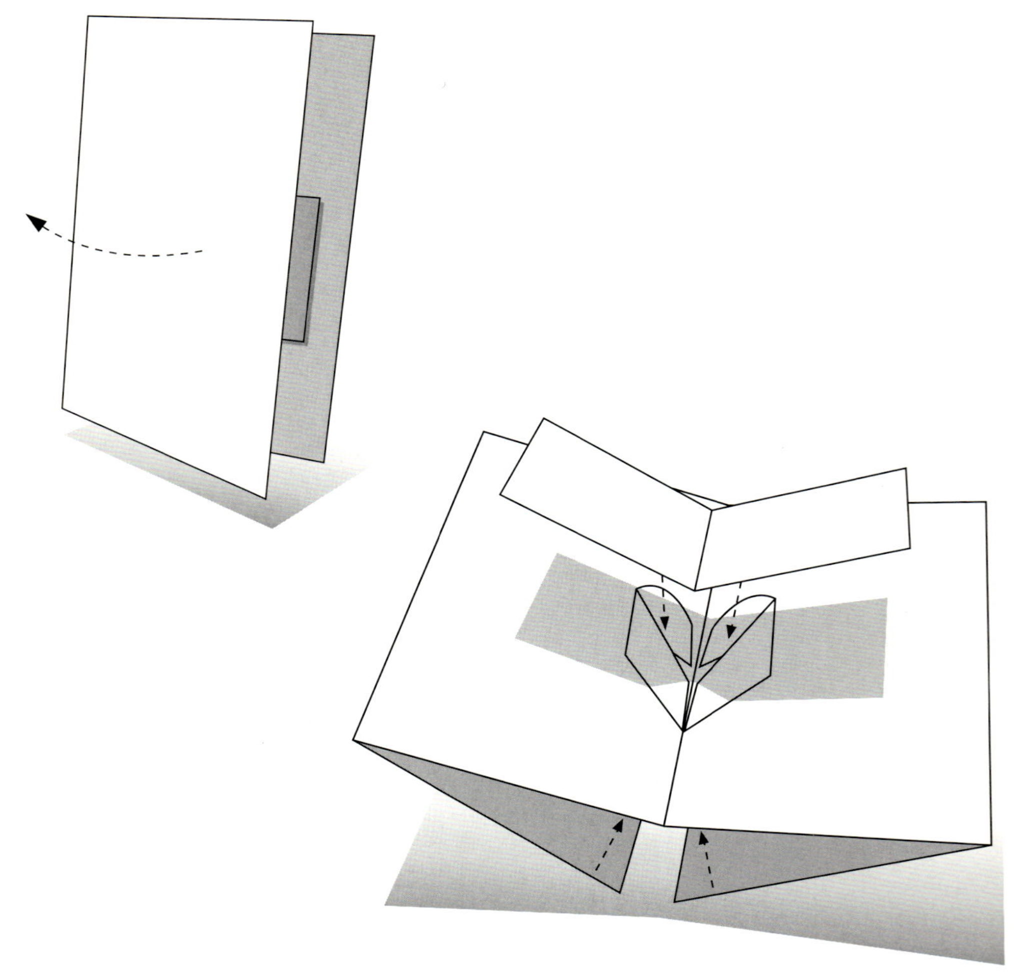

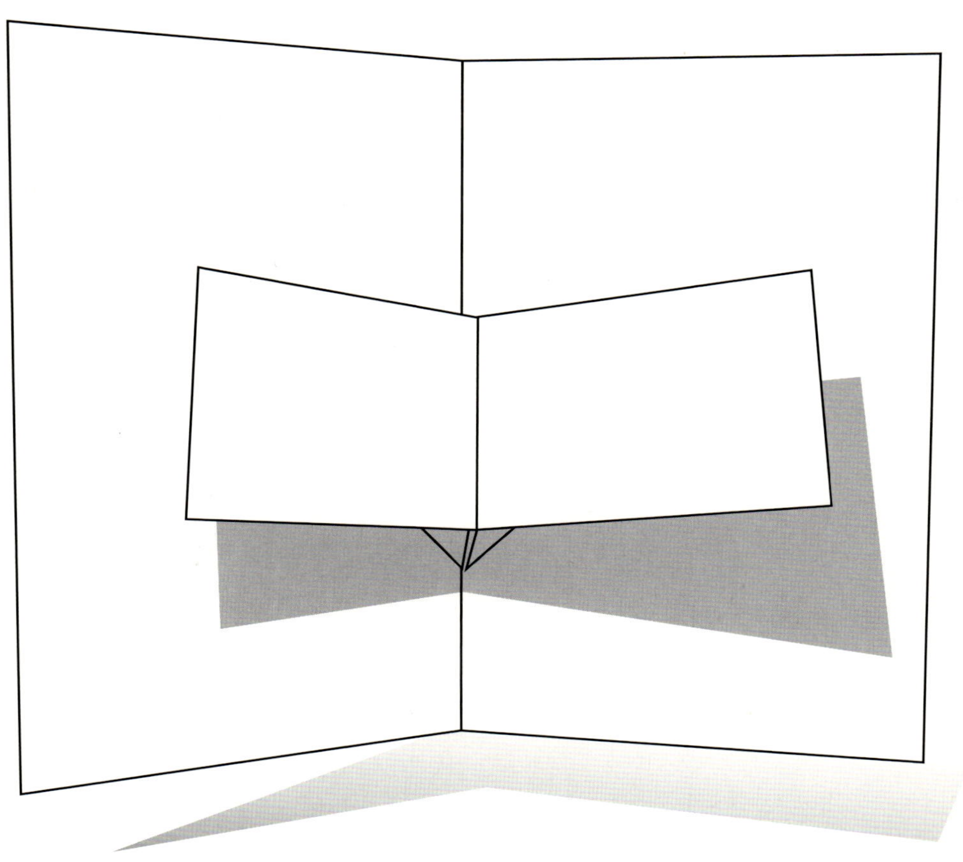

Envelopes

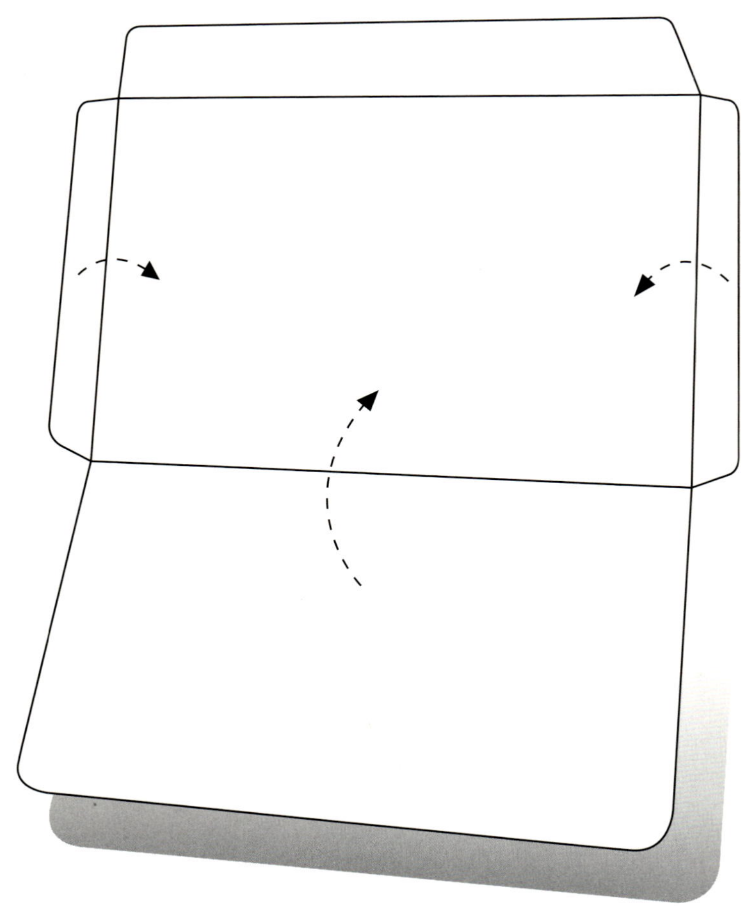

    Envelopes

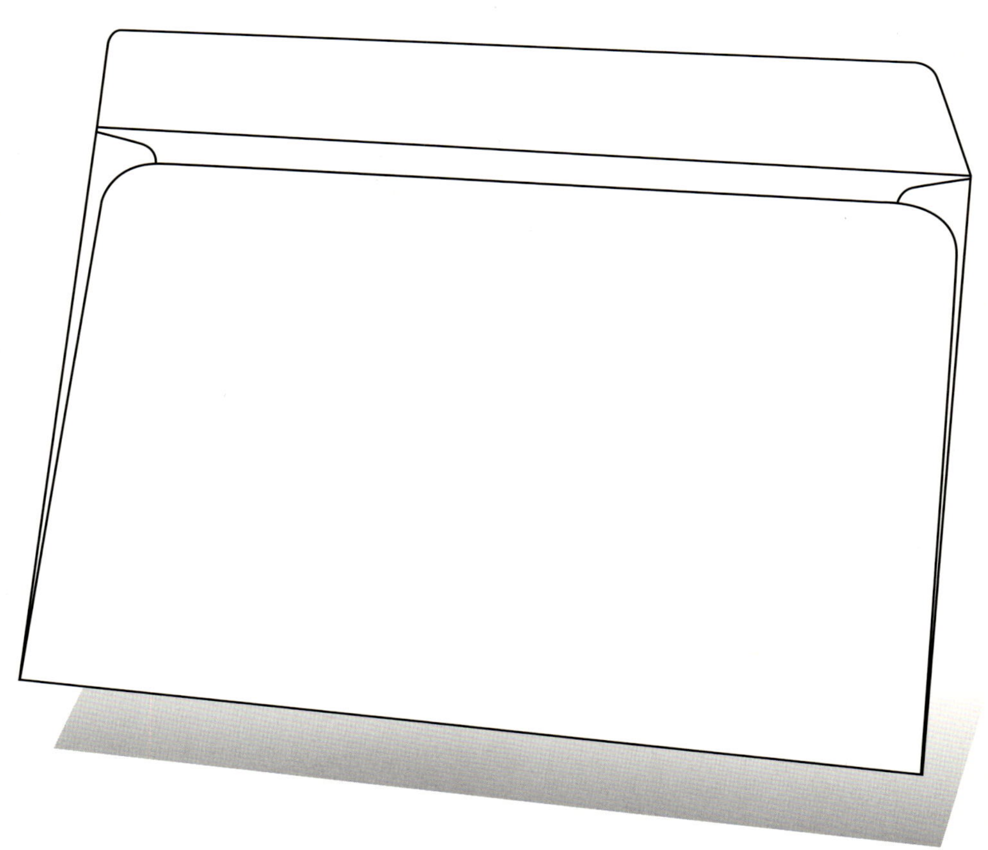

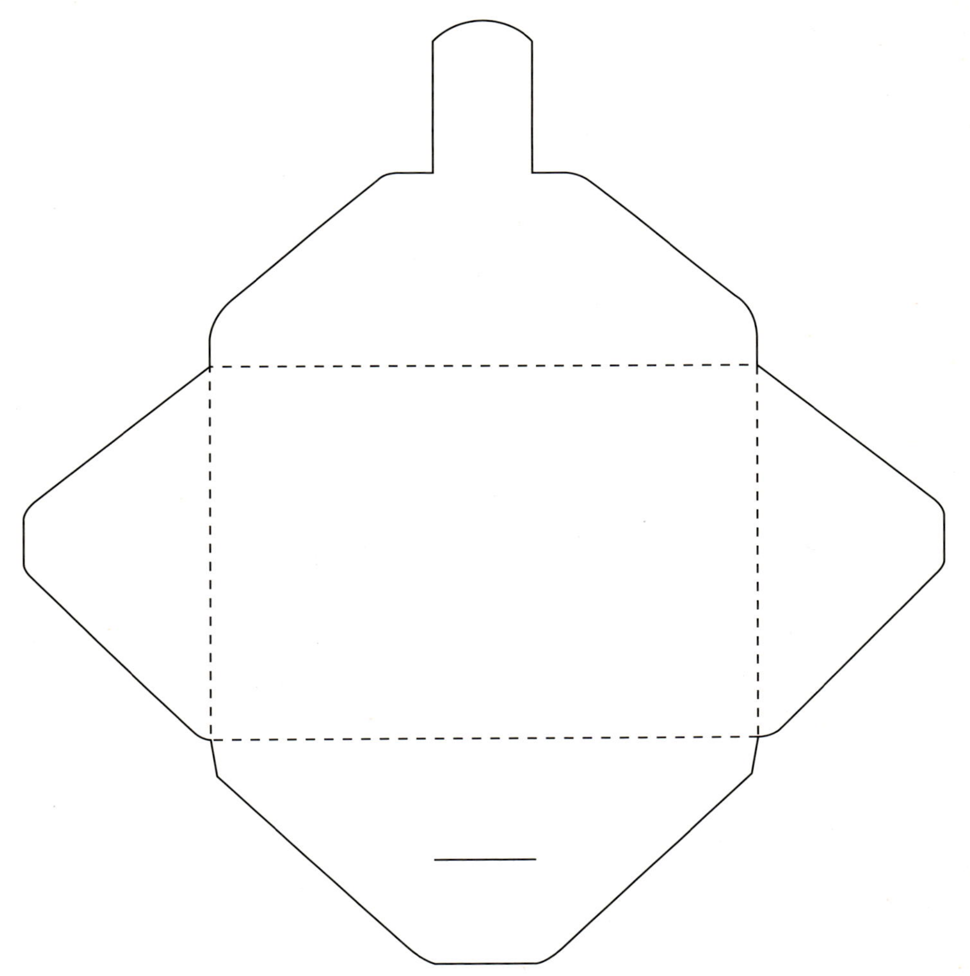

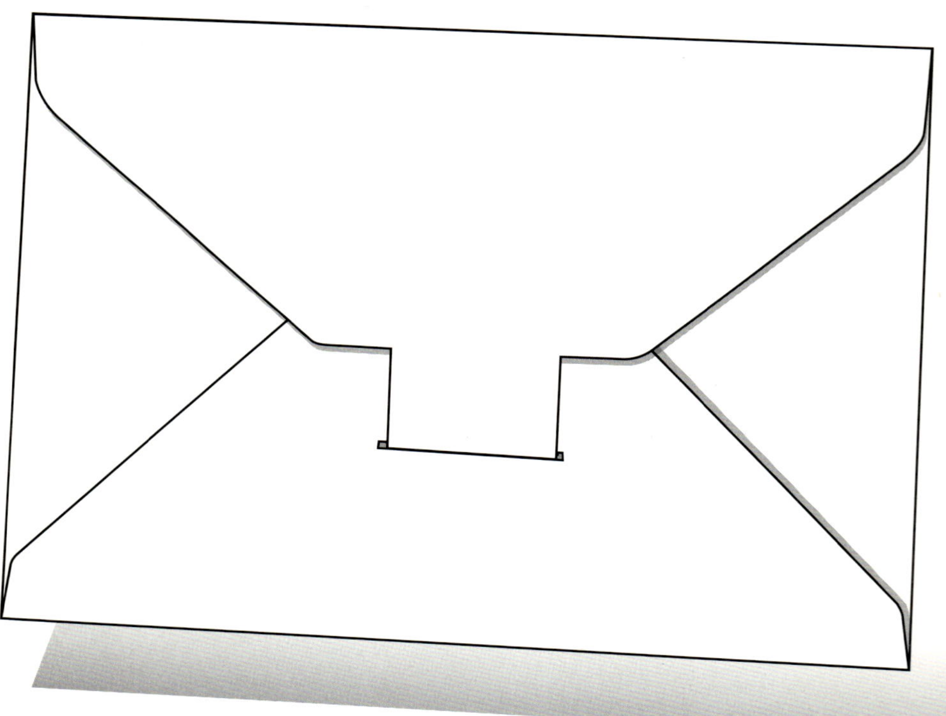

364   Envelopes

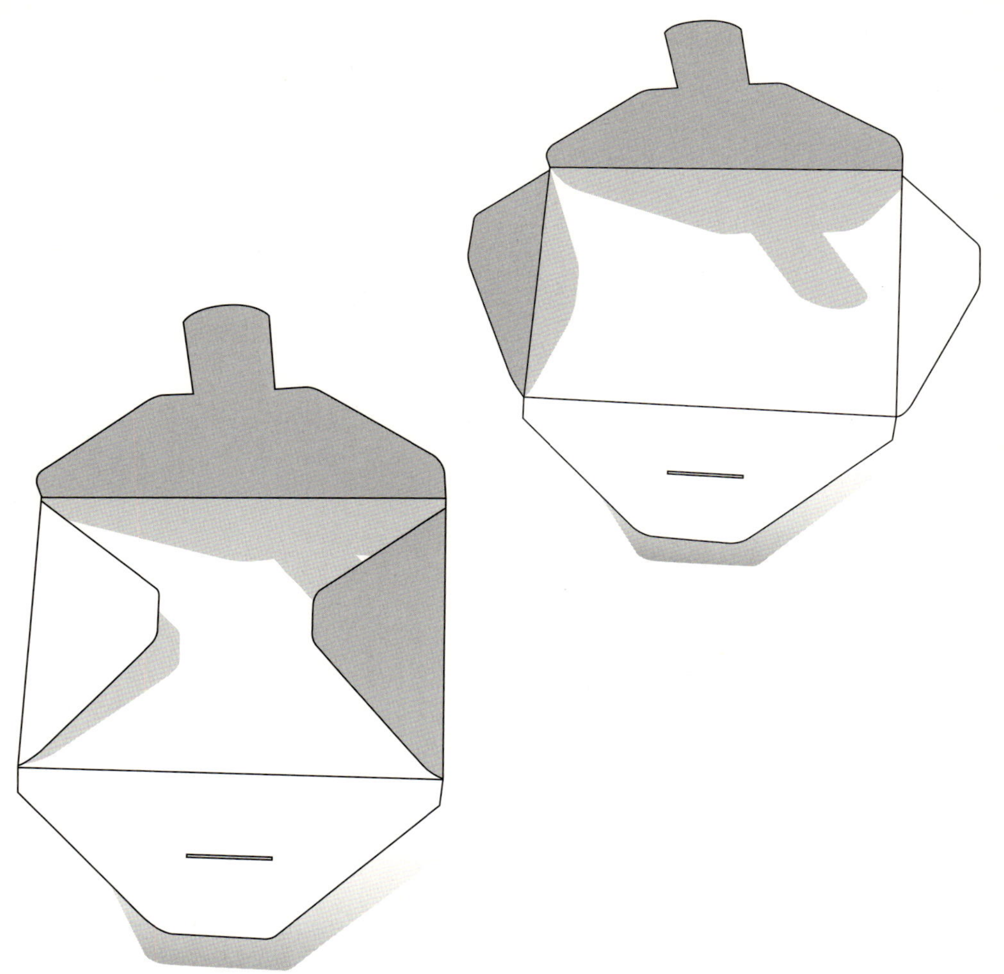

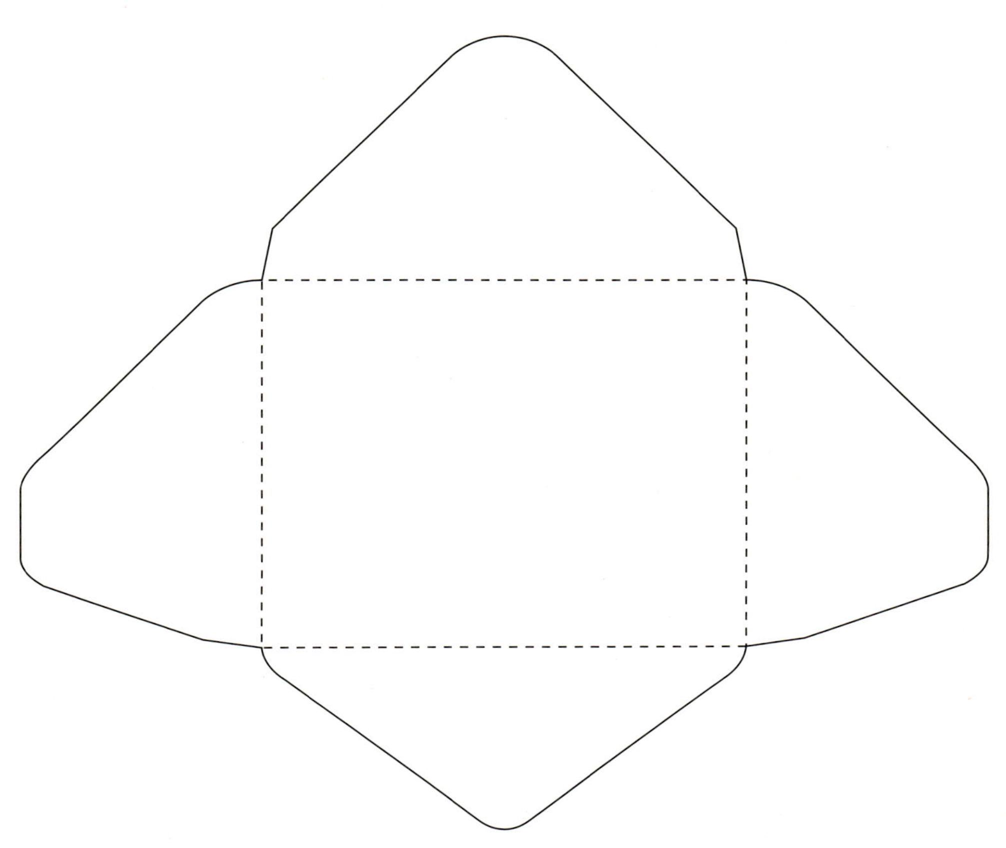

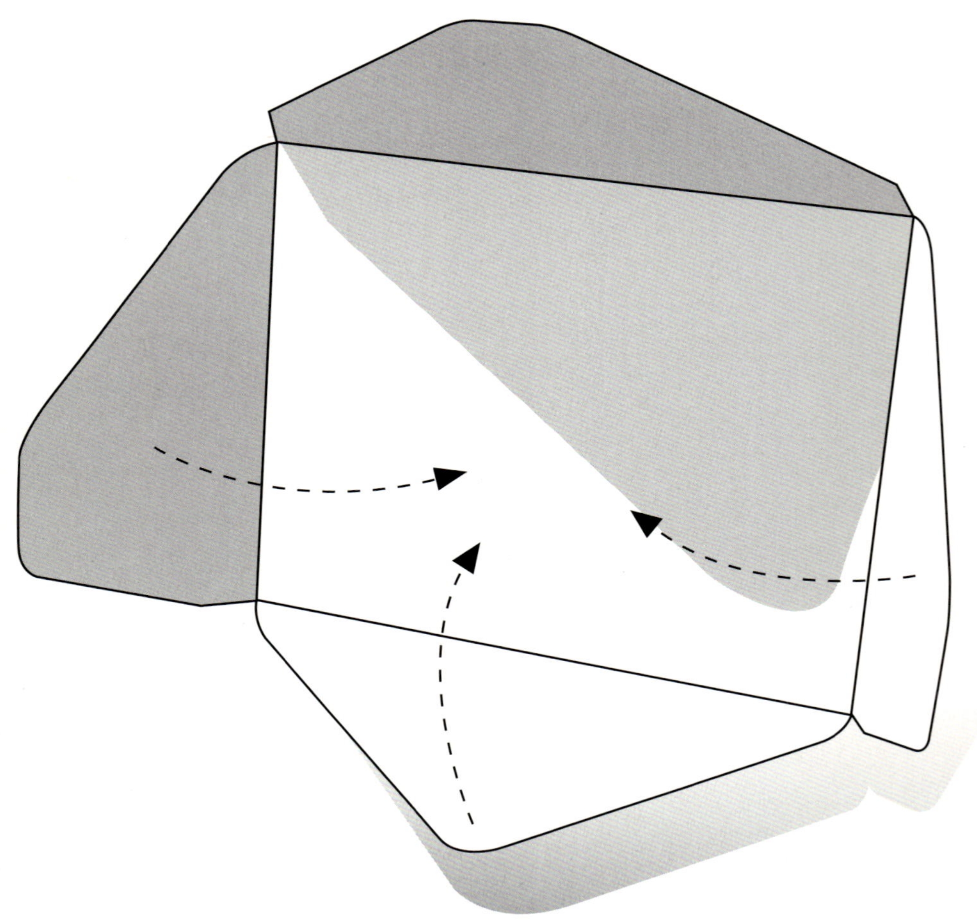

 Envelopes

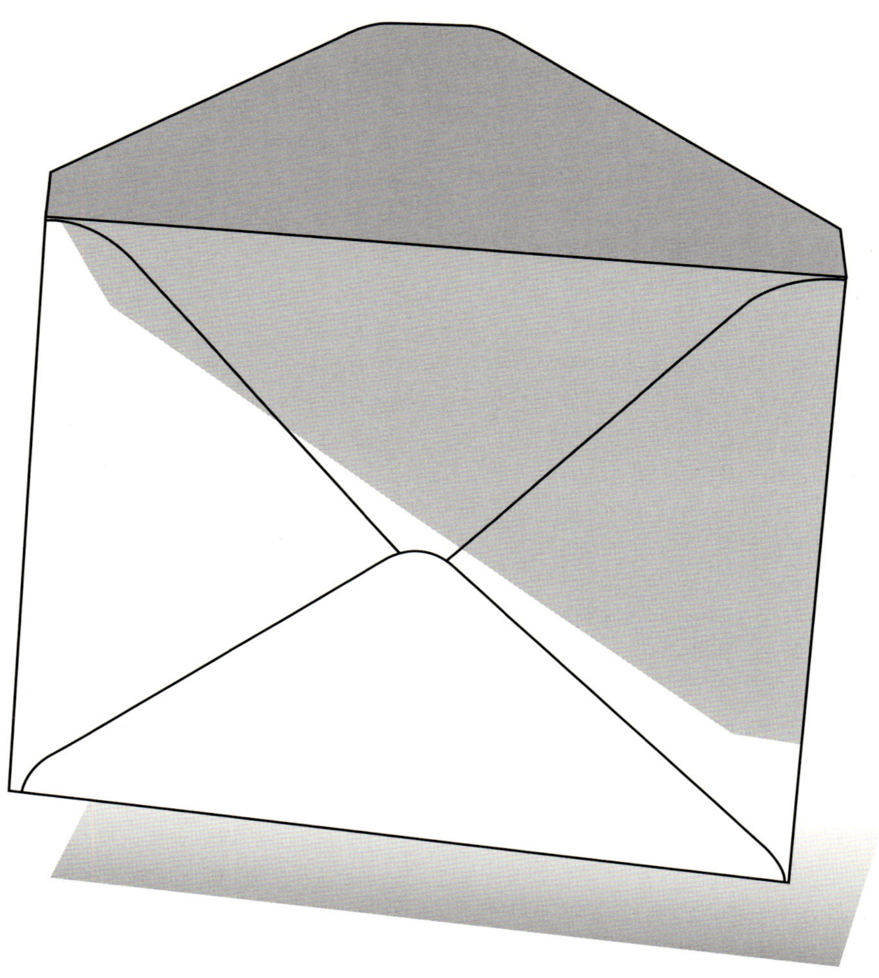

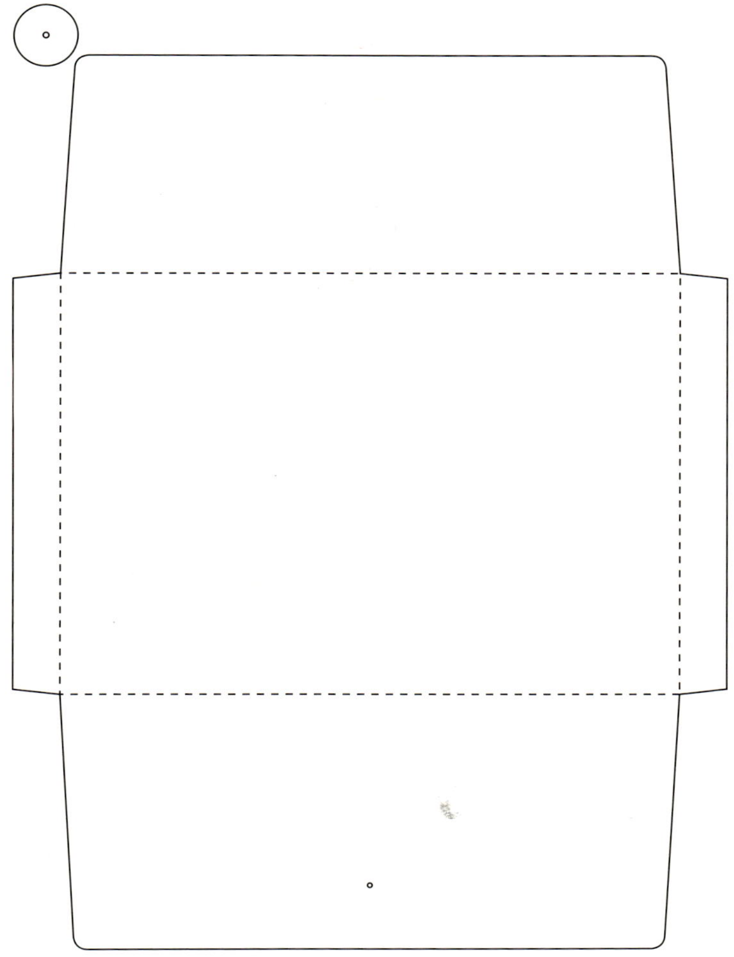

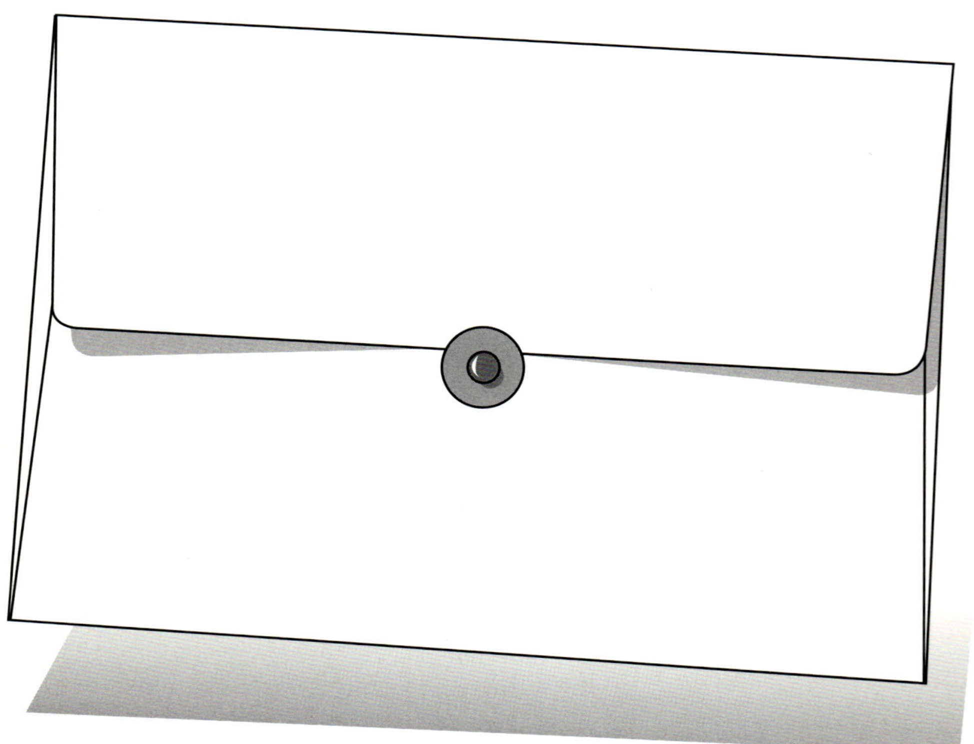

372   Envelopes

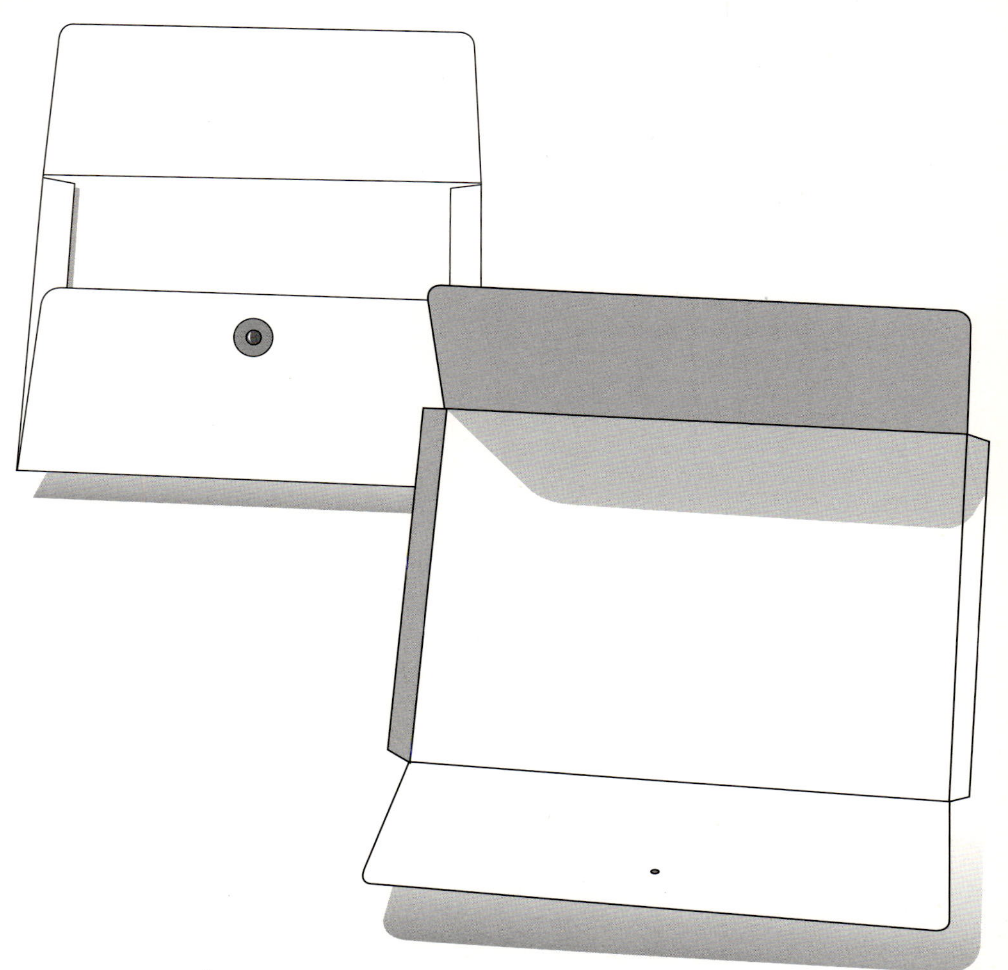

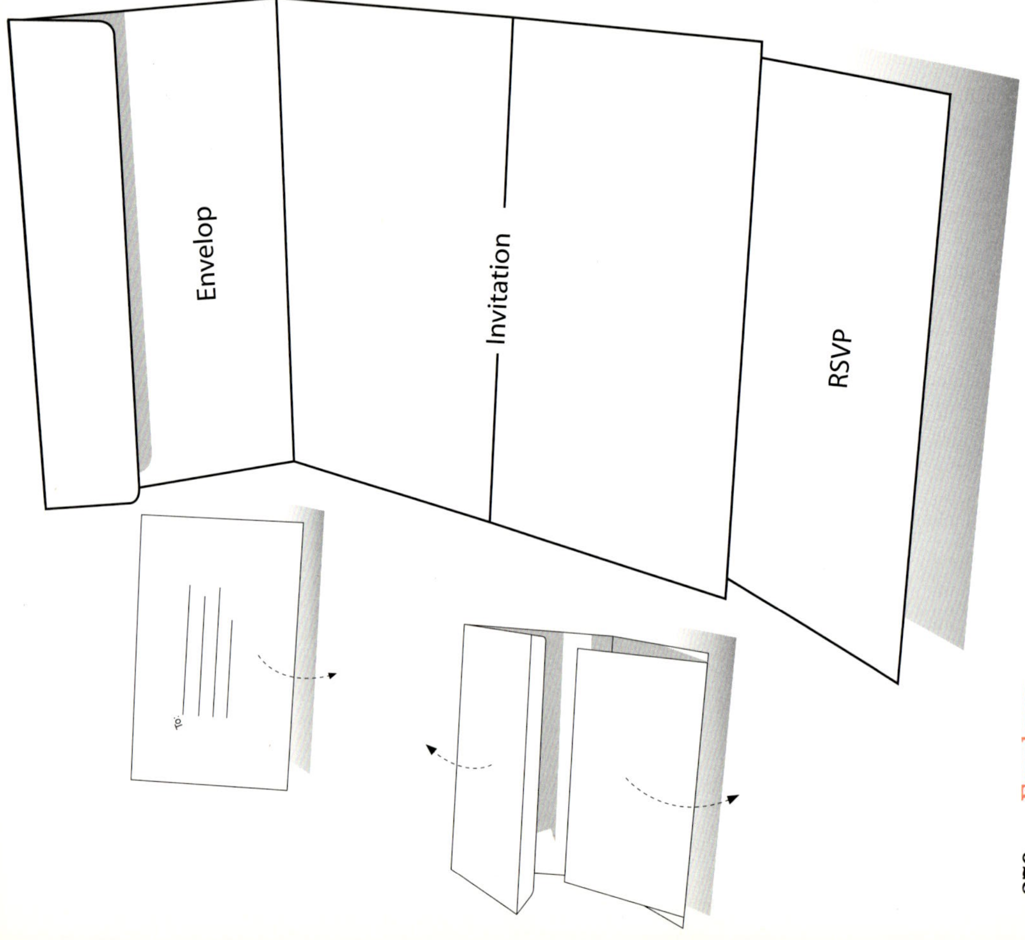

Envelop
Invitation
RSVP
To:

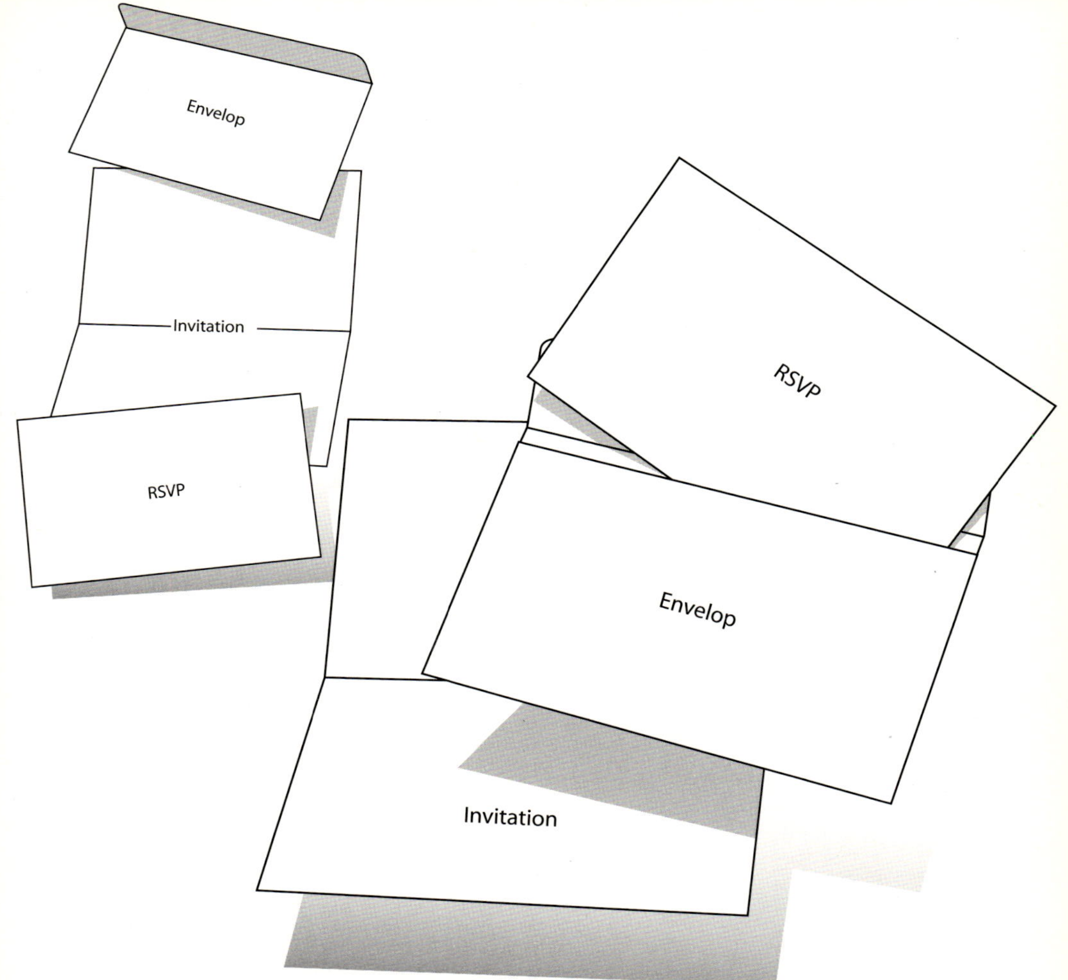

Envelop
Invitation
RSVP
RSVP
Envelop
Invitation

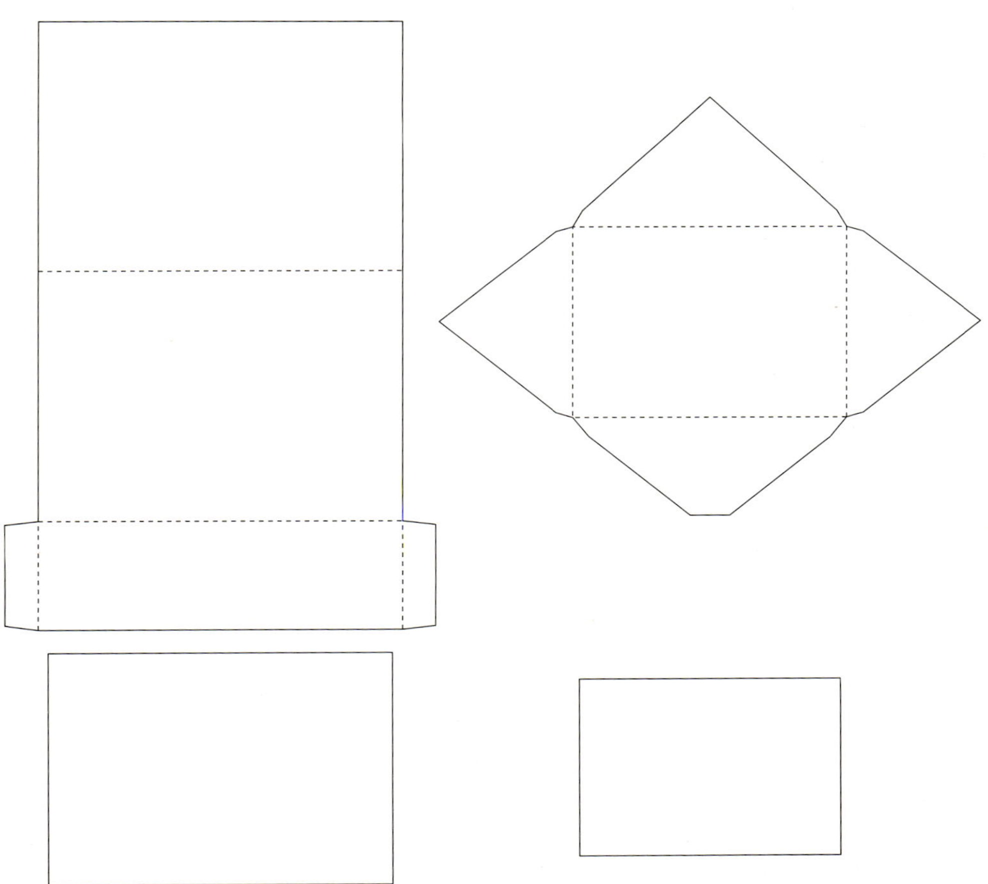

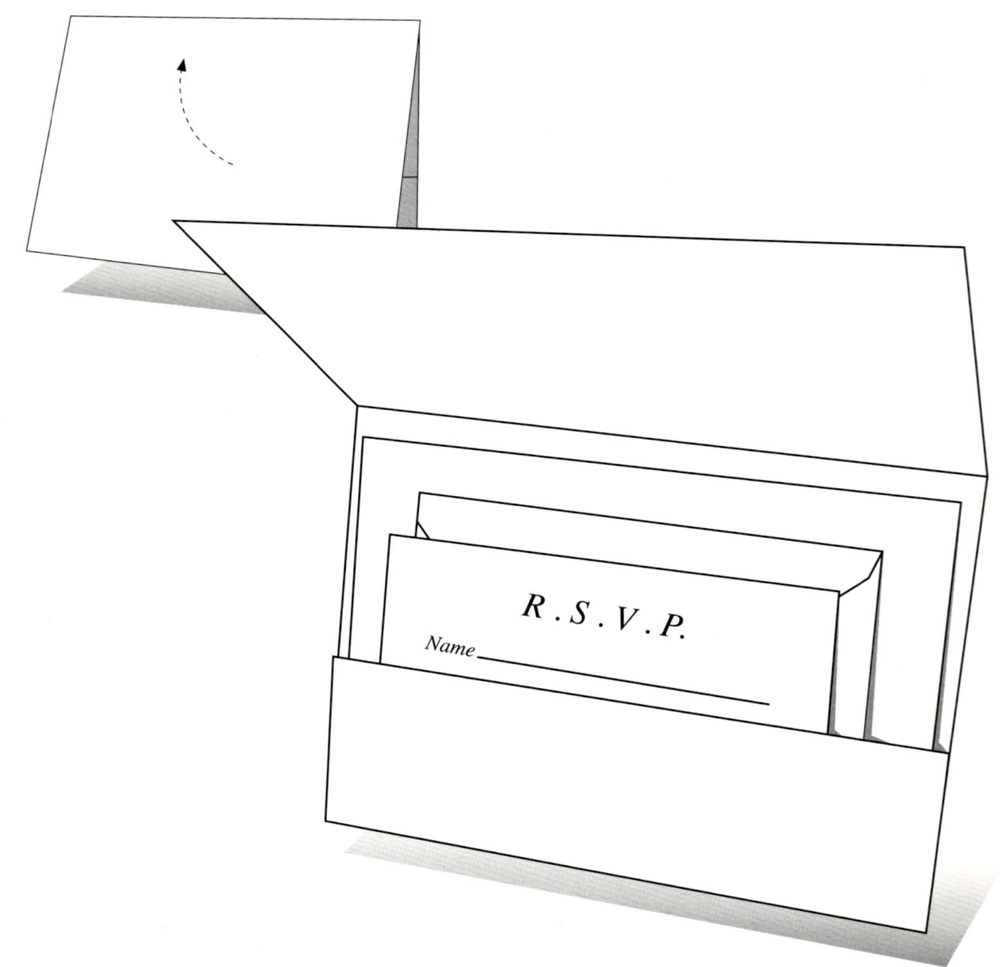
R . S . V . P .
Name

R . S . V . P .
Name

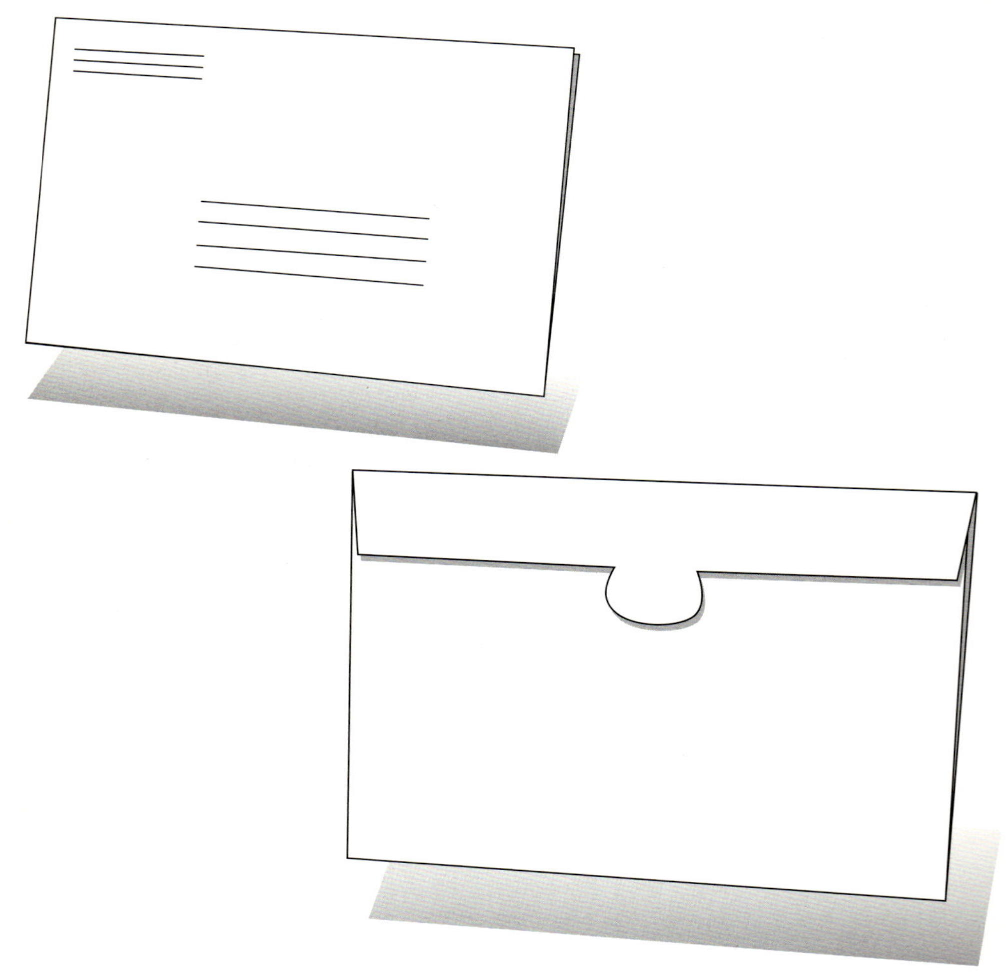

 Envelopes

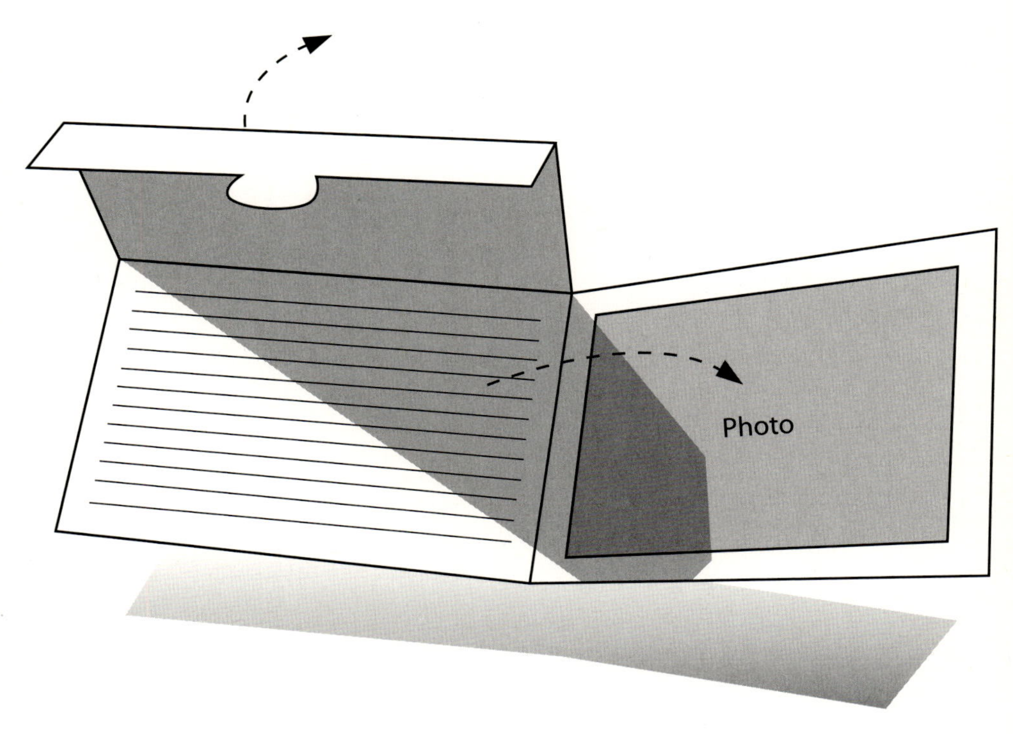
Photo

Miscellaneous

その他
Divers
Varios
Varie
Sonstiges

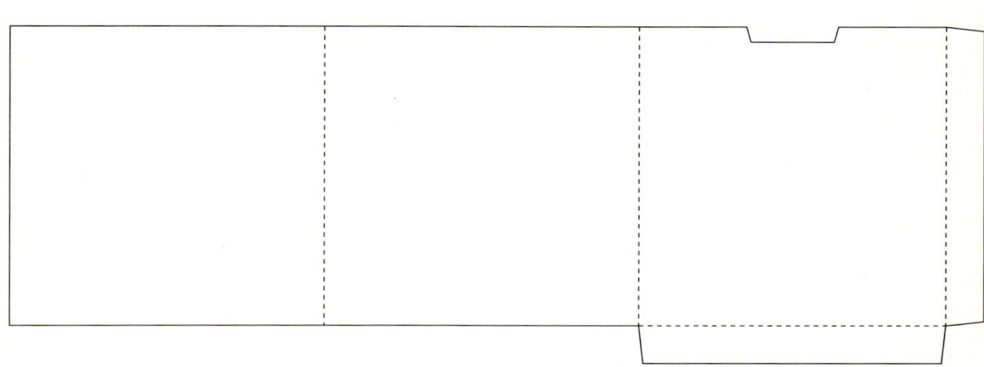

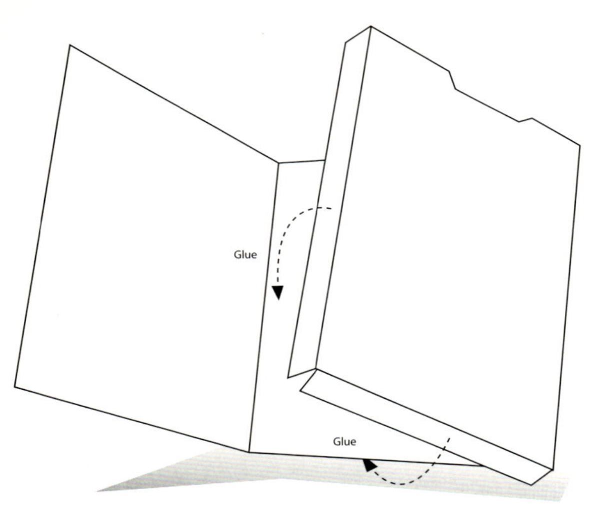

Glue
Glue

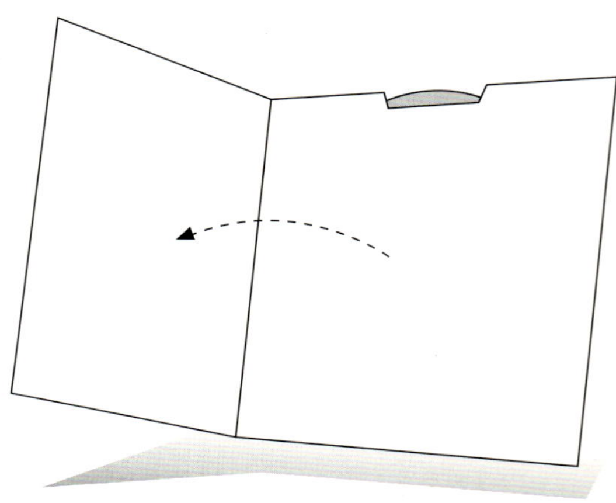

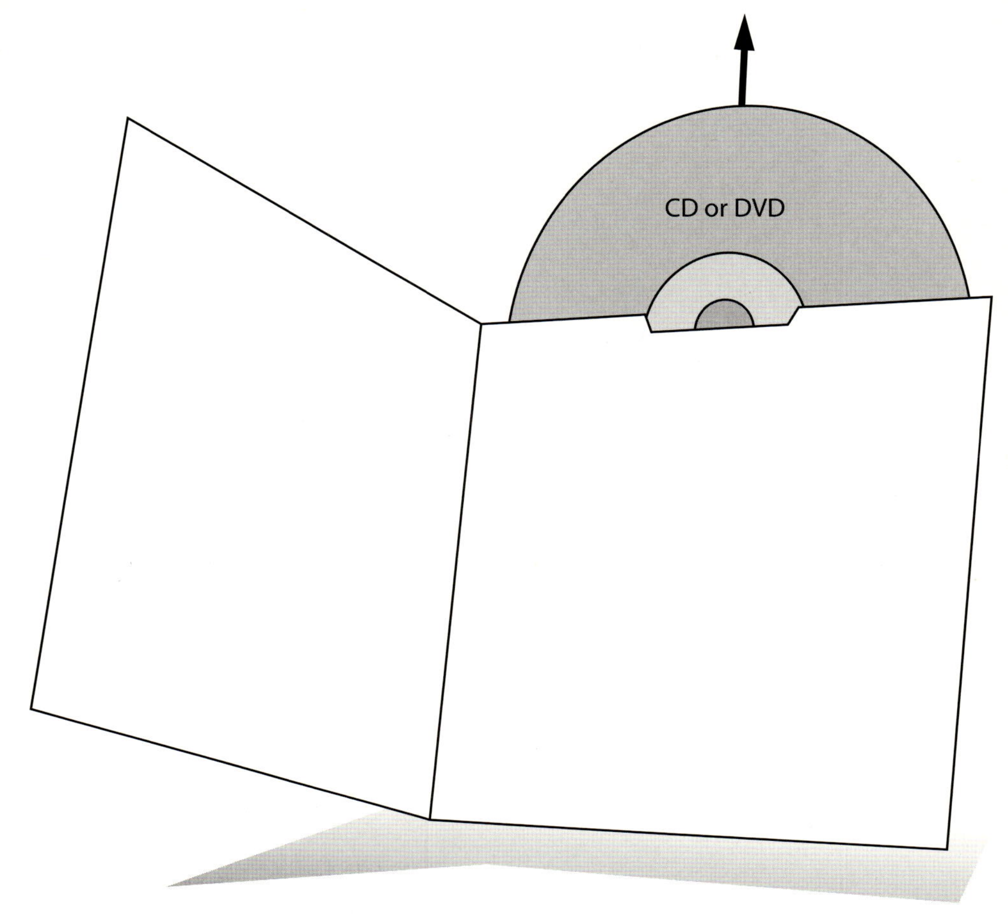

CD or DVD

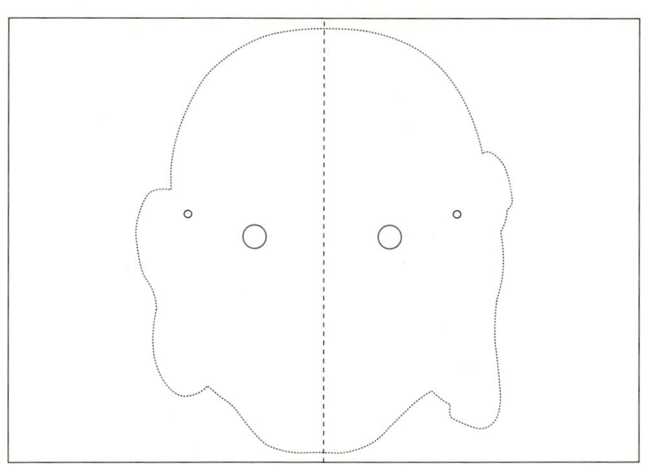

Happy
Birthday,
Matey!
Happy
Birthday,
Matey!

Happy
Birthday,
Matey!

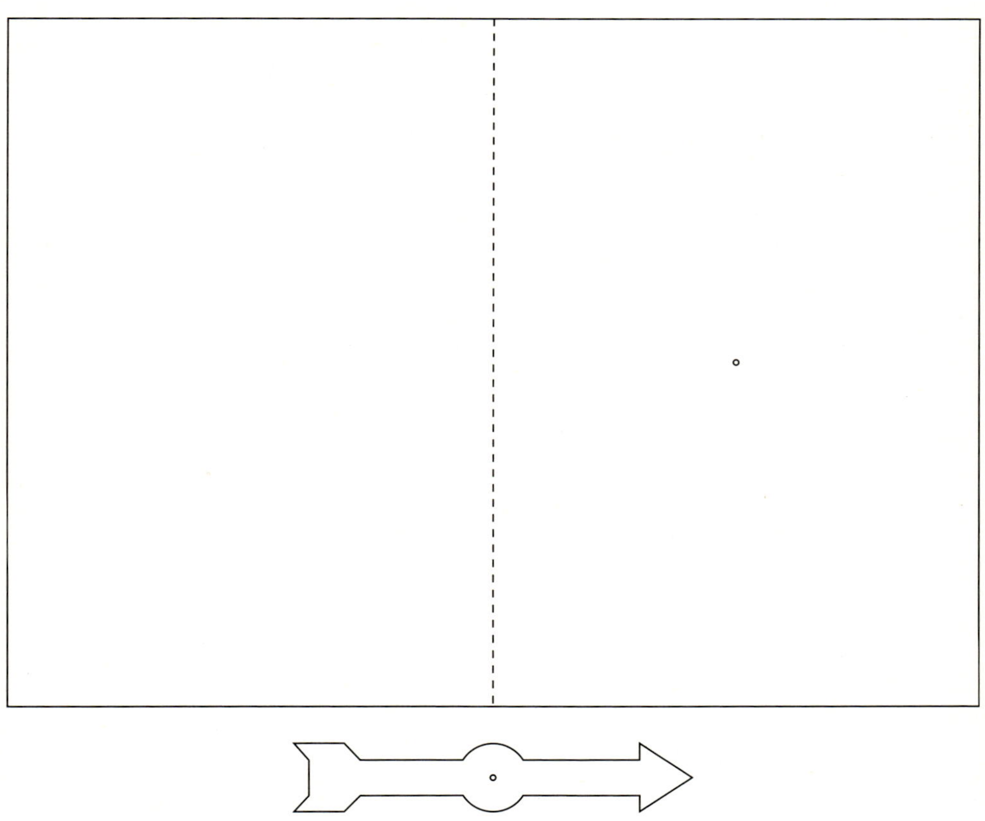

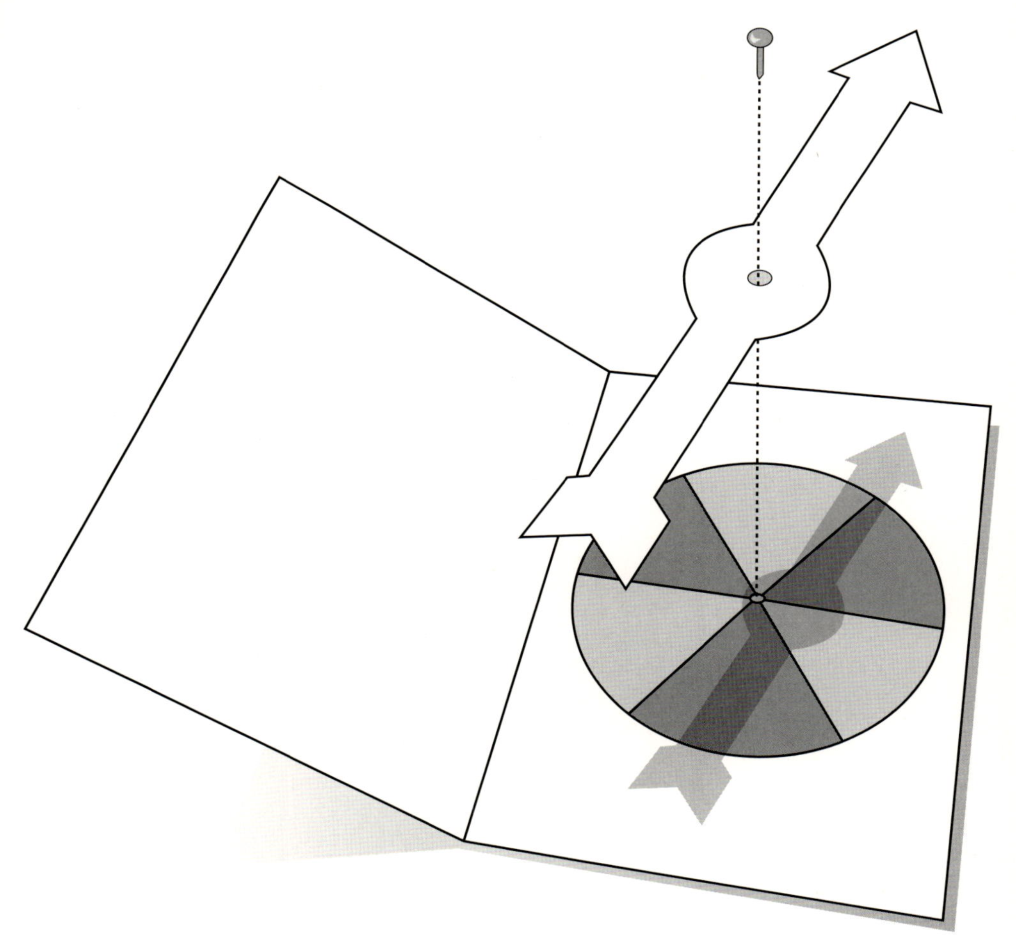

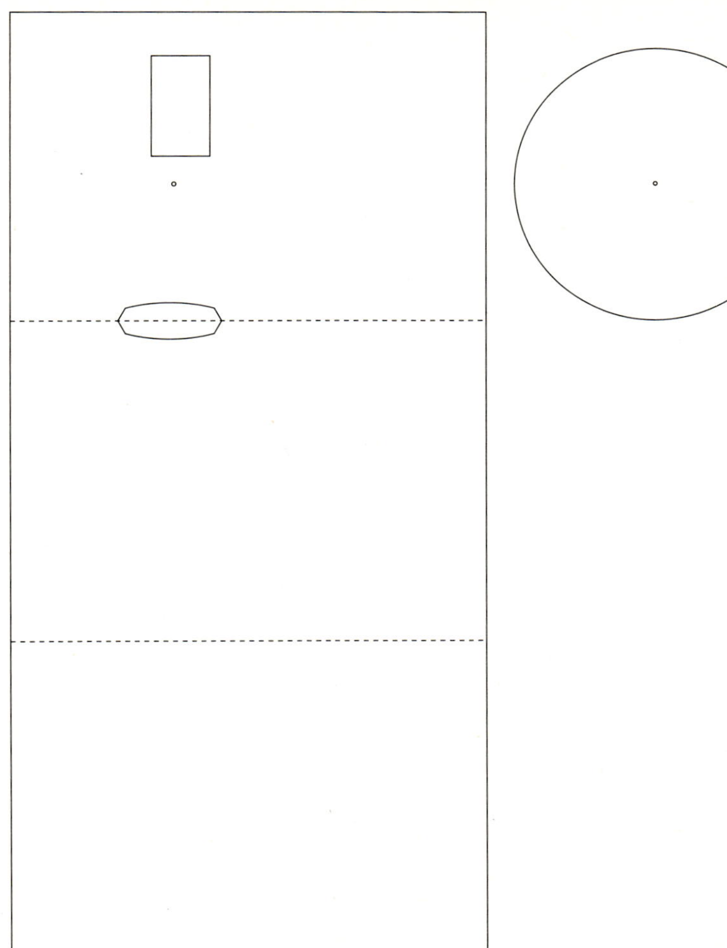

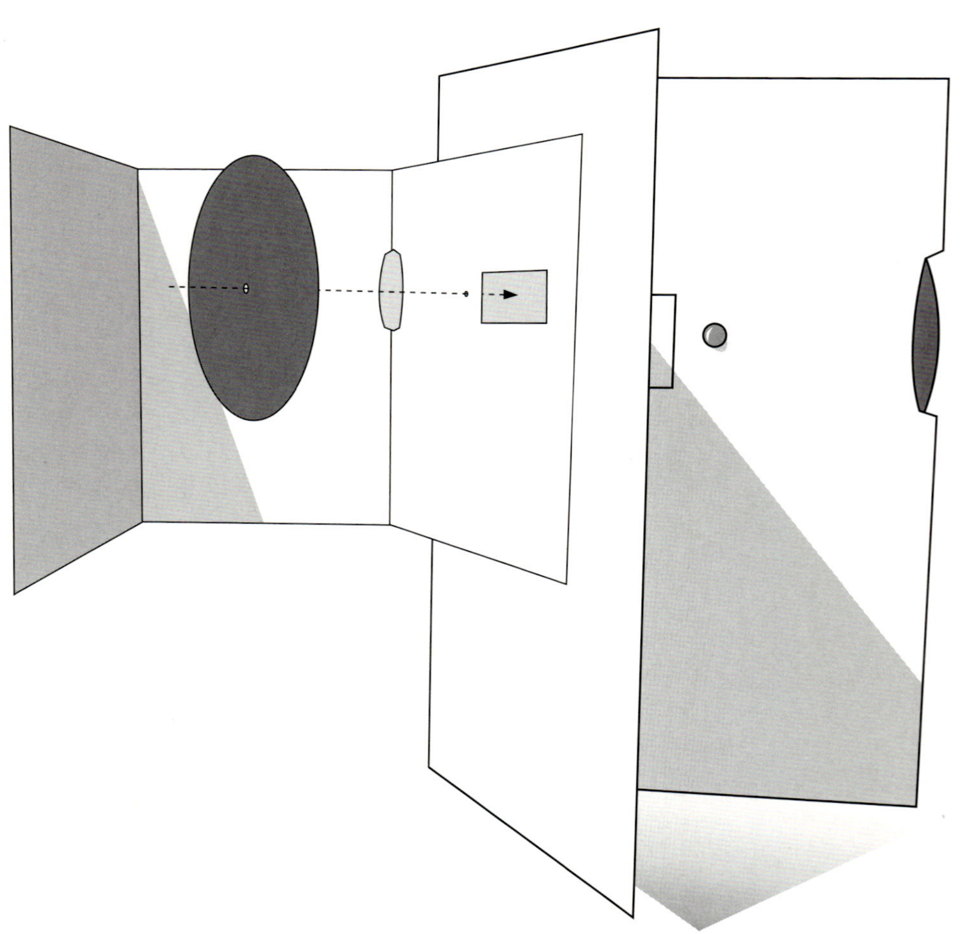

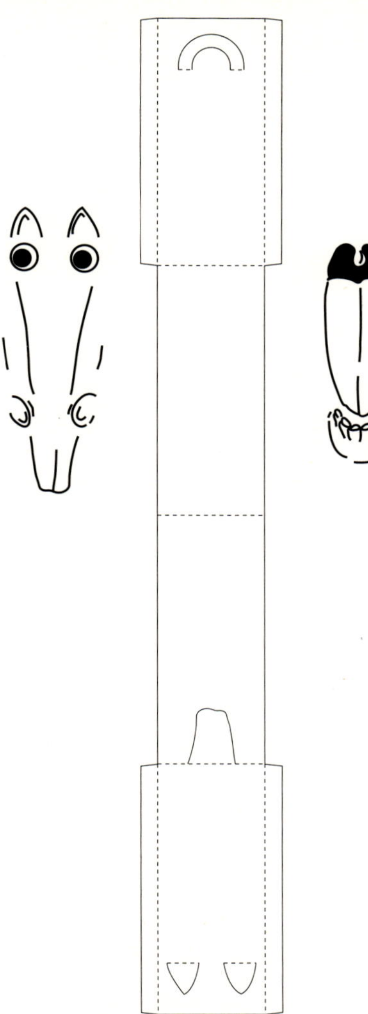

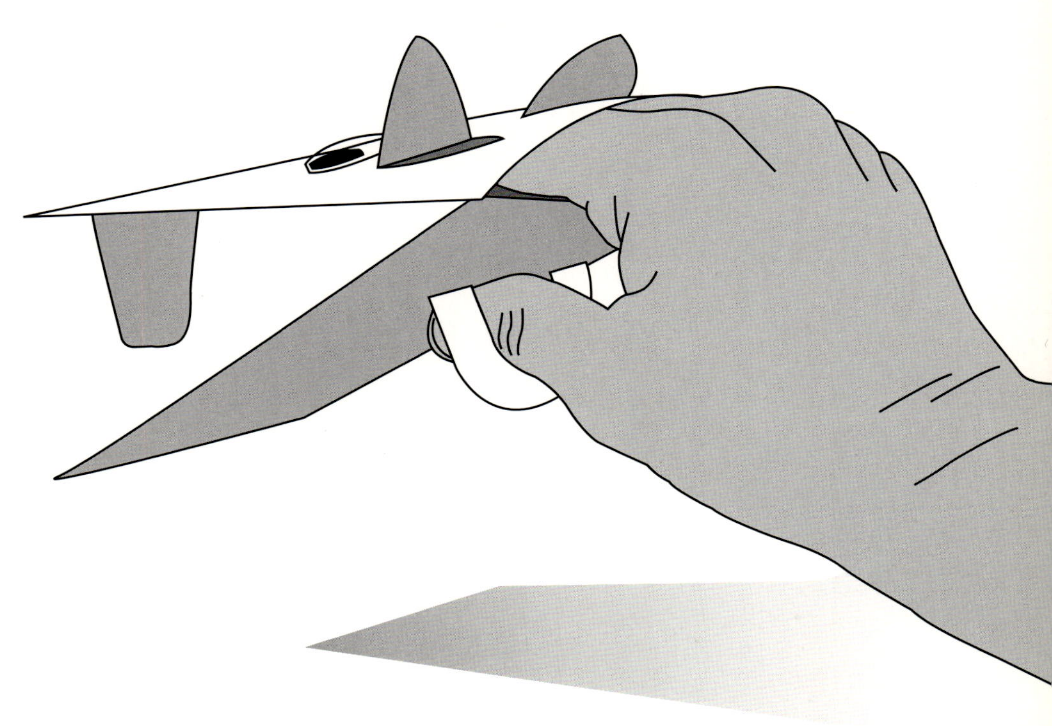

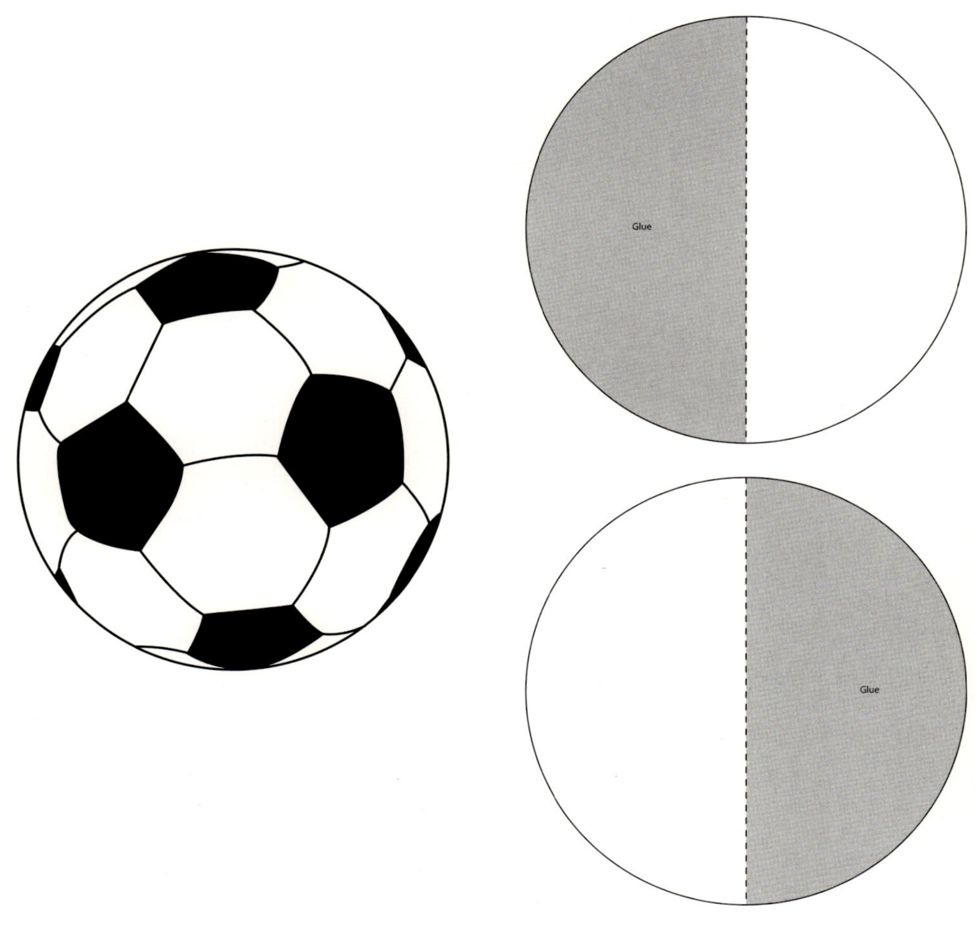

Glue
Glue

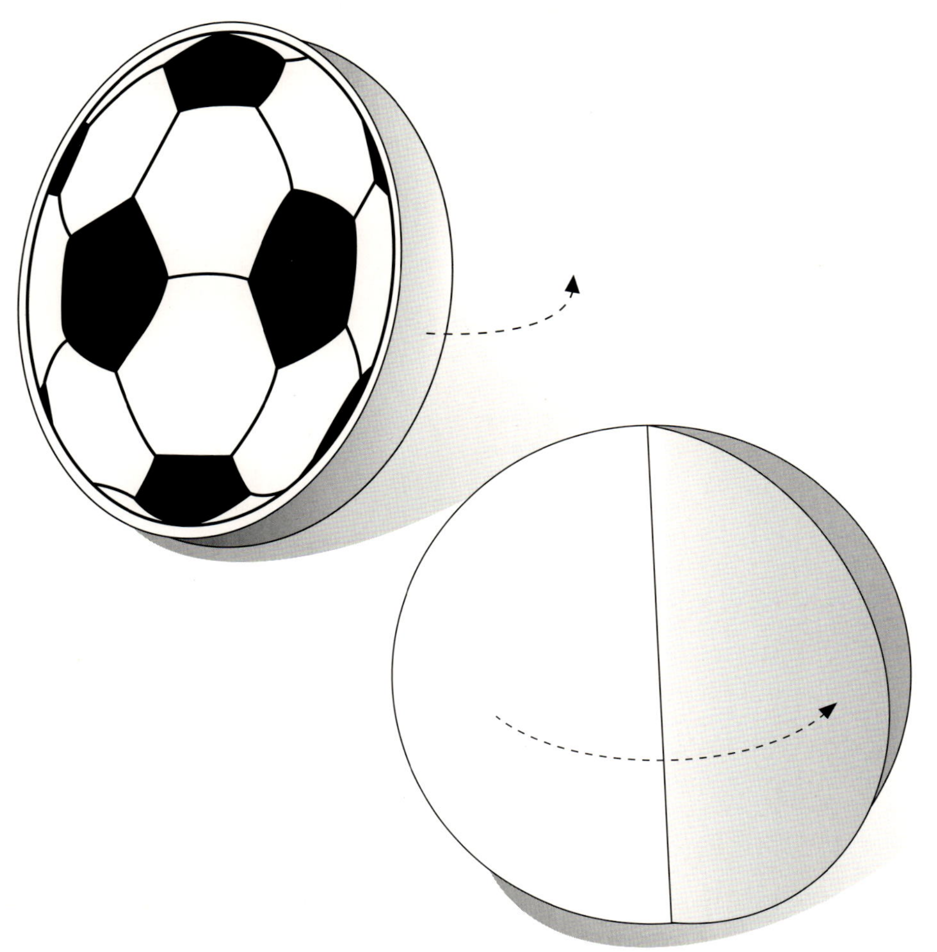

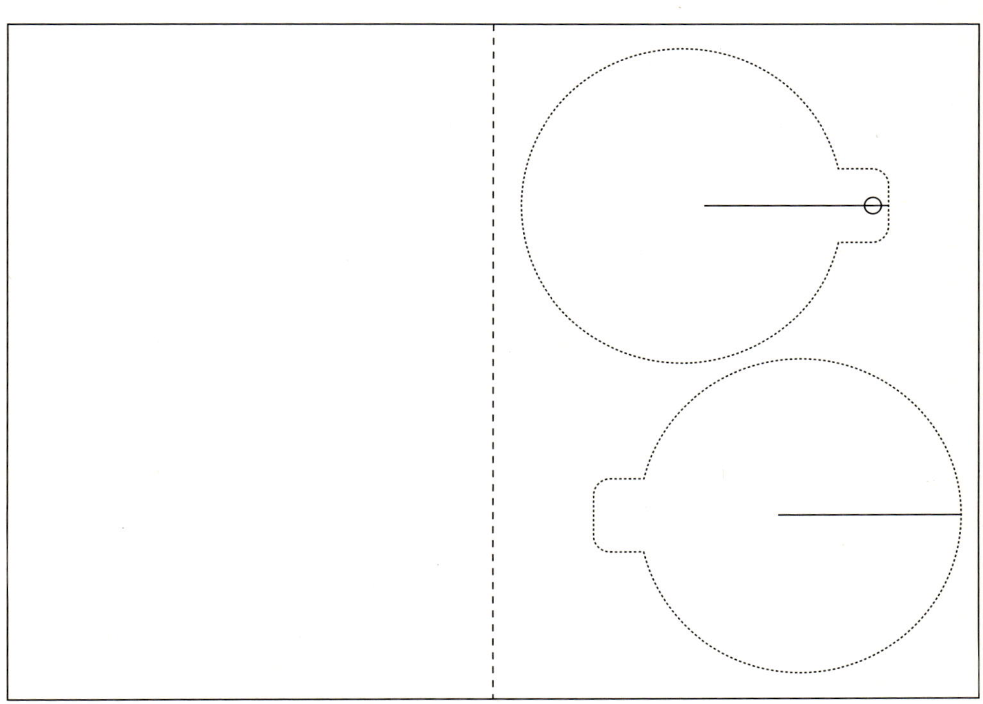

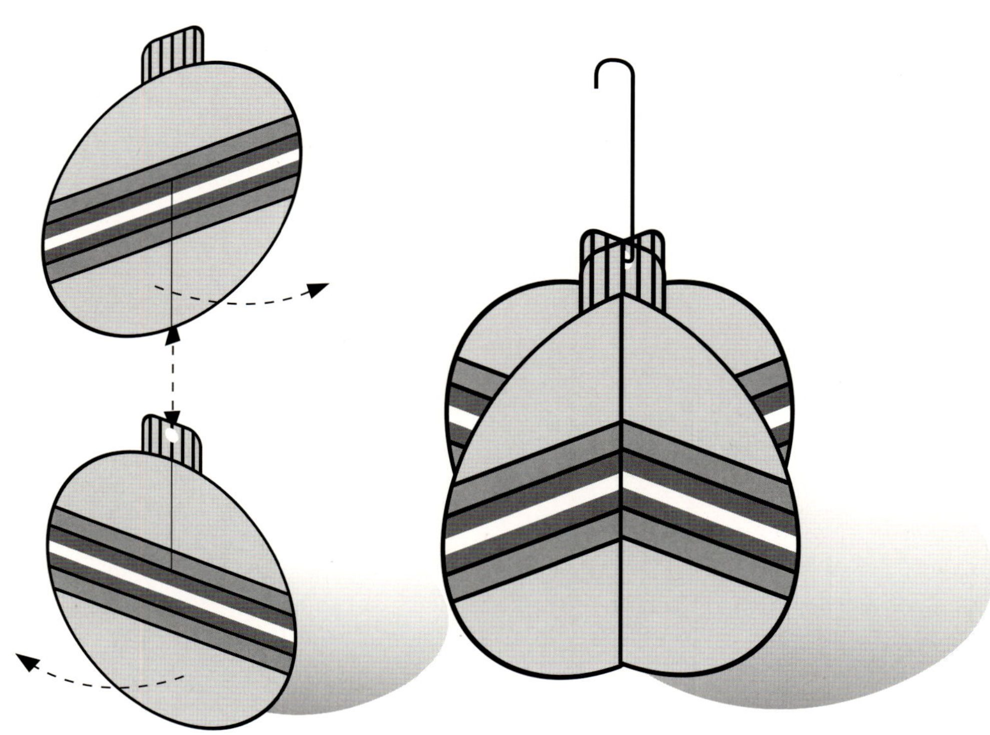

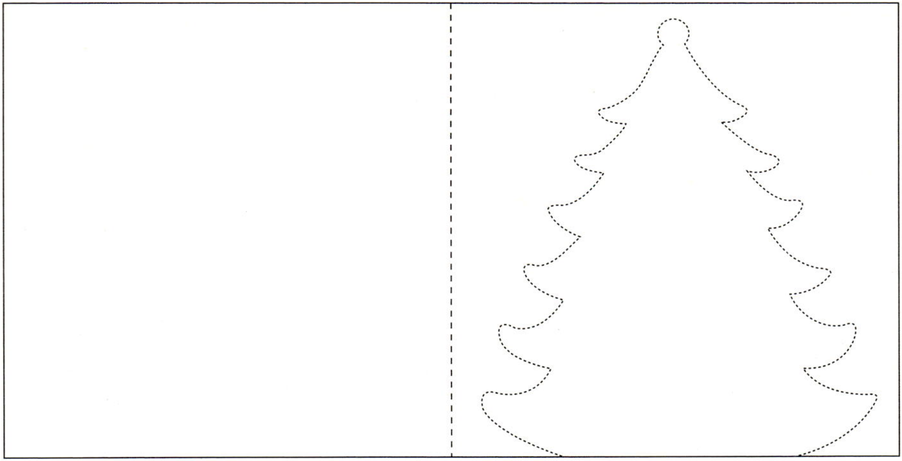

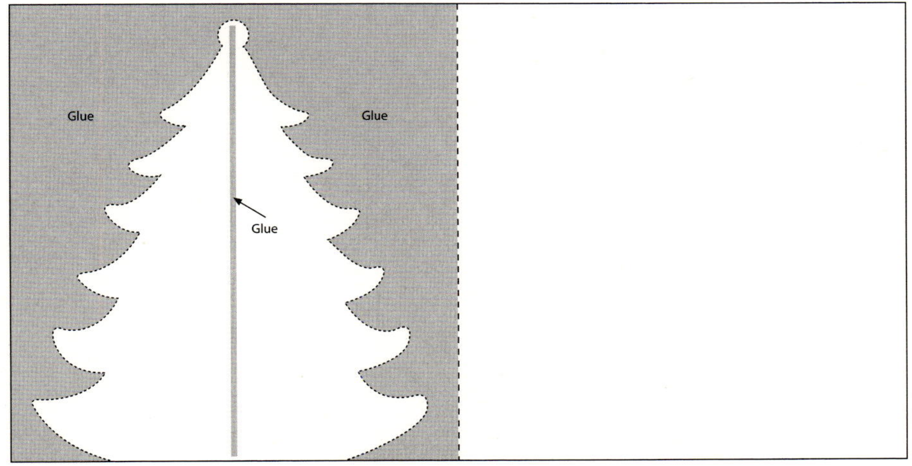

Glue
Glue
Glue

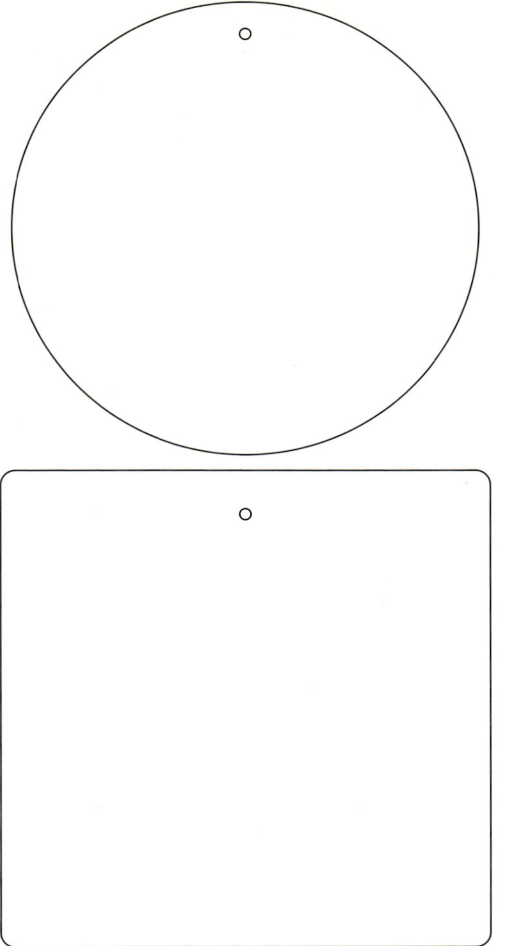

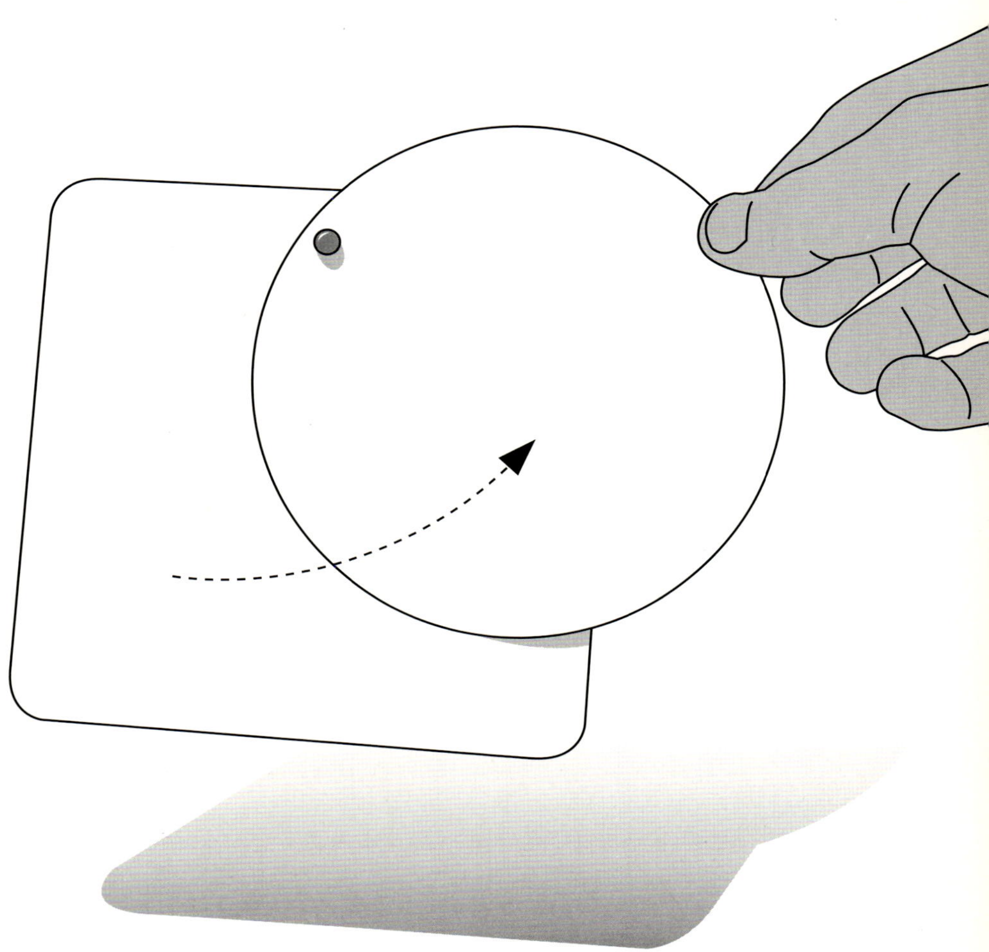

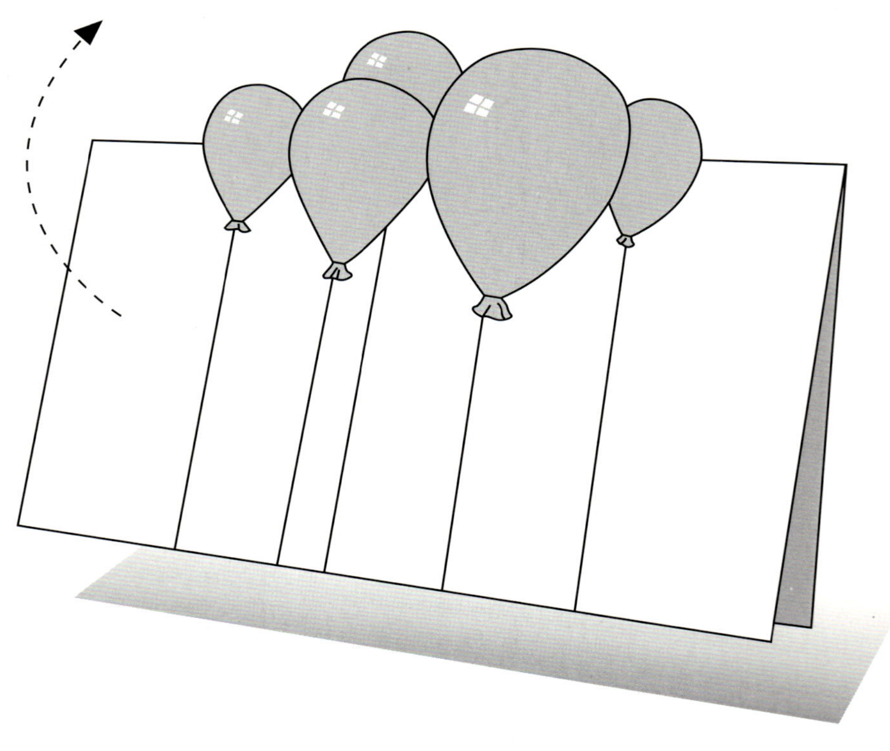

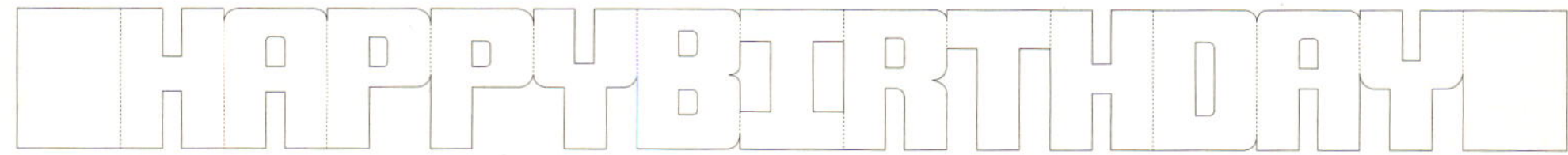
HAPPYBIRTHDAY

HAPPYB

H
BTHDAY!

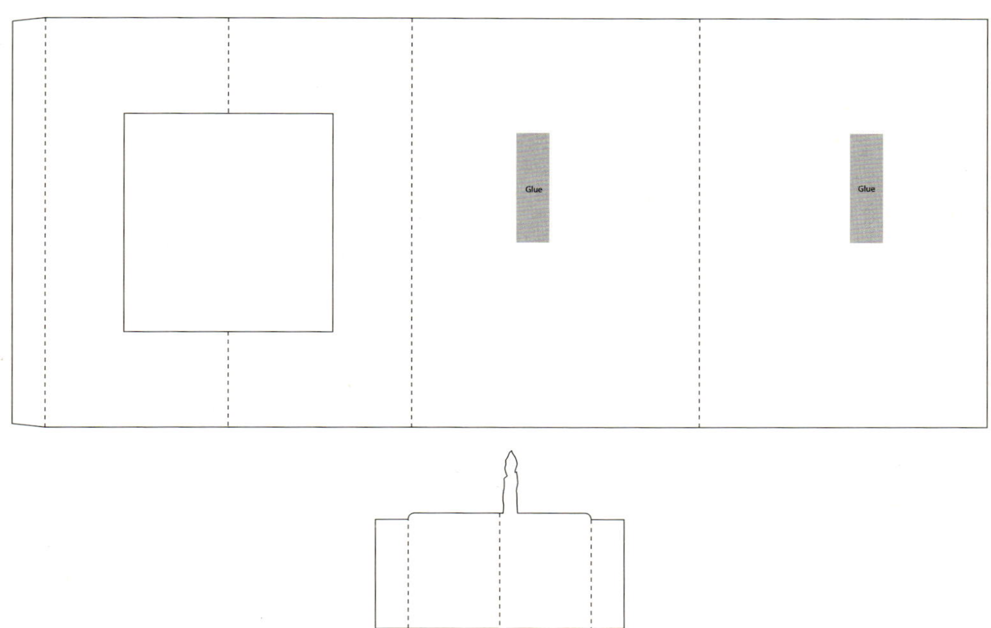

Glue
Glue

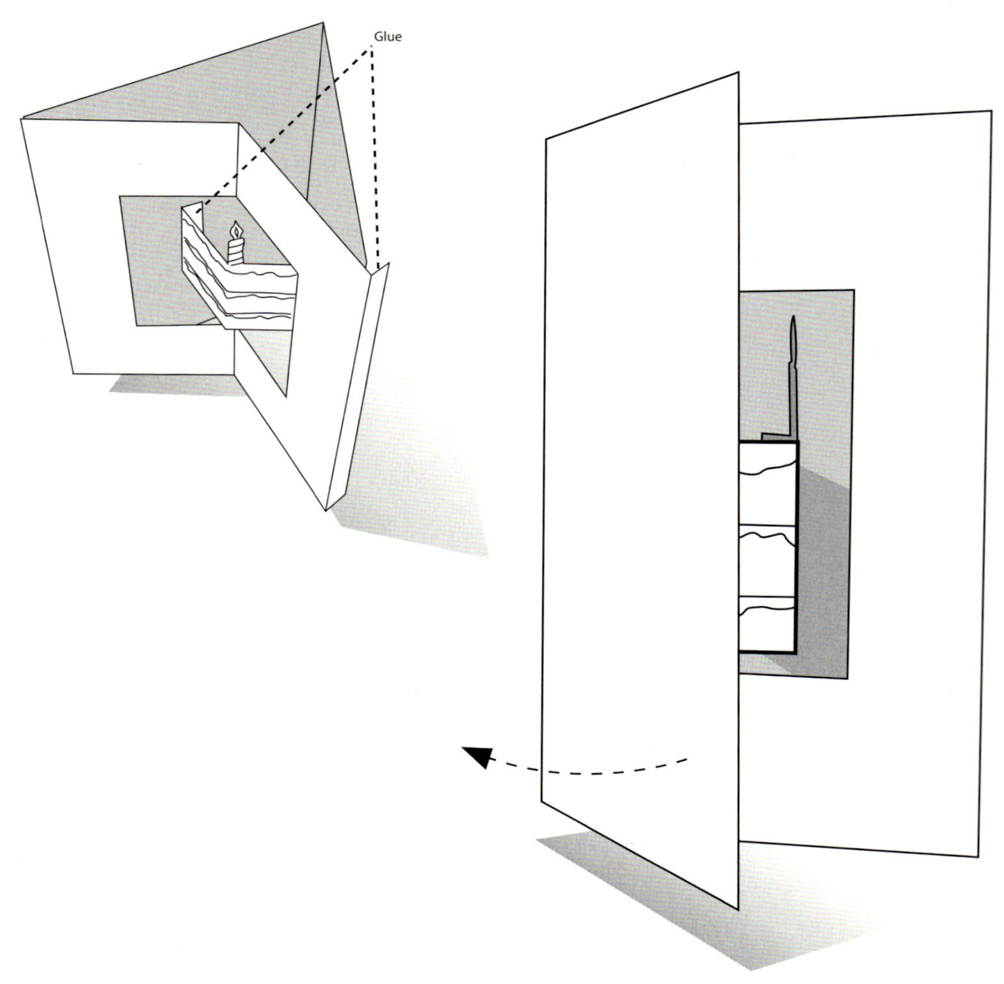

Glue

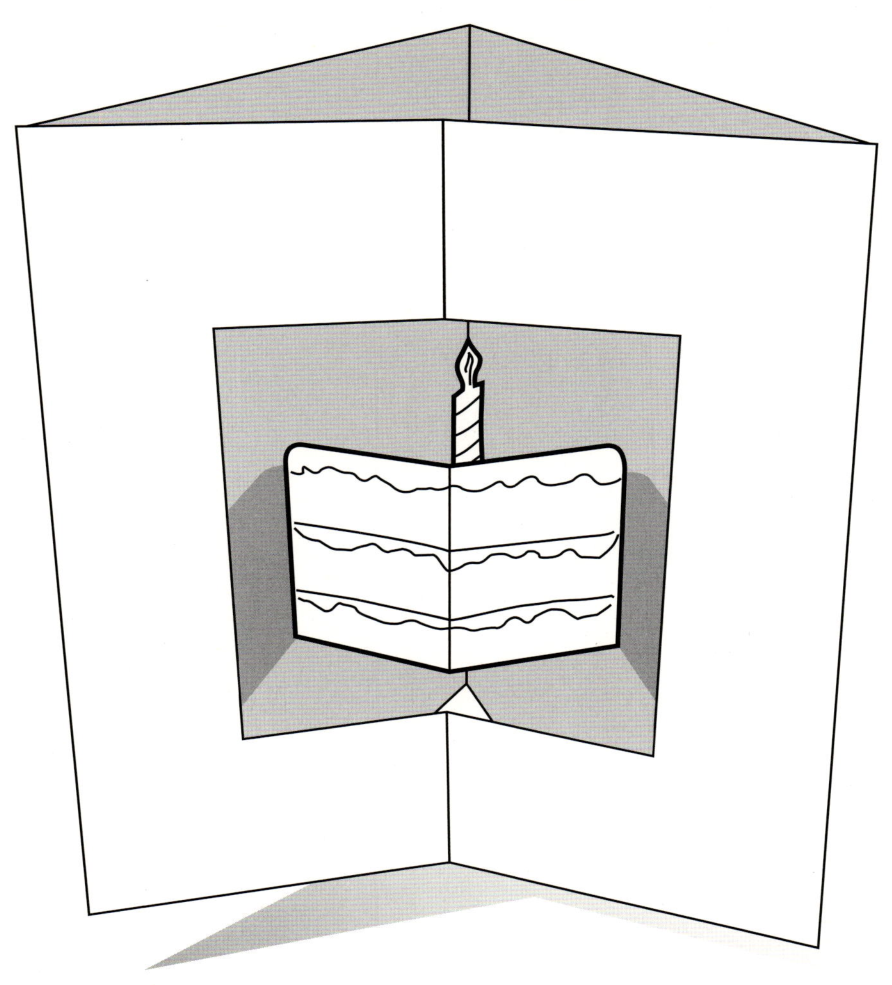

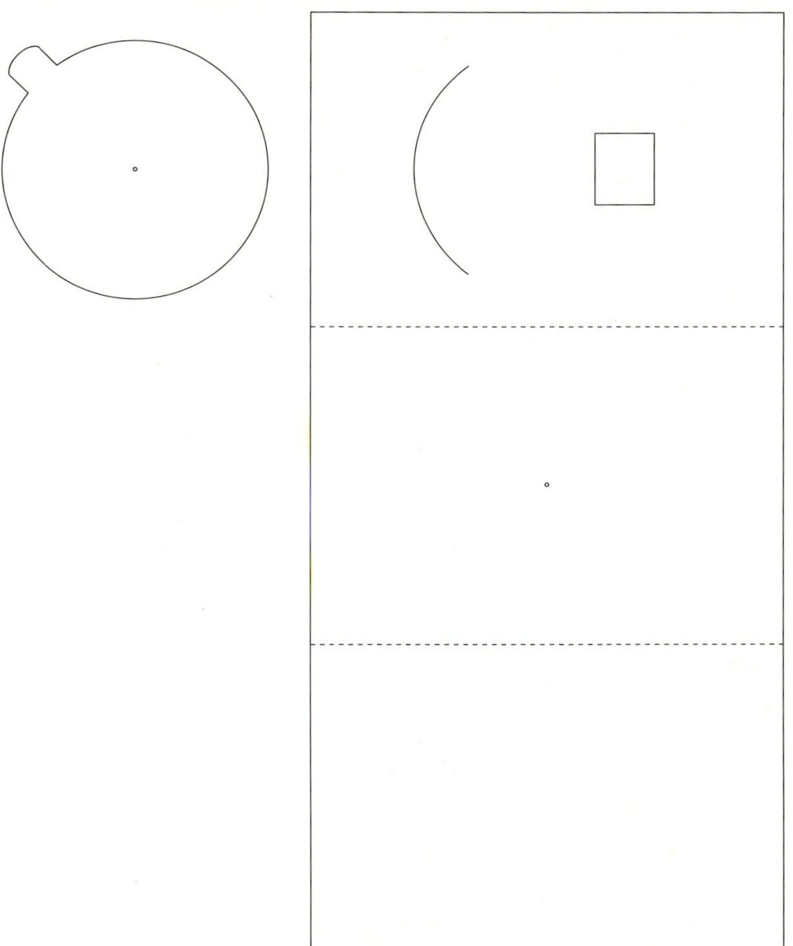

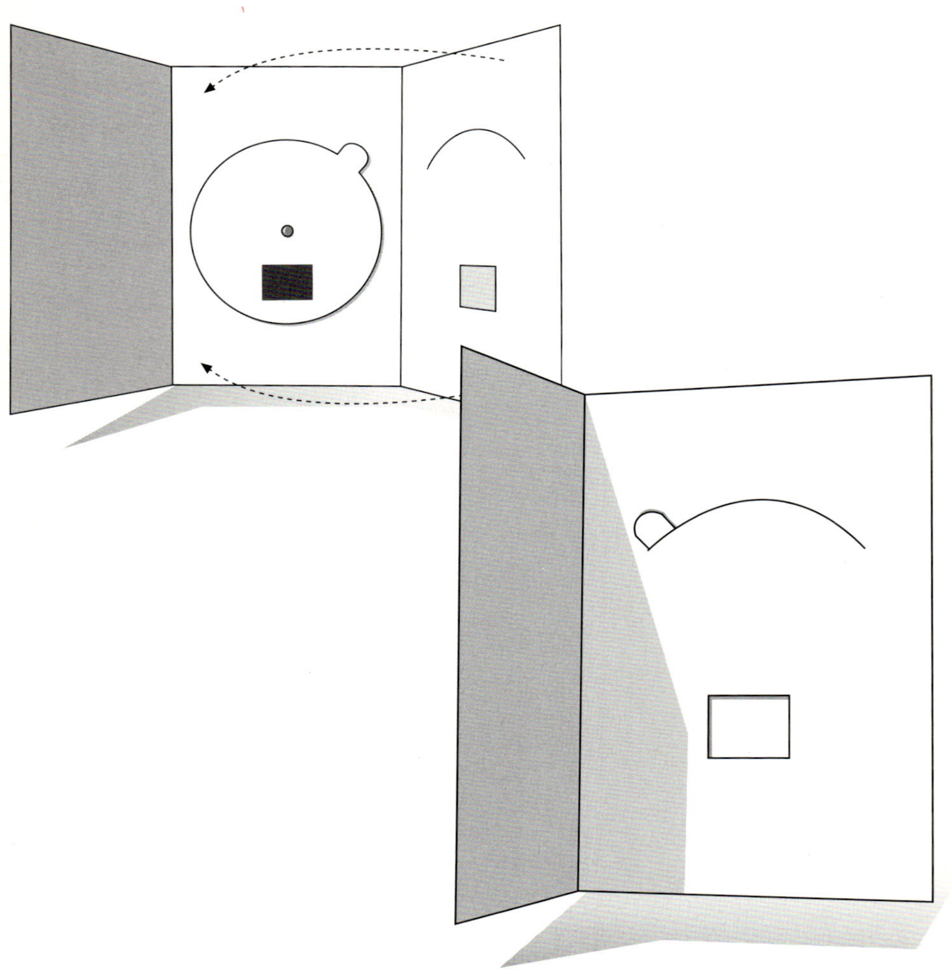

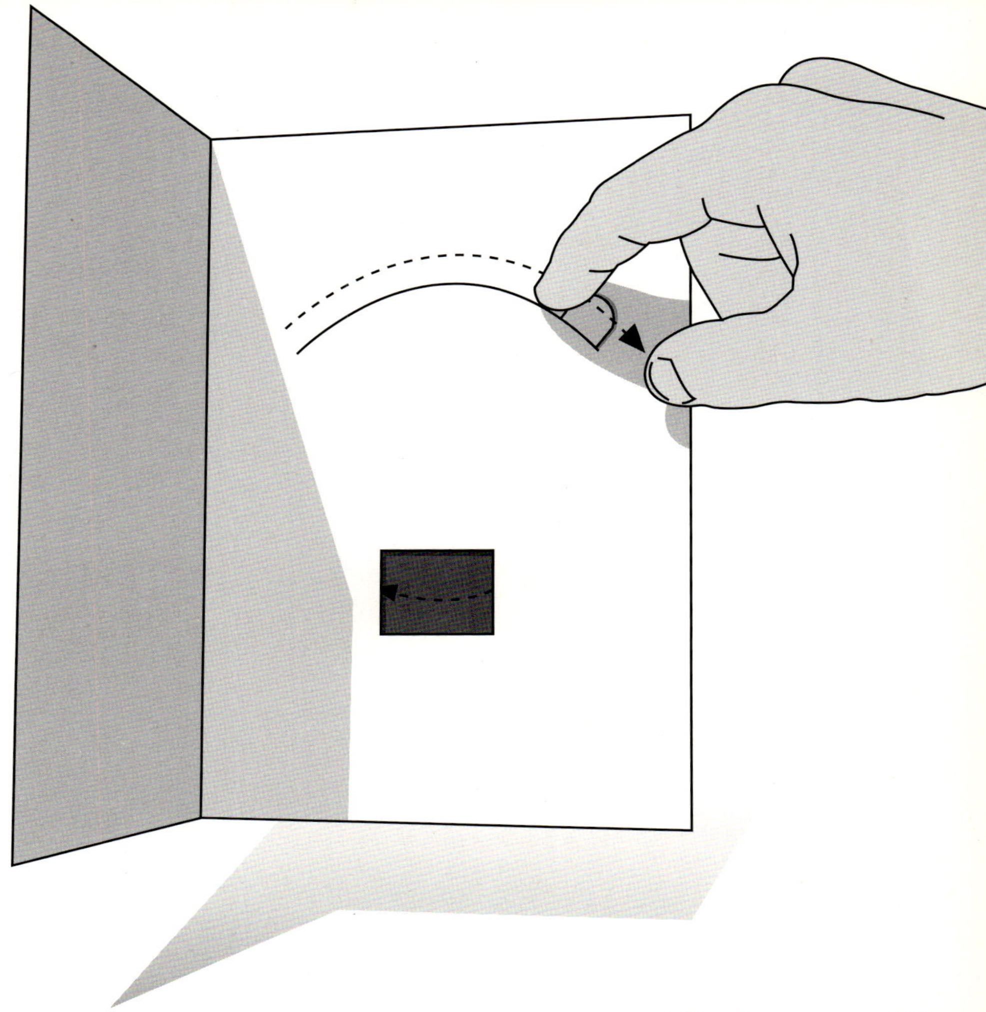

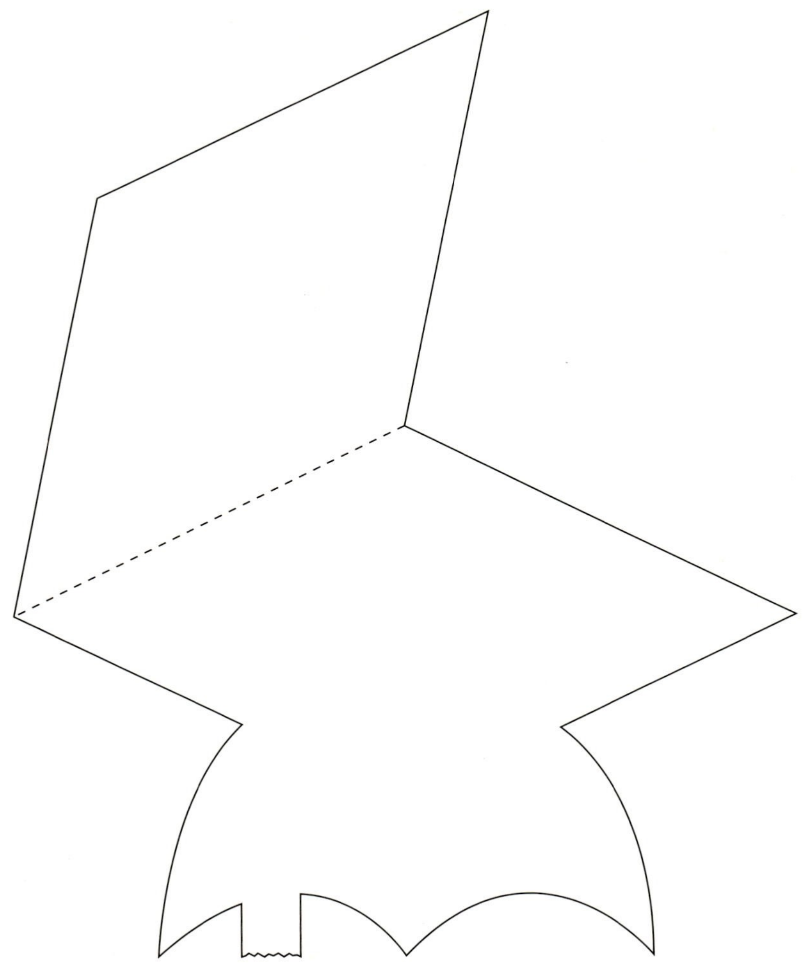

 Miscellaneous

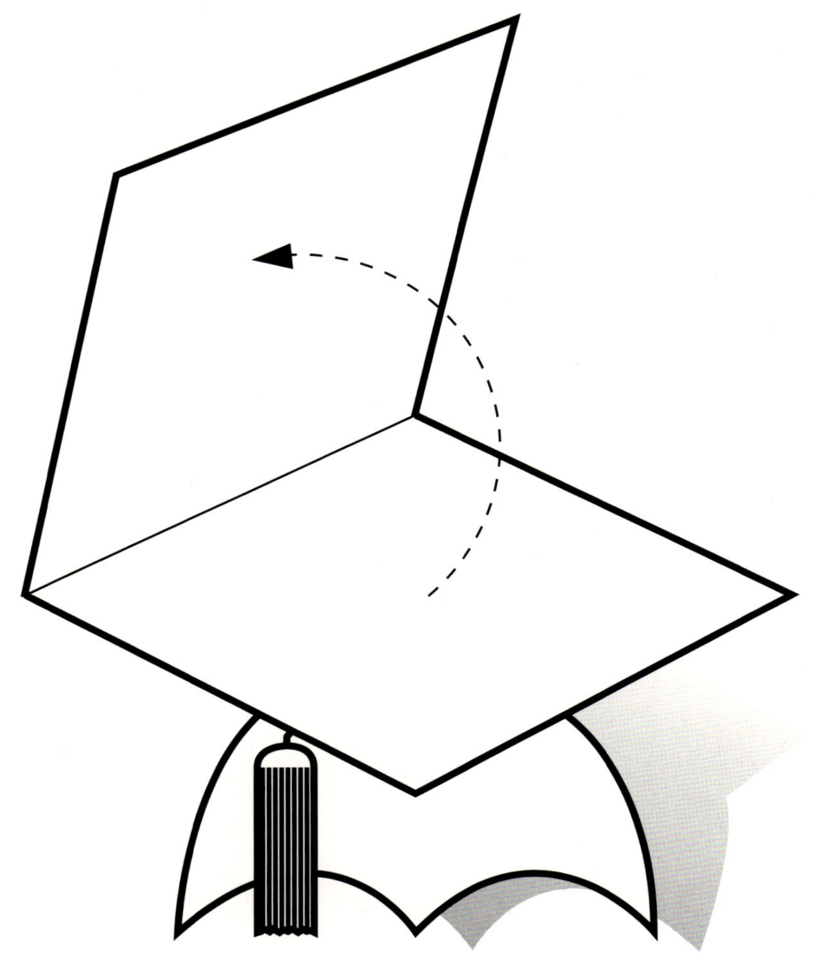

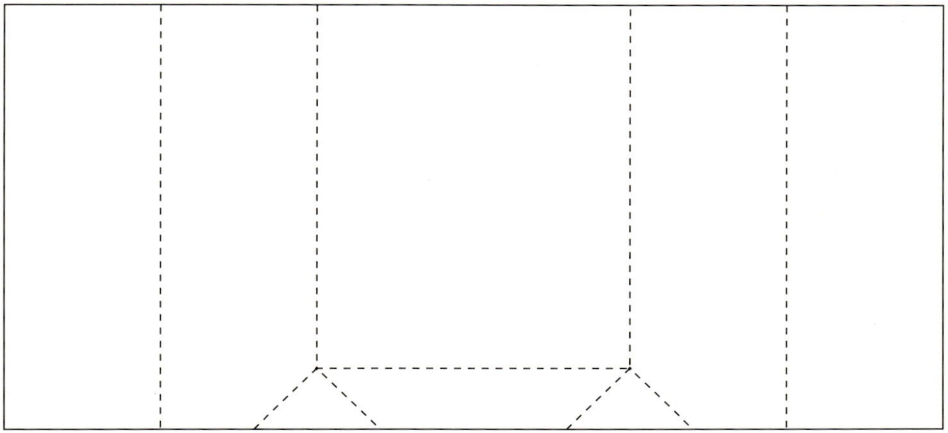

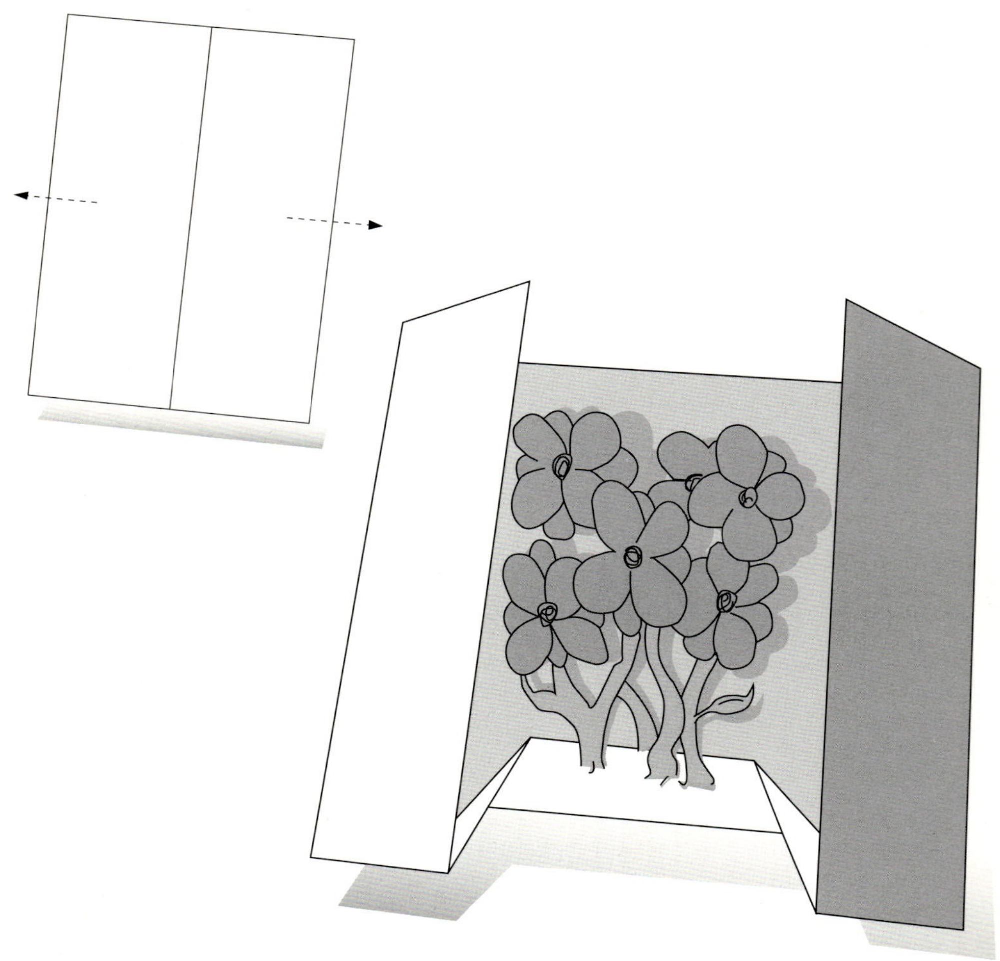

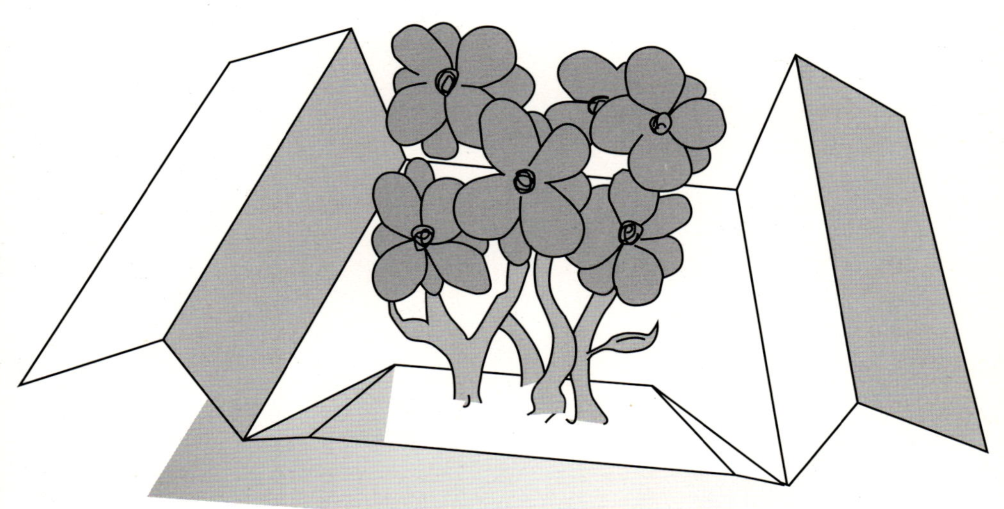